MOBILE LEARNING IN SCHOOLS

Mobile Learning in Schools explores the potential for using mobile devices in diverse school and college settings around the globe. It evaluates the exciting opportunities mobile initiatives bring and shares experience of where things can go wrong, in order to ensure that those embarking on new projects are fully informed.

Drawing on a wide range of international perspectives, it unpicks complex sociocultural issues, including lack of sustainability, behavioural and ethical concerns, and explores successful student learning. Key issues considered include:

- mobile learning in primary schools
- teaching and learning with mobile devices in secondary schools
- opportunities inside and outside school
- pedagogical principles and sustainability
- mobile learning for initial teacher training and CPD
- ethical considerations
- behaviour matters – disruption, plagiarism, cheating, cyberbullying
- assessing mobile learning.

With annotated further reading and questions to trigger reflection and further discussion amongst readers, this thought-provoking text provides a detailed survey of this often controversial topic. It is essential reading for all those engaged in understanding the potential for using mobile devices to support students' learning.

Jocelyn Wishart is Senior Lecturer in the Graduate School of Education, University of Bristol, UK, and has been Secretary of the International Association of Mobile Learning since 2010.

MOBILE LEARNING IN SCHOOLS

Key Issues, Opportunities and Ideas for Practice

Jocelyn Wishart

Routledge
Taylor & Francis Group

LONDON AND NEW YORK

First published 2018
by Routledge
2 Park Square, Milton Park, Abingdon, Oxon OX14 4RN

and by Routledge
711 Third Avenue, New York, NY 10017

Routledge is an imprint of the Taylor & Francis Group, an informa business

British Library Cataloguing in Publication Data
A catalogue record for this book is available from the British Library

Library of Congress Cataloging in Publication Data
Names: Wishart, Jocelyn, author.
Title: Mobile learning in schools : key issues, opportunities and ideas for practice / Jocelyn Wishart.
Description: Abingdon, Oxon ; New York, NY : Routledge, [2018] | Includes bibliographical references.
Identifiers: LCCN 2017020323 | ISBN 9781138690714 (hbk) | ISBN 9781138690721 (pbk) | ISBN 9781315536774 (ebk)
Subjects: LCSH: Mobile communication systems in education. | Education–Effect of technological innovations on.
Classification: LCC LB1044.84 .W57 2018 | DDC 371.33–dc23
LC record available at https://lccn.loc.gov/2017020323

ISBN: 978-1-138-69071-4 (hbk)
ISBN: 978-1-138-69072-1 (pbk)
ISBN: 978-1-315-53677-4 (ebk)

Typeset in News Gothic
by Cenveo Publisher Services

Dedication

This book is dedicated to my students, all those who, over the years, put up with me constantly trying out new technologies in teaching on them without a fuss and especially to those who joined in and encouraged me into more research.

Contents

Foreword

This book on using mobile devices in teaching for trainee teachers, CPD, teacher trainers and early career teachers, introduces mobile learning, its benefits and its challenges, via a range of pedagogic, technical, institutional, ethical and other issues. The book has been created in response to the need for a balanced overview of what can be a controversial question. Should we allow or even encourage our students to use mobile phones and tablet computers for school-work inside or outside the classroom?

It has been written by me, Dr Jocelyn Wishart, currently a teacher educator working at a research intensive, city university in the UK, and one of the first members of the International Association for Mobile Learning. I have long been involved in the research and development of ways in which digital technologies can support teachers and teaching and was one of the first to issue students, trainee teachers in my case, with personal digital assistants (PDAs, forerunners of today's smartphones) to explore their potential uses for teaching and learning.

The book includes many examples of both teaching practice and research projects that I have tried to source from across the globe in order to represent mobile learning practice in schools in diverse contexts. I have concentrated on using examples from either peer reviewed sources such as those published in academic journals, presented at international conferences or reports from national bodies. However, I have included a number of single teacher-based reports on the grounds that, if it worked for you in your classroom, I am likely to want to find out more and maybe try it out in mine. If research from your country is not included, I apologise, there wasn't space to include everything that is going on in this new and highly charged context. I apologise too, to those of you teaching children with Special Educational Needs, again there are many specialised apps and mobile learning activities for this group that I ran out of space to include.

Each chapter, except for the last, concludes with questions to trigger reflection and further discussion amongst readers. There are also some suggestions for further reading annotated with a few details about their background. My goal is that, for each reader, whatever their role, reading this book will raise their awareness of the potential for using mobile devices, even the students' own, to support student learning. However, the aim is also to share experiences of where things can go wrong and why mobile learning has become associated with unwanted behaviours in order to ensure that others taking onboard mobile learning initiatives are fully informed. If you would like to continue the discussion online I am @JocelynWish on Twitter and we can use the hashtag #mobilelearninginschools to link up our posts.

1 Introduction to this book

So, what actually is happening in respect of the use of mobile devices in schools today? Well, practice varies widely and is not really consistent even within school federations or districts, let alone countries. In 2015, two researchers, Clarke and Svanaes, working on behalf of an education research charity, pointed out that several countries have recently introduced large-scale mobile technology deployment schemes. These included Malaysia, India, Lebanon, Finland, the Netherlands, France, Northern Ireland, Scotland, Jamaica and Columbia. However, managing such large-scale deployment is not without its challenges and, in other countries including South Africa, Turkey, Thailand and the USA, such schemes have been delayed or even abandoned. Reasons for this include an inappropriate technical infrastructure, a lack of appropriate educational content, concerns for student wellbeing and cost. In these latter cases though, it appears that research was not used effectively to establish the parameters for successful adoption of technology in schools (Clarke and Svanaes, 2015). Hopefully this book will go some way to address that concern.

Currently, the mobile technology in schools spectrum includes: teachers using mobile phone video for professional development; schools that have been issued with a bookable class set of tablet computers such as iPads; teachers in schools where mobile phones are banned quietly suggesting students use their mobile phones to capture or support learning opportunities; students whose parents are required to supply them with tablet devices; and schools where students bring their mobile phones openly to class. It is recognised that teaching through mobile learning opportunities brings many challenges; indeed, Chapters 7 and 8 in this book discuss in detail both behavioural and ethical questions arising over the use of mobile devices in schools. Many schools and colleges, counties and states, even some countries, have banned mobile phones in their entirety. For some parents who consider such devices at best a distraction this is absolutely the right thing to do, yet for others, it is a waste of a valuable tool. Others focus on the fact that they can be used by parents or carers or even the school leadership to transmit essential information in an emergency. But what do the students themselves think?

In the USA, Thomas and Muñoz (2016) surveyed 628 high school students in a large urban school district to determine their perceptions of mobile phone use in the classroom. Their findings indicated that the majority of students (90.7%) were using a variety of mobile phone features for school-related work. This included everyday use of the calculator, accessing the internet, the calendar and the clock or timer. Also popular were educational apps, playing music and texting with email and watching video but were reported by fewer students. Student support for educational uses of their phones, however, was not universal. Only 73.8% of the students supported integrating mobile phones into classroom instruction, while 70.6% believed that mobile phones supported learning. It was clear that, while recognising their usefulness as educational tools, the students too had serious concerns about the disruptions caused by using mobile phones in the classroom and the potential for their inappropriate use. The same conflict reappears in schools across the globe. In a large-scale study of over 1,000 school students from South Africa, Porter et al. (2016) reported nearly three-quarters of them as saying that they have experienced some personal positive impact of mobile phone use towards doing well at school. However, only a slightly smaller proportion (70%) reported associated classroom disruption by their own or by another student's phone. In another recent but smaller survey, this time from Austria, Grimus and Ebner (2016) report students aged from 11 to 14 as recognising potential mobile phone-based learning opportunities such as internet search, use as a calculator, educational apps and tools, dictionaries and translators. Yet, by and large, the students did not associate use of their mobile phones with learning, with the majority reporting concerns over distraction and cheating. Though, that said, the boys also tended to report less handwriting and fewer books to carry as benefits. The situation is mirrored in Slovenia where, despite the fact that most of the students own a smartphone (and still more of them own a tablet), education that incorporates mobile learning is only spreading slowly (Ferko and Koreňová, 2015). Grimus and Ebner (2016) go on to note though that this is short-sighted; in Austria compulsory education ends at 15 and, if students haven't learned to use their phones productively by then, they are liable to miss out on lifelong learning opportunities. They conclude that students' perceptions of using mobile phone tools for formal and informal learning, as a part of their personal learning environment, needs to be part of education today. Indeed, UNESCO policy guidelines (West and Vosloo, 2013) suggest mobile technology is a powerful but often overlooked tool. It can support education in ways that were not possible before its arrival.

However, there are few studies that show measurable learning gains that can be confidently attributed to the use of mobile devices in schools and at least one, based on data from schools in four English cities, that found quite the opposite. When schools had a mobile phone ban in place there were associated small but statistically significant improvements in students' national test scores with the lowest-achieving students gaining twice as much as average students (Beland and Murphy, 2015). But then again, Cristol and Gimbert's (2013) evaluation study of 330 students from a Midwest US school district, though smaller, found statistically significantly higher recorded scores in state achievement assessments of students in the classes that utilised mobile learning devices on a regular basis. These included in reading and maths at 8th Grade and in social studies and science at 10th Grade. With these conflicting findings it appears that we need to look more closely at the different school policies and the actual types of uses being made of the devices. Interestingly, handheld tablet computers with much the same capabilities as smartphones usually gain a different reception. Haßler et al.'s (2016) critical review of research into the use of tablets by primary and secondary school children found the majority of studies described positive learning outcomes. Teachers in these studies appreciated in particular their ease of use, customisation and portability, alongside the integration of multiple features within a single touchscreen device.

In addition though, to these contradictory findings over attitudes to, practices with and opinions about the use of mobile devices in schools there has been long debate within the academic community as to what exactly mobile learning is and how to define it. I will detail this debate and its history in the next chapter; however, for the purposes of this book I am using the helpfully concise definition of mobile learning developed by Helen Crompton, an ex-school teacher now lecturing at a university in Virginia, USA, in which mobile learning is

> learning across multiple contexts, through social and content interactions, using personal electronic devices
>
> *(Crompton, 2013, p.4)*

These contexts can be real or virtual, thus mobile learning can be classroom based with, for example, the use of educational apps on iPads or outside class, capitalising on opportunities to capture and analyse data during field trips and museum or gallery visits. Chapter 2 also includes an introduction to the wide range of functions and tools on mobile devices that can and have been used to support learning, presenting the most characteristic opportunities in and challenges to their use. It is this wide range that also leads to the associated issues of distraction, disruption and possible behavioural or ethical concerns which have so concerned education professionals. These issues too are introduced.

In Chapters 3 and 4, to set the current scene for the reader, I present case study examples of the range of mobile learning initiatives that have occurred within the past few years in schools in different countries across the globe. These are organised as to whether they occur inside the classroom, outside class or, perhaps most usefully of all for the classroom teacher, bringing the outside, inside. For having students use mobile devices to deliver and/or capture task and context-relevant information at a particular location and then use that data to support a future lesson enables teachers to make the most of learning opportunities in authentic contexts. It does seem rather that science teachers have a head start in mobile learning here as many science curricula internationally involve students in considerable amounts of fieldwork which has always been supported with cameras, probes and other data logging devices. However, I have tried to include examples that represent a wider range of taught subjects. They include both teachers' own reports written up and published online for sharing with other practitioners and accounts of educational research-based initiatives taken from published academic journal papers or books.

Chapter 3 focuses on the background to using mobile devices in primary (elementary) school classrooms with younger students. At this age nearly all school-based mobile learning initiatives result from school- or district-based provision of mobile devices such as tablet computers like the iPad. Though, that said, only this week, I received a copy of the international journal *Technology, Pedagogy and Education* which includes a case study of the implementation of iPod Touches on a one-to-one basis in a Scottish primary school (Cornelius and Shanks, 2017). The researchers found that the students, by and large, used the devices sensibly and teachers' initial concerns about devices distracting students were not substantiated. The iPod Touches were quickly assimilated into existing classroom practice and the teachers' expectations in terms of them offering opportunities for resource provision, interactive learning and extension activities were fulfilled. However, some technical issues with the Wi-Fi provision remained and the hope that the initiative would lead to greater parental engagement with the children's' work was not realised. Teachers rarely set homework tasks that required the iPods and many students reported that they did not take the device home because they had an alternative device available there (Cornelius and Shanks, 2017). This study is an excellent example of the current 'glass half full or glass half empty' state of mobile learning in schools: it's nearly but not quite there and people's own views colour how they see it.

Chapter 4, which addresses mobile learning initiatives in secondary schools (middle, high and junior high schools), also includes bring your own device (BYOD) initiatives where schools capitalise on the increasing accessibility of using students' own mobile devices. Mobile phones have become widely available; World Bank data from 2015 shows an average 96.8% of the global population as having a cell phone subscription (World Bank, 2015). Though of course this is an average where people in some countries have more than one phone and, in others, none. The mean percentage of cell phone subscriptions per individual reported by the World Bank for high-income countries is 124% and, for low-income countries, it is 60%. In respect of children and young people it is most likely to be a parent or carer paying the phone bill; however, in Denmark, for example, a survey on behalf of the Groupe Speciale Mobile Association (GSMA) found over 80% of 9 year olds reported using smartphones (GSMA, 2015). This figure does illustrate one issue readers of this book need to bear in mind for, like some of the data sources used to evidence further chapters, GSMA could not be said to be entirely impartial. It is a trade body that represents the interests of mobile operators worldwide. However, even nonpartisan groups report high numbers of people with access to mobile phones; in 2016 the Pew Research Center calculated the global median average rate of ownership to be 88% (Pew Research Center, 2016). In addition, an earlier survey for the same centre had 73% of 2,000 US middle and high school teachers reporting that they and/or their students use their mobile phones in the classroom or to complete assignments (Purcell et al., 2013).

Chapters 3 and 4 also highlight differences between this BYOD model and providing tablets such as iPads on an 'organisation provided device' (OPD) model. There is much debate as to pros and cons of each; however, ultimately it depends on the school and its circumstances. Some initiatives whether BYOD or OPD have gone spectacularly wrong and in several cases the media has played a key role in magnifying individual concerns. For example, Male and Burden (2014) report an attempt to enable iPad purchase by parents for their children through a leasing scheme which fell foul of adverse media coverage based on the notion that education should remain free to students. Similarly, in New Zealand, Maas (2011) reports on the media headlines made across the country after a school told parents of all their Year 9 students that they needed to purchase an iPad 2. Another OPD initiative that made headlines was what has become known as the Los Angeles iPad debacle. Set up as a civil rights initiative designed to provide low-income students with devices available to their wealthier peers (Blume, 2015), the accompanying story of how insufficient technical planning for the hardware support networks and lack of engagement with the teachers and students who were to use the devices demonstrates well how mobile learning initiatives can go wrong.

In order to address this issue Chapters 5 and 6 discuss good practice in evaluating mobile learning and the necessity for accompanying teacher professional development with the aim of ensuring initiatives set off on the right foot. Chapter 5 focuses on how researchers have tackled the challenges arising when trying to follow learners, their learning activities and to identify any impact of the learning across locations within and beyond the school. As Sharples (2009) points out, such learning opportunities may involve multiple participants in different locations and who are using a variety of personal and institutional technologies that include home or classroom computers as well as tablets or phones. Nor does good practice have to involve an external evaluator; Kim (2014) found that teachers experienced in teaching with iPads regarded the ability to evaluate as a pedagogical skill needed to determine the usability of the iPads through assessing both teaching as a process and learning as an outcome. With this focus on ensuring good, or at least effective, practice Chapter 5 also includes an account of the learning theory principles that underpin the ways in which the different tools and functions on internet-connected mobile devices can support learning. These centre on the active, situated, authentic and visual learning opportunities often associated with the constructivist approach plus a greater role for the autonomous learner (with their device). Such principles are mirrored in the associated teaching practices and the three key pedagogical principles for mobile learning – collaboration, personalisation and authenticity put forward by Kearney et al. (2012) – are subsequently introduced.

Chapter 6 aims to exemplify the professional development needed for teachers so as to ensure their effectiveness in the case of a mobile learning initiative being introduced to a school together with any foreseeable challenges. So many research studies include the conclusion that further and often better training for the teachers involved would have made a big difference in how a school-based mobile learning initiative was received and implemented. It includes examples of professional development with both preservice teachers and experienced professionals faced with what is likely to be a profound change to their practice. Interestingly, O'Bannon and Thomas (2015) showed from a survey of 245 preservice teachers in the Midwest US that almost half the preservice teachers supported the use of mobile phones in the classroom whereas a quarter did not, leaving approximately one-third who reported they were uncertain. The preservice teachers perceived many features and/or functions of mobile phones as being useful in the classroom, but they identified access to the internet, clicker (classroom response system) capabilities, use of educational apps and use as an e-book reader as the most valuable. They perceived cheating, disruptions, cyberbullying and accessing inappropriate content as major barriers to the use of mobile phones in the classroom. These issues are all tackled in more detail in Chapter 8 of this book but first, what about the ethical considerations involved in using (and quite probably monitoring) mobile devices in the classroom?

Chapter 7 introduces the range of ethical questions that have impinged on mobile learning researchers' and practising teachers' concerns as they realise the extent of the opportunities afforded by mobile learning devices to merge public and private, real and virtual, home and school in what are hopefully 'seamless' (Milrad et al., 2013) learning opportunities. These concerns include boundary crossing for, as Pimmer and Gröhbiel (2013) note, mobile devices are easily carried between contexts, enabling information more usually restricted to one context to be accessed in another. Also privacy – as boundaries are crossed there are opportunities for teachers, or researchers observing students using their personal mobile devices, to infringe privacy. There is also ownership of data: whose data is on the mobile device or on the server and who owns it? This is a particular concern in respect of ownership of images and music and the need to obtain permissions from third parties. Then there is accessibility: students from different backgrounds may have more trouble than others sourcing a device or fielding data costs, and students' own awareness of their device capabilities such as what data is being logged by the different apps and who can view it. The chapter goes on to discuss support for teachers to address these concerns, firstly in the form of developing policy guidelines and secondly in the form of involving them in using ethics frameworks to generate their own scenario-based professional development.

Having a clear, up-to-date and well-communicated policy in place seems obvious; however, unless all stakeholders have signed up to it, it may well be a rod for the school's back. One target group, in my experience though, are clearly mindful of school guidelines and rules and that is student teachers. In an early exploration of the role of PDAs (personal digital assistants) in supporting learning to teach I found that the trainees were reluctant to use them as their students were banned by the schools from using mobile phones that were similar in appearance. So why are mobile phones banned, whether by the school, the district or even some countries such as Brunei and Sri Lanka? Chapter 8 discusses the issues of misbehaviour too often associated with mobile devices which range from small-scale disruption to active cyberbullying and include their potential use for cheating and downloading inappropriate material such as pornography. These issues, fed by all too frequent headlines in the media about students uploading and sharing images from the classroom, or downloading inappropriate material to show others in class, quite possibly lie at the heart of our difficulty in developing teaching with the support of mobile technologies. As Thomas (2008) points out, school personnel ban things they believe a) encourage students to adopt improper moral values or b) waste time that should be spent pursuing the school's learning goals. While both of these can be applied to the case of mobile phones teachers have not always had effective support or training for mobile learning.

One major factor in school-based teaching that teachers often prioritise over learning about new tools and pedagogies is the current assessment regime. Clearly, teachers internationally need to focus on preparing their students for their country's national assessments. These summative tests usually take place at key transitions such as between primary and secondary school or on leaving school in preparation for higher education or the workplace. However, Chapter 9 highlights the potential role for mobile devices in formative assessment through capturing a student's learning progress for teacher feedback. Such Assessment for Learning (Black and Wiliam, 1998) opportunities capitalise on the versatility of mobile phones or tablets running apps that can convert them into a variety of assessment tools. These include classroom response systems (clickers), creative multimedia tools to make slideshows, animations and videos or, more simply, the camera. As for summative assessment, Chapter 9 goes on to discuss the current international interest in what have become known as the 21st century skills and whether there is a need to develop new summative assessment mechanisms for the BYOD era. It concludes by considering the potential implications of using mobile devices on a large scale for digital assessment and the associated long-term data storage needed.

The final chapter, Chapter 10, aims to draw together the different themes addressed in the earlier chapters in order to identify clear recommendations for teaching learners equipped with mobile devices whether in the classroom or where the learners are truly mobile. For as Wang (2016) highlights, classroom teachers need information most of all, they are especially concerned about managing classes with mobile devices, evaluating whether a mobile learning initiative would be seen as worthwhile and worrying about its consequences. Moreover, they are concerned about how to refocus and optimise their teaching practice to include the mobile technology. Chapter 10, therefore, presents a number of conclusions for practice drawn from both the findings of the developments reported in the preceding chapters and other published experiences of mobile learning initiatives. It also acknowledges issues caused by the new technology itself failing, or being inaccessible to some, and considers three different possible future scenarios and their implications for teachers and teaching. These include: where all schools supply handheld devices, where schools allow students to bring their own and where mobile devices, whether phones or tablets, are banned from or unemployed in classroom use.

Questions

- What aspects of or support for learning do you use your own personal mobile device(s) for?
- Would you encourage your students to do likewise?
- Is the need to allow use of personal digital devices in schools inevitable?

Annotated further reading

- 21st-century technology in schools

Male, T. and Burden, K. (2014). Access denied? Twenty-first-century technology in schools. *Technology, Pedagogy and Education, 23*(4), 423–437.

In this journal article Trevor Male and Kevin Burden draw upon research that took place for three different commissioned mobile learning initiatives that took place during 2012–2013 to point out the accompanying challenges that stemmed from parents, schools, policy-makers and the students themselves. Firstly, there was the evaluation of a pilot iPad project in 11 Scottish schools that allowed students personal use of iPads including, in many instances, the right to take them home. Next they engaged in a similar evaluation in a major city in Scotland where three schools undertook a pilot project involving the use of personal Android OS or Windows-based digital devices (again, with the right to take them home). Both projects also employed interviews with head teachers and project leaders within the schools as well as online baseline and exit surveys of students, teachers and parents from which quantitative data were accumulated. Advisory staff and senior personnel from the local authorities involved were also interviewed. Quantitative data derived from these two evaluations were supplemented by a third survey conducted with a large comprehensive school in London. In total, 1,017 students, ranging from the final two years of primary school age through to sixth-formers, completed their online survey.

2 Introducing mobile learning and the associated issues

2.1 Early mobile learning opportunities

The concept of mobile learning came into being alongside the 21st century and was largely driven by the new learning opportunities offered by personal, portable technology that could connect to the internet via mobile phone networks or wireless networking. In schools in various countries innovative work with handheld mobile devices known also as personal digital assistants (PDAs), such as Palm Pilots (launched in 1997) and Windows Pocket PCs (launched in 2000), was taking place. These devices, forerunners of today's smartphones, had similar functionality but were slower with poorer battery life and lower screen resolution. In the USA, for example, over 100 teachers from different states participated in the Palm Education Pioneers (PEP) programme (Vahey and Crawford, 2002) and their reports were overwhelmingly positive about the use of PDAs in their classrooms. Approximately 90% of the teachers in the trial considered them to be an effective instructional tool. It was found that teachers who had explored using the handheld PDAs for science teaching or for writing-based activities reported them as the most effective in supporting learning.

In school science a typical lesson with the handheld PDAs centred on data logging, e.g. using sensors (known in the USA as probes) connected to a Palm Pilot. For example, Vahey and Crawford (2002) discuss an environmental study where the science teacher used sensing probes connected to handheld computers with a group of high school students to collect on-site data such as pH, temperature and dissolved oxygen content to determine the water quality at different points along a nearby river. Sensing probes can, of course, also be used with handhelds inside the classroom; Metcalf and Tinker (2004) report from the Technology Enhanced Elementary Middle and Secondary Science (TEEMSS) project that students' science learning was enhanced through the use of the probes and handheld computers. Here the focus was on data logging from practical experiments on forces and energy transfers conducted within the science classroom. Participating teachers reported that students engaged in watching the graphs appearing on the screen of the mobile device as data were recorded were clearly making connections between the observed phenomenon and the graph produced, which helped them to develop understanding and to confront misconceptions.

As for writing-based activities, reports from the PEP teachers highlighted the way having a PDA always to hand enabled effective note-taking with increased accuracy and legibility. For example, in a high school journalism class students used the handheld PDAs to devise questions for an interview, to research and store factual information on their subject and then later expanded on these notes to create an article for the school district newsletter (Vahey and Crawford, 2002). This increased the reliability of information being written up to the point where newsletter issues contained no factual errors. When the English department head evaluated the changed newspaper they reported an improvement in imaginative language or interesting sentence structures, although there was no observable decrease in grammatical errors. Also, by the end of the trial year, the teachers of the journalism class had begun using the handhelds as a device for communicating with the students about their work. Vahey and Crawford (2002) also highlight, in another initiative in a middle school, the way handheld PDAs allowed students who found writing difficult through dyslexia or sensorimotor problems to build upon the ideas that they had already typed, without the pain and frustration of rewriting the piece over again, using pen and paper.

Elsewhere the collaborative learning opportunities offered through using handheld PDAs to communicate via the school's Wi-Fi network were the focus of classroom research initiatives. In Chile, for example, Zurita and Nussbaum (2004) found that using a specially written app on their handhelds supported elementary school children (6–7 years old) working in small groups on either maths- or language-based problems through strengthening their ability to organise the material being learned, raising the level of social negotiation and communication among the group members (thus facilitating coordination between the task component activities) and encouraging the members' mobility within the classroom. In fact, when comparing the use of the handhelds for mobile computer supported collaborative learning (MCSL) to similar collaborative learning exercises using cards there were noticeable improvements in all aspects of the activities observed in both the maths and the language learning tasks.

In England, Becta, the public organisation funded by the Department for Education of the time that was responsible for promotion and integration of information and communications technology (ICT) in education, commissioned an evaluation of the early use of PDAs in schools (Perry, 2003). Over two phases this project involved 31 schools (2 infant schools with children of 7 years or under, 18 primary schools, that is for children under 11 years, 9 secondary schools with students aged from 11 upwards, a special school and a middle school). However, finding ways to use the PDAs in the classroom for supporting student learning was a challenge for the teachers in the schools involved. There were some positively reported examples such as note-taking on colours in the school garden for an English lesson on poetry writing and a family learning and literacy project that involved note-taking and making recordings and taking them home to continue with in primary schools. In secondary schools using a free app to monitor body fat in physical education in Years 10 and 11 (students aged 14–16) and using the camera for photos and video as well as note-taking in design technology were reported. However, the PDAs were used primarily by both students and teachers for administrative or organisational purposes, such as to do lists, homework deadlines, timetables and so on. While one teacher reported 'I would never willingly go without one now; it is my instantly accessible encyclopaedia, thesaurus, periodic table, diary, register/mark book, world map and even star chart!' (Perry, 2003, p.6) there were only a few users with this level of competence. It was clear that the amount of time each user had to explore the PDA had a direct impact on their amount of use of and commitment to PDAs. Many low-frequency users quoted a lack of training as the main reason for their lack of progress.

Other early worldwide mobile learning initiatives tended to focus on the potential for handheld mobile devices to support out of school learning. Malliou et al. (2004) describe how high school students in Greece and Crete used PDAs to enrich their learning during history field trips to museums and ancient sites such as the Parthenon. Handhelds were used by the students both to augment their understanding through accessing extra information when on site and to work collaboratively with a second, school-based peer group to capture relevant material to work further on when back in school. Similarly, in Sardinia researchers worked with teachers to add PDA-based quizzes to test students' new knowledge on a school history visit to an archaeological site (Pintus et al., 2004). The learning materials were triggered using GPS to identify when the student had moved into a 'hot spot'. It was reported that the students found it more interesting to have a direct contact with what they were studying and the competition among classmates to complete the quizzes was an exciting incentive. Researchers in Taiwan worked with elementary school students (Grades 4 to 6) at nearby bird watching centres (Chen et al., 2003). As well as having students use the PDAs to record what they saw, the teacher messaged them information and bird images to engage them in the activity. Students using this system were found, on return to the classroom, to have learned more than others using a standard guidebook. Secondary students in a similar project in Hong Kong used the 40 minutes' travel time between school and the bird watching station effectively to review video and other preparatory material on the birds they would see (So, 2004). In Singapore, Zhang et al. (2006) report primary school students who had not previously used handheld computers using PDAs confidently during an environmental awareness project that involved using the PDAs to record customer interviews and collect data on amount of packaging used at a local supermarket and a fast food restaurant.

Actually, as Mattila and Fordell (2005) remind us, a PDA-based learning environment includes the school, and possibly the home, computers as information can easily be transferred via Wi-Fi, GPRS or Bluetooth between all three. They describe how that, after visits to nearby locations of interest to the subjects being studied in school, Finnish primary school students (aged 11–12 years) were able to edit the observations they had recorded using PDAs and work together to construct mind maps on school desktop computers to show their learning in relation to the new observations and existing material. In the USA though a big draw for classroom investment in PDAs was the opportunity for 1:1 computing, and Eliot Soloway and colleagues at the University of Michigan designed a curriculum-based mobile learning environment (MLE) for Palm Pilots which was later enhanced and badged as 'GoKnow!'. It originally included a cut-down word processor, a sketching tool to create animations, a brainstorming tool, an archive and application manager to enable teachers to manage student files and simulation games (Vath et al., 2005). This became popular with early PDA users who were mainly from the USA but included a small international community. For example, Murray (2006) used Palm Lifedrive PDAs and the GoKnow! tools with Year 9 in an Australian grammar school for collaborative story writing and brainstorming in an English language curriculum enrichment course as well as for supporting them in organising their learning. This latter study also highlighted the key role played by the class teacher in whether the mobile devices were used effectively or not. They were also trialled successfully in the UK in the Bristol Hand-eLearning project reported on in the British Educational Communications and Technology agency's (Becta) overview of ways forward for using mobile devices in schools (McFarlane et al., 2009).

These small-scale early initiatives though were not sustained. Not only were they hindered by multiple technical issues but, having been triggered by developments in new technologies that enabled handheld, personal computing devices, they have been dogged by changes in available technologies ever since. With manufacturers following a business-led model ensuring frequent software updates and mobile devices changing almost annually it has been hard for curriculum-centred mobile learning projects to keep up. Also, as Ng and Cumming (2015) point out in the preface to their edited text on sustaining mobile learning, to bring about a mobile learning initiative, an educational institution is usually required to make a substantial investment. This will be in curriculum design, in technical support, in staff professional development and in supporting infrastructure (Wi-Fi and software applications) even if not investing in the mobile devices themselves. Yet the tremendous increase internationally in mobile phone ownership over the past decade (Pew Research Center (2016) report a global median average of 88% of adults as now owning a mobile phone) has led to increased numbers of 'bring your own device' (BYOD) schemes in schools. The Pew Research Center (2016) survey of 45,435 respondents from 40 different countries also found that a global median average of 43% report that they own a smartphone, and with younger people being more likely than older generations to own a smartphone, this can result in students having personal access to more sophisticated digital devices than the school can afford to provide.

However, returning to those early PDAs, even with their poor battery life and consequent data loss if their owner was not careful to keep them charged, the teachers in the PEP project reported that, when using them, students are 'more engaged in learning and often find their own ways to use the handhelds to support their learning, both in and out of class' (Vahey and Crawford, 2002, p.15). Vahey and Crawford (2002) go on to report that when students are also able to take handheld computers home, the enhanced access further facilitates students keeping their work organised and makes the handheld a more 'personal' device.

Thus in the examples presented above we can see the roots of mobile learning in schools; that is opportunities to use a portable, handheld mobile device with connectivity to other devices and the internet for schoolwork whether inside the classroom, at home or for field study. However, a shared understanding of exactly what constitutes mobile learning has been trickier to realise.

2.2 Characteristics and functions of mobile devices that support learning

Mobile technology-based educational opportunities and definitions of mobile learning are constantly evolving, as will be discussed in the next section of this chapter. However, they tend to fall into two groups: those that focus on the technology, the device being used and those that focus on the context and structure of the associated learning opportunities. So first, what is it about these devices that captures the imagination of so many education professionals but can alienate others?

Mobile learning pioneers John Traxler and Agnes Kukulska-Hulme highlight the following characteristics of mobile devices as being key to their ability to support, to enable and to enhance learning in and across different contexts.

- The essential portability of the device.
- Connectivity for spontaneous communication and collaboration.
- Beaming of stored information from device to device.
- Location-awareness, giving instant information about objects within sight.
- Portable sound-recording and voice-recording.
- Cameras for taking photos and making video clips.

(Traxler and Kukulska-Hulme, 2005 p.31)

Interestingly, Traxler and Kukulska-Hulme (2005) don't include what is probably the most frequently used aspect of connectivity – to access information on the internet for revision and research. They go on to highlight the importance of the Personal Information Management (PIM) functionality within most mobile devices which can easily be appropriated to support learning, for example, by providing course timetables and teaching locations, academic regulations, assessment rubrics and deadlines. At the next level of functionality, Traxler and Kukulska-Hulme (2005) describe various software applications (apps) that have specifically academic or pedagogic uses.

However, rather than list functions of individual devices and apps, I will introduce the learning opportunities or learning potentials associated with them for, as Wu et al. (2012) note, while past research tended to focus on mobile phones and PDAs, there is an increasing range of devices being utilised for mobile learning. It may add to the teachers' planning load, however, thinking through how the available technologies can be used to realise the intended learning opportunities will help focus on the pedagogy rather than the technology. Often such a learning opportunity linked to a particular characteristic or function of a mobile device is referred to as an 'affordance' after Gibson (1979) who pointed out that perception of an object leads to some course of action in relation to it. For example, a camera on a mobile phone is said to 'afford' learning opportunities that are supported by having a visual record, e.g. height of plants in a science investigation or artefacts viewed on a museum trip. In a recent investigation Parsons et al. (2016) asked primary and secondary teachers participating in a part-time post graduate certificate course in digital and collaborative learning in New Zealand about the affordances of mobile devices for learning. They found that amongst the 72 respondents, as shown in Figure 2.1 opposite, most use of mobile devices by teachers outside specific apps for teaching results from learning opportunities linked to using the camera.

Just under half of these teachers, who were, admittedly, motivated practitioners seeking to learn more about using digital technology in teaching, reported regularly using mobile phones with their students at least 10% of the time in their classroom teaching. Over two-thirds of them had used tablets at least as often.

There is also a myriad apps that are specifically designed around the 1:1 affordance of mobile devices allowing teachers to include an extensive range of elearning opportunities in the classroom via mobile devices. In particular, using class sets of tablets has become popular in schools in countries where Wi-Fi in schools is accessible and affordable. Teachers appreciate in particular their multiple functions: in one Portuguese language teacher's class, for example, students have researched information on the web; consulted online dictionaries, answered quizzes and taken tests; taken and shared their notes and ideas; read literary works; created concept maps and collaborative word clouds; discussed via chat; written short stories; created videos and taken pictures to illustrate their work; accessed email to send and receive school messages and

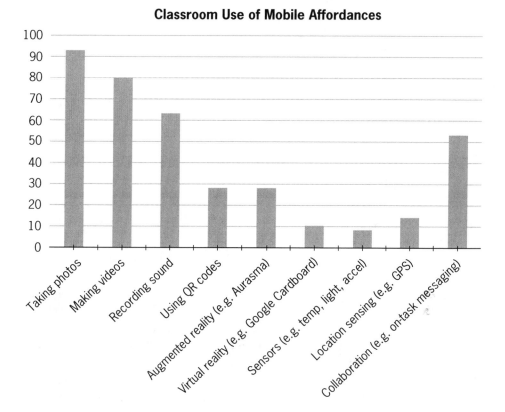

Figure 2.1 Potential affordances of mobile devices for school-based learning

work and created QR codes with slogans (Moura, 2015). Many similar examples will be described in the following chapters of this book; however, first, I want to clarify what we understand by mobile learning.

2.3 Defining mobile learning

There have been a number of attempts to define mobile learning in the past two decades stemming from the almost simultaneous development of mobile learning in schools and colleges and mobile work-based training opportunities. Pioneers from both higher education and business introduced us to the term 'mobile learning' in the year 2000. In the UK, Mike Sharples published a framework for the design of personal mobile technologies for lifelong learning (Sharples, 2000) in a well-established academic journal. In the USA, in an online magazine targeted at the 'New Economy', Clark Quinn announced a working definition of mlearning (short for mobile elearning) – using a Palm OS personal digital assistant as a learning device (Quinn, 2000). So, for Quinn, mobile learning was elearning delivered via mobile computational devices, which, at the time, were Palms, Windows CE machines and some digital mobile phones. However, Sharples' work focused more on the role of the learner than the technology and, with colleagues, he developed the definition of mobile learning to be used by MOBIlearn, the first large international research project to explore the landscape of and potential for mobile learning. This was:

> Any sort of learning that happens when the learner is not at a fixed, predetermined location, or learning that happens when the learner takes advantage of the learning opportunities offered by mobile technologies.
>
> *(O'Malley et al., 2003, p.7)*

This was insightful as the technology available in mobile devices changed rapidly over the following years; however, the contrast in the two approaches has been an issue for researchers seeking clarity over the concept of mobile learning ever since. Another early authority, Agnes Kukulska-Hulme, recognised the challenge as she wrote in her introduction to the first *Handbook of Mobile Learning* edited with John Traxler:

> Readers will probably position themselves differently in their own definitions of mobile learning, as indeed do the various contributors to this book: there are many ways to conceptualize, theorize about and experiment with mobile learning.
>
> *(Kukulska-Hulme and Traxler, 2005, p.5)*

Yet, by and large, the community of researchers and innovators in mobile learning have not been content with this eclectic approach and continued to define and redefine mobile learning. Changes to these definitions have been regularly prompted by the ever-increasing range and contexts where mobile devices can be used. There is also a lack of shared agreement over terms with researchers using m-learning or mlearning interchangeably. Brown (2005) describes this expanding context as the background to his placing of mlearning firmly as a subset of elearning but one that provides 'more mobility, flexibility and convenience' (p.10).

One of the most widely cited definitions gains credence from the authors' association of it with their aim to develop a widely applicable theory of mobile learning relevant to the broad range of learning opportunities available in the 21st century. Sharples et al. (2007) point out that the first step in developing a theory of mobile learning, surely, is to distinguish what is special about mobile learning compared to other types of learning activity. Their obvious answer is that it starts from the assumption that learners are continually on the move. Thus their definition of mobile learning as:

> the processes of coming to know through conversations across multiple contexts amongst people and personal interactive technologies
>
> *(Sharples et al., 2007, p.4)*

reflects the dynamic, changing nature of mobile learning contexts and the authors' conception of learning as an interaction within a system.

Other definitions, not unsurprisingly, also reflect their authors' predominant conceptions such as this one emphasising productivity by Wexler et al. (2008) that was aimed at elearning professionals in the USA and presented in a report for the elearning Guild exploring what mlearning is, why it matters and how to incorporate it into a learning strategy. Thus the elearning Guild defines mobile learning (or m-learning) as follows:

Any activity that allows individuals to be more productive when consuming, interacting with, or creating information, mediated through a compact digital portable device that the individual carries on a regular basis, has reliable connectivity, and fits in a pocket or purse.

(Wexler et al., 2008, p.7)

Another US-based professional association, Educause, that was formed to serve the interest of the higher education information technology community also starts their definition of mlearning with a technological focus; however, it then moves on to restate the importance of mobility emphasising learning opportunities outside the traditional classroom.

Using portable computing devices (such as laptops, tablet PCs, PDAs, and smart phones) with wireless networks enables mobility and mobile learning, allowing teaching and learning to extend to spaces beyond the traditional classroom. Within the classroom, mobile learning gives instructors and learners increased flexibility and new opportunities for interaction. Mobile technologies support learning experiences that are collaborative, accessible, and integrated with the world beyond the classroom.

This definition also includes mobile technology enabled collaborative learning experiences, a notion also introduced by Sharples et al. (2007) as a new pattern of mobile learning. However, for Educause the focus on mobility of mobile learning as 'an essential defining attribute – is beyond dispute' as Oller (2012, p.1) pointed out in a research bulletin on the future of mobile learning created specifically for Educause.

However, this view is not endorsed by all within the mobile learning community. John Traxler, in reflection on both the content of this debate and its length, notes, 'After extended discussions within the mobile learning research community about the definition, it is probably just "learning with mobile devices"' (Traxler, 2011, p.4). Though he then immediately defines four key ways in which mobile learning opportunities can enhance, extend and enrich both the concept and the activity of learning itself. He labels the first as contingent mobile learning and teaching, where learners can use personal, mobile devices to react and respond to their environment and their changing experiences both inside and outside the classroom. This would include subject specific apps and virtual learning environments (VLEs). The second is situated learning, where learning takes place in surroundings that make learning meaningful. Traxler (ibid.) exemplifies this with the examples of learning religious studies while visiting temples, mosques, churches and synagogues or learning about biodiversity on a field trip. This links to his third category of mobile learning opportunities, which are those that enable authentic learning, where learning tasks are meaningfully related to immediate learning goals. This could include recording data, whether from sensors, the camera or making notes to support project-based learning. The fourth is context aware learning, where learning is informed by information on the history and/or surroundings of the learner, for example, in art galleries, botanical gardens and museums that is delivered via their device.

Other areas noted by Traxler (2011) where mobile learning is enriching the learner experience include location-specific student support systems such as the open source Mobile Oxford and

My Mobile Bristol applications. These systems enable students at Oxford and Bristol universities in the UK to find any information they need, such as, for example, which bus to take them to the library holding the book they want at a particular moment in time, even allowing for multiple buses and multiple copies of the book being lent and returned at different libraries. Schools have yet to emulate this; however, many offer learning management information and tools via VLEs that are mobile device compatible such as those based on the Frog or Moodle learning platforms.

This wealth of learning opportunities afforded via mobile devices goes some way to demonstrate why the community has found it so hard to settle on a single, agreed definition of mobile learning. One of the latest, devised for UNESCO, tries to cover these multiple aspects.

> Mobile learning involves the use of mobile technology, either alone or in combination with other information and communication technology (ICT), to enable learning anytime and anywhere. Learning can unfold in a variety of ways: people can use mobile devices to access educational resources, connect with others, or create content, both inside and outside classrooms. Mobile learning also encompasses efforts to support broad educational goals such as the effective administration of school systems and improved communication between schools and families.
>
> *(UNESCO, 2015)*

Others have even announced that mobile learning is undefinable. Winters (2006), reflecting on the Big Issues in Mobile Learning workshop held by the pan-European Kaleidoscope Network of Excellence in 2006, reports 'there was general agreement that a precise definition of mobile learning is unattainable' (Winters, 2006, p.6). The expert group discussions moved on instead to propose four key characteristics of mobile learning. These included:

- that it enables knowledge building by learners in different contexts;
- that it enables learners to construct understandings;
- mobile technology often changes the pattern of learning/work activity; and
- the context of mobile learning is about more than time and space.

This stands in stark contrast to a recent, much more succinct, definition put forward by Helen Crompton in her historical overview of mobile learning in the recent, almost encyclopaedic, *Handbook of Mobile Learning* published by Routledge. She defines mobile learning as

> learning across multiple contexts, through social and content interactions, using personal electronic devices.
>
> *(Crompton, 2013, p.4)*

Others take a different approach, aiming to frame (Koole, 2009) or categorise mobile learning (Park, 2011), thus avoiding the need to first wrestle with a definition. Koole's model, developed as a basis for assessing the effectiveness of mobile devices for distance learning, makes it clear that she defines mobile learning in terms of three distinct aspects: the device (technology and usability), the learner (their knowledge, experience and attitude) and the social (sociocultural context). These aspects overlap and considering what happens at the intersections of these aspects will usefully inform the design of different mobile learning opportunities. For Koole, therefore, mobile learning is a combination of the interactions between learners, their devices, and other people. However, this conceptual model does not acknowledge the potential mobility of the learner whose technology enables them to use information and data from one context in another.

Park's (2011) aim is similar to Koole's (2009) in that the purpose of her categorisation of the educational applications of mobile technologies is to support instructional designers of open and distance learning in understanding the concepts of mobile learning and how mobile technologies can be incorporated into their teaching and learning more effectively. This categorisation is based on a modified approach to transactional distance theory that includes opportunities for social mediation as a separate dimension to the transactional distance between learner and the source of that which is to be learned.

Transactional distance itself is a concept based on the pedagogical, psychological and geographical space between instructor and learner introduced to distance learning by Moore (1997). It centres on the interactions between the learners, the learning resources, their tutor or instructor and their environment. The transactional distance itself is controlled and managed by three interrelated factors: (1) the taught programme's structure; (2) the dialogue that the teacher and learners exchange; and (3) the extent of the learners' autonomy. To this Park (ibid.) added a third factor, social mediation, acknowledging the potential for collaboration via mobile technologies. Whether learners are working individually or collectively in a group was termed individualised mlearning or socialised mlearning respectively. This results in four categories: (1) high transactional distance socialised mlearning in classroom-based, group activities; (2) high transactional distance individualised mlearning where there is instructional support or tightly structured content and resources such as in 'flipped learning' homework tasks set to prepare students for a lesson; (3) low transactional distance socialised mlearning which as loosely managed, unstructured group work is rarer; and (4) low transactional distance individualised mlearning such as outside classroom, individual informal learning opportunities such as those involved in Citizen Science projects. Yet, as Park (ibid.) herself acknowledges, though it is obscured by the emphasis on creating the four-category model, transactional distance is, in fact, a continuum rather than discrete categories.

The approach of expanding the concept of mobile learning into a continuum was also taken up by Sharples (2013) in an overview of mobile learning research and practice written for the distance education community in China. He moves away from seeking to define what has, despite the efforts described above, become a nebulous concept that is difficult to seize and presents mobile learning on a continuum. This continuum or dimension, as Sharples (ibid.) labels it, extends from enhancing classroom learning via devices such as handheld response systems and tablets to learning as part of everyday life through informal communication and knowledge sharing by mobile phone. Thus it extends from curriculum-led learning opportunities in a fixed setting to informal, highly mobile learning opportunities. However, on closer inspection it actually comprises two dimensions, from the formal (curriculum based) to the informal (interest or hobby led) and from fixed (in a classroom) to mobile (in the field, crossing contexts) that can be represented orthogonally as shown in Figure 2.2 overleaf.

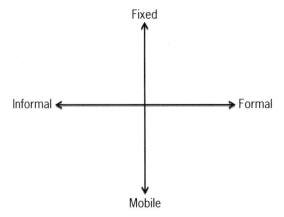

Figure 2.2 Two possible dimensions of mobile learning

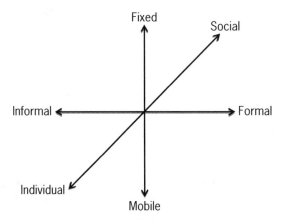

Figure 2.3 Three possible dimensions of mobile learning

If we add in the individualised-socialised dimension as proposed by Park (2011) we have a three-dimensional model that encompasses a myriad opportunities to engage in learning via personal, mobile technologies as shown in Figure 2.3 above.

However, this book focuses on formal learning environments in schools worldwide so we will be discussing both individual and collaborative mobile learning opportunities as well as those taking place in the classroom and outside school on location. While school learning environments vary massively both within and between countries, they share key features. These include a set curriculum that guides the organisation of teaching schedules where learning is assessed at certain key points through national qualifications and a focus on behaviour as well as learning itself. These can act as constraints on the way mobile devices are used in schools, if they are at all, for, in quite a few regions, concerns over or potential issues with using mobile devices have led to their exclusion from schools. These, and other challenges to the use of mobile technology in schools, are introduced in the next section.

2.4 Issues in mobile learning

Potential issues with and challenges to implementing mobile learning in schools were also identified in the early years. The small size of mobile devices and their portability, their key affordance for mobile learning, also means a number of design compromises. This is particularly obvious when considering how a mobile phone outputs information, on screen or via a speaker. While today's smartphone screen resolutions are around ten times as good as that of the early PDAs the screen size remains small and capable of displaying only limited information. Though as to whether this issue impacts on learning depends very much on the user's perceptions and the task at hand. Van t'Hooft (2006) reports younger children as having less trouble with small screens and, in an overall report of the same study, Swan et al. (2005) note how receptive elementary school children were to using the PDAs. Students said that they preferred using the mobile devices over writing by hand and that using them for writing assignments made the work 'easier' and 'more fun'. This was especially true of less able students. Today, with larger devices such as iPads and other tablet PCs being trialled in schools, screen size is much less of an issue; however, the device will no longer fit into a pocket. This can be an issue too for the new 'phablet' devices that are halfway between a phone and a tablet in size.

Educational apps can get around the screen limitation on small devices by providing key information via sound; however, the small speaker on board a typical mobile device means it needs either to be held to the head to hear audio or used with earphones. This type of information delivery is useful for location-based mobile learning where learners are moving around particular sites, e.g. for history or geography, though we should be mindful of safety considerations. Listening to a recording may impair attention to other incoming sounds such as those made by traffic. When evaluating a mobile city game, designed to teach 13 year olds about history through visiting key locations in Amsterdam, Huizenga et al. (2009) ensured that the teams of students were accompanied by adult guides to oversee their safety.

Information input appears to be less of an issue, especially now touch screens have led to the demise of the, all too easily lost, PDA stylus. Even in the early studies (Swan et al., 2005; McFarlane et al., 2009) it was frequently found that students would use mobile devices willingly to make notes, take pictures and record audio or video. Though, that said, teachers should note that they are not suitable for entering text in quantities. Syvänen and Nokelainen (2005) introduce us to the need to plan mobile learning opportunities around both technical usability (ease of operating the device) and pedagogical usability (effective instructional design) to take account of the special features of mobile learning materials and environments. Apart from ongoing concerns over battery life, most of the early technical usability challenges have been met and many students come to school with relevant experience gained with iPods, Kindles and games consoles as well as phones. However, issues for pedagogical usability reported by Syvänen and Nokelainen (2005) such as learner control, motivation and methods for providing feedback still form a central challenge.

Control itself is a key issue for mobile learning with teachers fearing a loss of control over student learning where they cannot physically see what is on the screen of a student's mobile device (McFarlane et al., 2009) and learners regularly reporting improved engagement through the increased levels of autonomy presented. As early as 2002 Mike Sharples (2002, p.518) pointed out that using handheld mobile devices in school may become a 'zone of conflict between teachers and learners, with both trying to wrest control, not only of the physical device but also the opportunities it affords for managing and monitoring learning'. Mifsud (2002) highlights the impact of the prevailing culture that still exists in many school classrooms, where communication is mainly 'controlled' by the teacher and punctuated by raised hands from students wishing to contribute to a school- or classroom-related discussion. She points out that using mobile devices challenges 'this power that the teacher has over communication – easily seen in the students' sending of messages to each other, across the physical boundaries of the classroom, and without the "permission" of the teacher' (Mifsud, 2002, p.114). Occasional inappropriate use of handhelds was one of the drawbacks reported by teachers in the final Palm Education Pioneers' Report (Vahey and Crawford, 2002). Examples cited included games being played during class time, downloading inappropriate materials and inappropriate use of beaming (for passing notes, cheating on tests and 'copying' by handing in assignments beamed from other students).

More recently, cybersafety concerns such as children sharing personal details and images, accidentally accessing inappropriate material and even online or phone-based cyberbullying have arisen. Indeed, West (2012) points out that online safety is often cited as one of the reasons mobile technologies should be banned from schools; however, he goes on to point out that 'the reality is that mobile devices are so powerful and widely available that students will use them regardless of whether schools decide to embrace them' (West, 2012, p.15). He notes that teachers are best placed to help students learn to embrace mobile learning opportunities responsibly and safely. West's (ibid.) conclusions are informed through a review of more than 60 mobile learning initiatives from Africa, Asia, Europe, North and South America conducted for UNESCO. Research for this review even identified several examples of how mobile phones have been employed to improve student safety.

For example, instant communication via mobile devices can help protect students when a school needs to go into 'lockdown' because of a perceived threat, particularly important should an emergency situation arise between lessons. Other examples presented by UNESCO (West, 2012) are more commonplace: schools around the world send text messages to parents informing them when children are absent, alerting parents to a potentially dangerous situation, and mobile phones have been used in various projects to inform young people about safe sex and the dangers of drugs. It is thought that mobile devices are especially effective for these types of messages because

> they are usually private; students can read, for example, informational text messages about an issue that is culturally or socially sensitive without others being aware of what they are doing.
> *(West, 2012, p.15)*

In a review of, mostly US-based, journalistic accounts, survey data, published reports, interviews and his own focus group data to explore how personal mobile technology is changing the educational experience, Katz (2005) classifies problems generated by mobile phone use by students in educational settings into four groups. These are: disruption of class; delinquency (theft and bullying); chicanery (cheating and plagiarism); and erosion of teacher autonomy. Yet these groupings largely result from student behaviour and not the technology per se and we need to look to more effective teacher professional development to enable them to work confidently and competently with mobile devices so as to ensure their potential to support learning effectively is realised.

Indeed, West (2012) emphasises that teachers are crucial to mobile learning, pointing out that most of the mobile learning projects reviewed for UNESCO required more expertise and skill on the part of teachers, not less. The associated need for supportive professional development was clearly demonstrated in a number of the early mobile learning projects projects (McFarlane et al., 2009) and it is good to see that lessons have been learned. For example, West (2012) describes the Text2Teach initiative from the Philippines, which employs mobile phones along with video clips to help primary-school teachers plan and deliver engaging lessons aligned with national curricula. Pedagogical training, not technical know-how, constitutes the central focus of this programme with the trainers showing teachers how to integrate the videos into lessons in ways that facilitate inquiry-based and collaborative learning. Though, that said, overcoming technical issues is also covered. In addition, each video is accompanied by a suggested lesson plan, intended to reduce rather than add to teachers' workloads. Teachers are encouraged to use the mobile phones and social media to share ideas, discuss problems and quiz other colleagues in the Text2Teach programme with the aim of building communities of practice. Teachers report liking the programme because it makes their challenging jobs a bit simpler.

Providing feedback and assessing learning are also central to the role of teachers. Syvänen and Nokelainen (2005) included methods for providing feedback to students under pedagogical usability issues relevant to mobile learning, for some early projects (Vahey and Crawford, 2002; McFarlane et al., 2009) reported problems with teachers' access to students' digitally produced work. Either they couldn't see the work on the mobile device screens to check it or easily access student document files once submitted. Seeing what is being displayed on a student's mobile device can still be an issue; however, school investment in VLEs and teachers' increased experience with computer file structures means accessing student work is no longer problematic. Other ways of providing formative feedback have taken off with both tablets and mobile phones being widely used with apps such as Socrative or Kahoot as classroom response systems in schools (Admiraal et al., 2016) and teachers collating their students' mobile phone video clips to review later (Ekanayake and Wishart, 2014a). Online quizzes and revision websites are also popular with many, such as BBC Bitesize, specifically tailored for delivery via mobile devices.

There is also the issue of assessing or evaluating the impact of the mobile devices themselves upon learning. Sharples (2009) points out that this is problematic because the very nature of mobile learning means the learning under scrutiny may be spread across locations and times. Not only that but evidence may be distributed between a variety of personal and institutional technologies as a student moves from mobile device to desktop or laptop computer at home or at school. The learning itself may weave between informal and formal settings and, as Syvänen et al. (2004) found, can be fragmented, especially with young children who are inexperienced mobile device users. Sharples (2009) adds that because of the personal nature of mobile devices evaluating mobile learning initiatives may present particular ethical issues.

Indeed, potential ethical considerations as well as concerns over the inappropriate use of mobile technology have existed for some time across all levels of the educational system (Andrews et al., 2011). Andrews et al. (2013) point out that the design of mobile devices themselves – multifunctional, internet connected, highly portable and used both inside and outside school – is an obvious contributing factor that creates opportunities for privacy infringements as well as lowered control over student behaviour. Aubusson et al. (2009) add that the much smaller size of mobile devices compared to traditional cameras makes them more portable and unobtrusive, making surreptitious recording more likely than was possible with the older technology. Again, because of their size, theft and loss of mobile devices is not unusual, compromising data security (Wishart, 2009). Such ethical considerations, both real and perceived, have impeded the adoption of mobile learning as quickly or as broadly as might have been expected (Andrews et al., 2011). At its extreme this takes the form of the complete banning of mobile phones in many schools in the UK, USA, India, Australia and elsewhere (Garrett, 2010; Hartnell-Young, 2008). In these cases, the emphasis is usually on harm minimisation. Although this then raises further questions such as whether reacting in this way is neglecting the professional responsibility of educators to promote learning approaches that have been shown to benefit a wide range of learners, including students from disadvantaged backgrounds and developing countries (Andrews et al., 2013).

The issues described above – continuing professional development, assessment for and evaluation of mobile learning, ethical considerations and the associated potential for disruption – are discussed in more detail in the following chapters of this book using illustrations from more recent mobile learning initiatives in schools across the globe.

2.5 Conclusion

Thus, despite the potential for mobile devices to support a broad range of teaching and learning activities both inside and outside school, their involvement in teaching has been dogged by teachers' concerns over potential for misuse. This book will go on to address the issues surrounding mobile learning initiatives in more detail; however, first, in the next two chapters, a range of the ways in which schools internationally have implemented mobile learning in recent years whether through providing tablets such as iPads on an 'organisation provided device' (OPD) model or enabling connectivity and support for a Bring Your Own Device (BYOD) model, will be presented to illustrate the context for the later chapters.

Questions

- When you used a mobile phone or tablet to help you with finding something out, revision or recording information for later use, was that mobile learning?
- What teaching or learning opportunities would you consider to be 'mobile learning'? What defining characteristics, if any, do they share?
- Your students are bringing simple mobile phones with cameras to school; will you encourage their use to support learning or ensure they are kept out of sight? Why is that?

Annotated further reading

- The 'Big Issues' Report

M. Sharples (Ed.) (2006) *Big Issues in Mobile Learning: Report of a workshop by the Kaleidoscope Network of Excellence Mobile Learning Initiative.* Nottingham, UK: University of Nottingham.

This report presents the outcomes of a series of discussion workshops held in 2006 at the University of Nottingham, UK for dozens of European researchers in mobile learning, especially those belonging to Kaleidoscope (a European Community (EC) funded Network of Excellence). It comprises a series of chapters written by the workshop leaders detailing the themes that appeared in the different discussions. These included: What is mobile learning? How to enhance the experience without interfering with it? What are the affective factors in learning with mobile devices? How can we address the conflicts between personal informal learning and traditional classroom education? What are appropriate methods for evaluating learning in mobile environments? How should learning activities using mobile technologies be designed to support innovative educational practices? How can we integrate mobile devices with broader educational scenarios?

- UNESCO series: Exploring the Potential of Mobile Technologies to Support Teachers and Improve Practice

West, M. (2012) *Mobile Learning for teachers: Global themes.* Paris: UNESCO.

The above reference points to the overview report of a series of publications commissioned by UNESCO, the United Nations body responsible for coordinating international cooperation in education, science, culture and communication. The series sought to better understand how mobile technologies can be used to improve educational access, equity and quality around the world. It provided a, then current, snapshot of mobile learning efforts around the world intended to provide policy-makers, educators and other stakeholders with a valuable tool for leveraging mobile technology to enhance learning. The full series comprised fourteen individual working papers; this overview integrates and synthesises the themes found in the five papers that examined how mobile technologies in different geographical regions can support teachers and improve their practice. The regions included: Africa and the Middle East, Asia, Europe, Latin America and North America.

- Handbooks of mobile learning

Z. L. Berge and L. Muilenburg (Eds) (2013). *Handbook of Mobile Learning.* New York: Routledge.
Y. Zhang (Ed.) (2015) *Handbook of Mobile Teaching and Learning.* Springer International Publishing.

Edited handbooks such as these comprise multiple chapters from a wide range of authors from different countries and educational contexts, most of which describe a research initiative of some kind. The Routledge one has 53 chapters, the Springer one has 63 and, while they tend to focus on higher education, several chapters in each are relevant to school-based teaching and/or teacher training. Their comprehensive nature means they include sections on mobile learning theory and instructional design in addition to case studies of a variety of initiatives. The Springer one though aims to focus on mobile technology use in education in Australia, China, India and the USA. In addition to these two, there is a further handbook on the way, the *International Handbook of Mobile and Ubiquitous Learning,* again to be published by Springer and to be edited by X. Ma, S.Yu, M. Ally and A. Tsinakos.

3 Current and recent mobile learning teaching and learning initiatives in primary schools

3.1 Introduction

So, what actually is happening in schools today with respect to the use of handheld mobile devices to support learning? The picture is extremely varied with some schools and even states or countries banning mobile devices and with other schools encouraging students to bring their own devices and enabling internet access for them through the school's Wi-Fi network. Other schools and even city-wide groups of schools have taken the decision to control the technology to be used at source and have provided tablets such as iPads for student use. Whether these can be used by students outside of school hours again varies with the school or district's approach. Often parents are asked to contribute to the cost of purchase or insuring the devices. As Crompton and Burke (2015) point out, it very much depends on the culture of the school; however, mobile technologies are presenting schools with the need to consider change to their structures and educational practices.

This chapter, therefore, presents several case studies intended to provide an overview of recent and ongoing mobile learning and teaching initiatives to set the scene for the reader. These examples have been sourced from the many made publicly available through presentation at educational research conferences, on school websites, in blogs and newspaper or journal articles. They have been selected to provide a wide representation of school teaching subjects and a range of countries. These case study examples of mobile learning activities are further sub-divided into whether they are targeted at work inside or outside the classroom and whether or not they focus on using the devices for collaboration, thus following the dimensions of mobile learning introduced earlier in Chapter 2, Section 2.3.

Younger children attending primary or elementary schools are less likely to have access to their own mobile phones. The British national body that oversees electronic communications services, Ofcom, collects data annually on children and young people's media literacy and online access. In late Spring/early Summer 2015, 1,379 at-home interviews with parents and children aged 5–15 were conducted, analysis of which showed that the likelihood of owning a smartphone increases with the age of the child (Ofcom, 2015). Just 4% of 5–7 year olds reported owning a smartphone, rising to one in four of 8–11 year olds (24%) and to seven in ten 12–15 year olds (69%). Smartphone ownership is more likely amongst girls than boys aged 8–11 (29% compared to 19%) although there are no observable differences between genders amongst 12–15 year olds. The numbers of school children owning mobile phones in the UK have actually fallen slightly since 2010 when the proportion of those owning basic, not internet enabled, phones was higher; however, portable tablet computers are now owned by two in five (40%) 5–15 year olds. Ownership of these is also higher amongst 8–11 year olds (43%) and 12–15 year olds (45%) than 5–7 year olds (29%). These trends are repeated in other countries. The Groupe Spéciale Mobile Association (GSMA), a trade association which represents the interests of mobile operators worldwide, reported survey data on children's mobile phone use in Belgium, Denmark, Ireland, Italy, Portugal, Romania and the United Kingdom – comparing it with that of children in Japan (GSMA, 2015). In all eight countries, children's smartphone usage rate tends to increase with age, with Denmark showing a particularly high smartphone usage rate of over 80% at age 9. This may be explained by the Danish government's BYOD educational policy. In Denmark many educational services are delivered by the schools via Learning Management Systems (LMS), which provide students with access to online- and mobile phone-based tools and materials to support study. Denmark was also one of the seven European countries participating in the Net Children Go Mobile Project funded by the Safer Internet Programme of the European Commission (EC) (Mascheroni and Cuman, 2014). The proportion of children surveyed for this project who reported being encouraged to use smartphones daily at school varied from 1% in Ireland to 4% in the UK, Belgium and Portugal, 6% in Italy, 9% in Romania to 13% in Denmark. Mascheroni and Cuman (2014) also conclude that the children's, teachers' and parents' comments offered in the accompanying interviews seemed to suggest more reasons for using mobile technology in school than to avoid it. The arguments presented in favour of using smartphones in class were diverse, including health or ecological issues such as the opportunity to replace numbers of heavy, paper-based books with a single device and motivational reasons such as the opinion that smartphones and tablets are more engaging for children as well as reasons linked to enhanced learning.

3.2 Inside school

However, understandably, given teachers' and parents' concerns over mobile phone use by young children, many primary schools considering this potential of mobile devices to enhance learning have chosen to invest in lightweight tablet computers as a classroom resource. In England the British Educational Suppliers Agency (BESA) annual report on tablets and connectivity in schools for 2015 records that 71% of the 335 primary schools surveyed are making at least some use of tablets to support learning (Connor, 2015). Over one-third of the primary schools that have adopted tablets indicated that the integration of these into lessons is currently either good or excellent, though at present the tablets are most likely to be shared by the different classes, meaning that the full potential and efficient use of tablets is not necessarily being achieved. As for choice of device, the report records that, in England, the Apple iPads were the preferred option for 57% of primary schools. Similar patterns of digital technology adoption are found in the other regions of the United Kingdom where more detailed evaluations of iPad use by primary schools have been carried out. For example, Beauchamp and Hillier (2014) conducted an evaluation of iPad implementation across a network of six primary schools with varied catchment areas on behalf of the local authority (the body responsible for local schools) in Cardiff, Wales. Also data from five primary schools in Scotland informed one of the earliest academic investigations into how the use of tablet devices such as the iPad impacted on teaching and learning (Burden et al., 2012).

The main focus of Beauchamp and Hillier's (2014) study was to explore how the iPads were introduced and implemented, as well as to assess the impact they had on the attitudes and motivations of teachers, parents and students. Professional learning was central to the successful introduction of the iPads with teachers reporting that training on a range of different apps was useful as they provided activities for a variety of ages and abilities though some teachers seemed overwhelmed by the variety of apps that were available. A number of teachers also highlighted the usefulness of the more informal in-class training that they later received from their students themselves. As for impact, while the teachers did not mention any positive correlation between iPad use and academic attainment, there were three areas that were singled out for perceived, positive impact. These were support for assessment for learning opportunities; encouraging engagement and motivation; and providing access to the curriculum for different learning styles. As well as the variety of available apps, the multimodal capacity of the iPad and the ability to use the camera and iMovie to record videos both in class and other areas around the school were key to all three of these areas. This was even noted by a Year 5 student: 'It is so fun because you can do everything on [the iPad] … you can read books, play games, get images, record videos all on one piece of technology' (Beauchamp and Hillier, 2014, p.26).

The results of their evaluation confirmed the earlier results from Scotland where Burden et al. (2012) found that the introduction of iPads into the classroom engaged both teachers and students equally well with many members of school and Local Authority management teams commenting that the deployment and effective use of iPad technology had been the most easily accepted, successful and problem-free initiative they had ever witnessed. Case study examples of the use of iPads in primary schools from different countries will now be presented alongside those describing other mobile technologies in the following sections of this chapter to give the reader a sense of the wide range of their potential uses.

Collaborative group work using iPads: Raising standards in boys' writing using gaming

This case study, taken from a range presented on a blog written by David Andrews, a primary school teacher in Hull, UK and a writer for the *Guardian* (a national newspaper) Teacher Network, follows in the footsteps of all those who have used computer games to inspire learning through collaboration and writing (Bober, 2010). The school was targeting the need to improve boys' writing and the case study describes how one app was used to encourage boys to write for different purposes with confidence, in an appropriate style for each purpose and with a strong level of knowledge (Williams, 2012). It was triggered by the teacher observing how confident and knowledgeable children using iPads in another Year 6 class (aged 10–11) were in terms of speaking about their work, and that this clarity and depth had a direct and hugely positive impact on the children's writing.

The chosen app, Bike Baron, was already popular with the current class, also in Year 6. It is a fun, motorbike riding simulation where players get to test their prowess on a motorbike. They roll, flip, tumble and speed their way through sequences of ramps, loops and levels. The children worked in groups of four to each school-supplied iPad over the course of three weeks with each specific task and writing purpose introduced alongside an objective for children to complete on the Bike Baron game. The lessons followed a similar pattern, starting with game play (taking it in turn), followed by individual writing then group discussion generating peer feedback and reviewing their progress. The different writing tasks were:

- to recount where the students were asked to retell their experience of a single difficult jump or ramp in the game from the point of view of the rider;
- to report, that is to describe how things are for a motorbike stunt rider, for example, the safety equipment needed, their attitude and skills plus the risks they face;
- to instruct, the students had to discuss and write about how the Bike Baron himself could avoid injury when completing a jump or loop;
- to explain, after taking notes as they take turns on the game, students wrote out an explanation of its controls and key features;
- to persuade, where the students were asked to write a piece arguing why people should take up stunt biking and;
- to discuss, students were set the task of weighing up the pros and cons of including stunt biking as an Olympic sport.

Once the lessons started all the children involved really engaged with the game quickly. The short, moderately challenging levels and simple controls proved popular as did the variety of courses and the high frequency of dramatic crashes. In the teacher's view, the portability of the iPad, its ability to be passed round a group and having a screen large enough for spectator viewing made gameplay on an iPad ideal for this type of activity. Talk amongst students was encouraged and the need to collect examples of language used and points made in the subsequent discussions on the note-taking sheet provided was emphasised. Once the allotted time for gameplay had elapsed the students were ready to write. The teacher reported that the quality of the resulting written work for all types of writing was very good and reflected improvements in standards for all those involved. In fact he was surprised by the pace with which children were able to write when they wanted to.

Later, in a refinement of the activity, the students took screenshots as they played the game. These screenshots were imported into the Strip Designer app to create a sequence of comic strips, with captions describing the Bike Baron's thoughts and feelings at various stages of the course. The students then used their comic strips to support writing their recounting of events from the Bike Baron's perspective. This integration of different apps, making a variety of uses for the mobile device, is also characteristic of 1:1 mobile learning tasks as described in the next case study which features a suite of apps that were used for a few minutes in class every day to reinforce learning basic maths skills.

Using drill and practice apps 1:1

Many primary level teachers have capitalised on the consistent finding that using handheld mobile devices is motivating for students in order to engage them in learning drills such as those needed to cement phoneme-grapheme bonds in learning to read and number bonds or multiplication tables for learning maths. In one example, Kiger et al. (2012) describe how 3rd Grade students at a Midwestern elementary school in the United States using free apps such as Multiplication Genius Lite, Pop Math, Brain Thaw, Multiplication Flashcards To Go amongst others outperformed their peers using traditional flash card and maths games.

In this carefully set up study it was pre-arranged that all students would practise multiplication for 10 minutes each day (with two classes using iPod Touch devices and two similar, comparison classes using traditional means). Also that teaching of multiplication facts would be consistent across all the four participating classes. The two classes using iPod touches were initially supported by a learning resources teacher who introduced an app a day for students to learn and use. Typically this introduction went along the lines of rolling the cart with 24 iPod Touches into the classroom followed by an overview of the application, using a document camera to project the screen of the iPod Touch. The cart itself held the mobile devices plus an Airport Extreme wireless hub and laptop computer to store, charge and sync them. The learning resources teacher was careful to emphasise the goal of each application as they showed the class how to operate it. Students then retrieved their allotted iPod touches from the cart and started working on the application as soon as they got to their desks.

Students following the mobile learning initiative used the iPod touch devices and math apps to practise multiplication each day for two months. Teachers often directed students to use one or two specific apps during the 10-minute period. On occasion, students were asked to focus on a specific multiplication table using a particular app. Other days, students self-selected the application. In the comparison classrooms students practised multiplication for 10 minutes each day using more traditional techniques such as flash cards, math games, fact triangles and number sequences. Sometimes students chose their desired method of practice, and other times classroom teachers directed practice. In the final post-intervention multiplication test it was found (controlling for prior student achievement, home iPod Touch use and previous teacher) that the students who had been using the iPod Touches outperformed the comparison students. The difference was even clearer when only performance on the most difficult multiplication test items were compared.

The same research team also reports how other classes used the iPods to reinforce key learning (Herro et al., 2013). For example, the kindergarten classes augmented their learning of letter and sound recognition with simple apps, such as ABC Flashcard, by tracing the letters with their finger, listening to phonetic pronunciations, and identifying objects with beginning letter sounds. However, we should note that such simple learning drills do not generally capitalise on the range of functionalities afforded by a smartphone and also run effectively on the cheaper mobile phones which are available widely, including throughout developing countries.

In one example from Sub-Saharan Africa, Jere-Folotiya et al. (2014) report on the use of GraphoGame, a cell phone-based literacy game, by Grade 1 students in Zambian public schools. GraphoGame is an online environment for learning letter-sound correspondences developed in Finland. In this study a version created for the medium of first-grade instruction, ciNyanja, was mounted on Nokia cell phone handsets with headphones. Playing GraphoGame itself involves repeated trials in which the player must choose, from 2 to 8 alternatives, the letter that corresponds to the phoneme s/he hears from headphones. It adapts to the progress of the students to keep their success rate high (>80 %) and proceeds from easy to differentiate phonemes to more difficult ones, before moving to larger units such as letter combinations of two, three or more. It was presented to Grade 1 students at their schools in multiple short sessions (no more than 9 minutes) spread over several consecutive days amounting to a total average exposure time of about 1.5 hours. Results showed that playing GraphoGame produced significant improvements in the performance of the students who were exposed to it, that this improvement was most prominent when both students and their teachers played the game and the teachers were introduced to the phonics approach so that they would not provide incompatible instruction.

However, while clearly enjoyed by students and catered for by a vast range of easy-to-use, multimedia apps, it is arguable as to whether such mobile device-based drill and practice inside class is truly mobile learning. As in the previous Bike Baron case study no one went anywhere. The next two case studies focus on school-based learning activities where the main focus for the students was on using mobile devices outside the classroom.

3.3 Outside school

Taking younger students outside school can be difficult with the cost of both transport and the extra staff needed to ensure safety. Taking students on field trips or allowing costly equipment to go home is understandably a concern for many teachers; however, as these next two case studies from Singapore and Sweden describe, this can result in effective learning opportunities. The first focuses on home-based learning activities and the second on learning stimulated by a visit to a local attraction.

Personalising inquiry learning through using HTC smartphones 1:1

This case study, based on an evaluation of a primary science class mobile learning initiative in Singapore reported by Looi et al. (2011), describes how personalised learning underpins the design of a smartphone-based 'toolkit' created to scaffold Grade 3 students' inquiry-based learning. Stimulated by successes in earlier mobile science learning work with older students (such as the Personal Inquiry (PI) project (Sharples et al., 2015)), Looi et al. (2011) set up a 'mobilised Grade 3 science curriculum'. This involved providing a mixed-ability Grade 3 class of 9 year olds with HTC TyTyn smartphones and the researchers and teachers working together to design an activity-based curriculum with the aim of making mobile learning the routine for the science lessons, and preparing students for out-of-classroom, self-directed learning. Apps on these Microsoft Windows-based smartphones included a camera, a calculator, a calendar, mobile web internet access, Mobile Word, Excel, PowerPoint and the GoKnow MLE (Mobile Learning Environment) comprising concept mapping, animation and project management tools. Each project centred around planned home and informal activities as well as class field trips to the zoo, the horticulture park and a probiotic drinks factory. According to Looi et al. (2011) the MLE provided the infrastructure to develop each project with driving questions, activities and learning resources making each project 'a container of related and interdependent learning tasks' (Looi et al., 2011, p.273). Each task was intended to be an instantiation of how the affordances of mobile computing enable personalised learning from the four facets reported by Looi et al. (2009). These are: (1) allowing multiple entry points and learning pathways; (2) supporting multimodality; (3) enabling student improvisation in situ; and (4) supporting the sharing and creation of student artefacts on the move.

For example, the project on body systems starts with students reading an overview on their phones which shows them its objectives, what is expected from them in learning about the body system. The students started the inquiry by playing a cooperative game to identify the parts and functions of five body systems. They helped one another to identify the parts correctly, and the teacher played the role of a critic to ensure that the students had identified the correct body parts and systems. Each student was then tasked to conduct an experiment during eating at home with the help of his or her family members. Using the smartphone, the students video-recorded the experiment and used their recording to support later class discussion with their classmates and teacher. From this activity, the students learned that digestion starts from the mouth and how the teeth in the mouth help in the digestion process. After that discussion, the students were required to do online research on digestive systems using their smartphones and to update their notes showing how their learning was progressing. Reading these helped the teacher to identify learning gains and rectify gaps in the conceptions of the students. The students then created animations of digestive processes using Sketchy to illustrate their under-standing and used a rubric to help them self-assess the quality of their work. Before the teacher commented on their work, the students evaluated one another's work using the same rubric. The teacher also shared these artefacts created by the students and at the same time offered suggestions to improve the students' work. The project lessons culminated in an unusual 'teach-your-parent' activity. The students were tasked to ask their parents what they know about the digestive system and to identify gaps in their parents' knowledge. They then had to teach the parents what they thought the parents did not know and to interview their parents again to check their understanding. Key parent–child interactions were video- or voice-recorded using the smartphone. Each student shared the audio or video recording of his or her parent–child interac-tions with a partner, and together they discussed and reflected on their own understanding of the digestive system.

Following up the children's learning for the purposes of the evaluation showed that the students in this class gained the highest exam scores of all the mixed-ability classes in the school in the annual P3 year-end science exam. Also the students were positive about the experience with around 80% of the students reporting that the HTC smartphone helped their learning both in (84.6%) and out of class (78.9%). Furthermore, 62% of students thought that, by using the smart-phone, they better understood the science concepts learned and also understood better how things they learn in class were connected to their daily life. The class teacher reported that she had learned that the teaching of science was not necessarily confined to the textbooks which she had previously relied heavily on. In addition, the researchers observed that, when teaching the 'mobilised curriculum', she was inclined to give students more time to construct their own under-standing rather than feed them with information. However, readers should note that implementing the one project extended the allotted classroom hours for learning the body systems beyond the limited 4–5 hours of class time to over 3 weeks. We are not informed as to how this extension affected other compulsory topics.

While the intention behind this exemplar case study was to enhance opportunities for personal learning it is clear that both group discussion in class and family discussion at home still fea-tured strongly. In the next case study discussion is central as students work together in small groups to co-create multimodal digital stories inspired by visiting a local landmark.

Collaborative digital story creation using iPods during a school visit

This initiative formed part of an EC-funded research project exploring lifelong learning through opportunities for collaborative creativity (Nordmark and Milrad, 2012). It comprised a three-day intervention where the researchers took an active role in supporting a primary class teacher with the introduction of mobile digital storytelling. The intervention involved 24 children aged 9–12 from a local elementary school in the south of Sweden and their teacher. Stakeholders in addition to the researchers included the local museum organisation of Kulturparken Smaland and a professional actor from the local theatre company.

The activity itself was set at the now ruined castle of Kronoberg, which was once a defensive stronghold. Over three days, one each on preparation, the visit with associated story creation and reflection, the school children worked in groups of three to collaboratively plan, collect, create, edit and produce their own stories of the castle, its inhabitants and its surroundings, inspired by the various on-site activities. Each group was assigned one iPod Touch and each child had sole responsibility for one specifically designated aspect of the story creation: 1) images/live content; 2) sound/voiceover; and 3) notes and group activity documentation. For image capture and story creation, the children used one of two different off-the-shelf apps created for mobile storytelling; Story Kit or StoryRobe. Requiring further documentation was an attempt to make the students aware of and reflect on what choices and decisions they made and why, issues they had to consider when they reassembled for the story creation. During the actual visit local historian guides and actors in relevant costume reported for the children on both battles and everyday life in the castle. The children listened, took photos, recorded facts and participated in the different prepared activities, continuously gathering material for the story creation later the same day. Later, when writing their story using their chosen app on the iPod, the children had to discuss, reflect and argue for their content and their standpoints in order to make the final story a cooperative production representing the input from the whole group. On the next day the children watched the stories in school and discussed issues related to the story creation and production, the collaborative process and their general views of the activity.

The researchers report that the students showed sincere interest in taking part in the activity and were able to handle the apps easily. They acted very responsibly, both in regards to participation and attention, as well as in gathering and sharing ideas, facts and images for the afternoon story creation session, and all seemed eager to finish the assignments and tell their stories. It was also clear that the creation of individual roles within the group motivated the students' work ethic and promoted their feeling of responsibility for their work, as well as the importance of finishing the assignment. In particular they were interested by the publication and dissemination of the finished work. Questions like 'where will they be stored?', 'who will be able to see them?', 'will they know my name?' and 'who made which story?' were common. Lastly, while the software chosen, either StoryKit or StoryRobe, ran satisfactorily even though it had not been adapted or revised in any way, StoryKit ended up as the less popular option. This was mostly due to its rather basic output format, which mimicked that of an ordinary book, rather than taking the advantages of the multimodal approach digital storytelling offers.

As demonstrated in both the case studies above, it is important for any class teacher to integrate learning from any such external class activities including fieldwork and homework into their students' everyday curriculum. Doing so enables teachers to capitalise on the essential portability of mobile devices which, alongside extensive memory capacity, enables them to transport different media between locations. This portability is a key affordance of handheld mobile devices thus enabling mobile learning opportunities that cut across contexts as described in Chapter 2. The following section, therefore, reports two more case study examples where primary school students have been specifically tasked with using school-supplied mobile devices to capture information outside school for use in their lessons.

3.4 Bringing the outside inside

During her investigation into Sri Lankan teachers' use of mobile devices in teaching science one of my doctoral students (Ekanayake, 2011) coined the phrase 'bringing the outside inside' as a means of describing the way in which teachers were using the cameras on their mobile phones to capture local, topic relevant images to show their students. The students too were occasionally sent outside with one camera phone per group to the school grounds. One of the teachers reported:

> in this lesson students brought the images of mutual relationships *[in ecosystems]* that they had observed, understood and experienced in the school environment. Therefore it was easy to construct the lesson inside the classroom with active student participation.

Another teacher, also participating in this investigation, worked similarly but with younger, Grade 6, students using mobile phones to take pictures to support the construction of a biological key to identify plant leaves as described in the following case study.

Using camera phones in small groups: 'The diversity of leaves'

This 80-minute lesson based on the standard science curriculum in Sri Lanka was conducted for Grade 6 students, aged 10 to 11. It has been included here with the other primary school case studies because of the children's age even though, in Sri Lanka, Grade 6 is the first year of secondary school. The teacher used the following steps to create a three-part lesson.

1. Engagement: The teacher introduced the lesson and the concept of 'diversity' as a whole group discussion with the help of a PowerPoint presentation. While listening to the teacher introducing the topic, the students sat around desktop computers in small groups to view the PowerPoint presentation on the computer screens.

2. Lesson development: The students were formed into groups of about six, each group was given two mobile phones and a worksheet with instructions to collect images of different leaf colours, shapes, edges, and whether they were pinnate or non-pinnate, from the school garden. The mobile phones had been loaned from one of the mobile phone operators in Sri Lanka.
    The students then went outside to photograph the leaves. During this time they used the captured images on the mobile phone to support both group discussions as to their progress on the task and discussion with the teacher or other students when they needed to ask for assistance or further details. Also the teacher reported that having the images available enabled her to assess on the fly. For example, after viewing one group's images she directed them to plants growing outside the principal's office.
    After returning to the classroom the students shared their images amongst the groups using Bluetooth. Then the teacher introduced the concept of using a dichotomous key to classify

the plant leaves. Each group next constructed their own dichotomous key based on the images they had in their mobile phones and presented it to the class. After each presentation, the teacher highlighted the important points for the students to note.

3. Evaluation: The teacher assessed the work carried out by each student group based on their presentation and examining the images saved on the mobile phones. She found she could correct the students' misconceptions about the leaf structures as a direct consequence of the potential of the mobile phone to capture and store the students' observations activities and re-viewing/replaying them when required.

In summary, Ekanayake (2011) concludes that having access in class to the images they had taken outside enabled the students to connect their science learning to authentic examples and the teacher to assess their progress; in particular, promptly addressing any misconceptions spotted. However, as already discussed, many primary schools are reluctant to allow students to bring their mobile phones into school and also, where primary schools have purchased expensive tablets to be shared between classes, it is not always the case that the school will allow these tablets to go far from the teacher's sight. Though, as the following case study from an Apple Distinguished Educator shows, there is a wide range of opportunities for using tablet computers to link the outside world to school work taking place in the classroom.

Using iPads 1:1: 'The Secret Garden grows into an immersive experience'

This is one of a range of detailed case study examples published by Apple showing the work teachers they endorse as 'Apple Distinguished Educators' have conducted in their schools (Sparkes, 2016). In this case Rhiannon Sparkes, an elementary school teacher in Quebec, Canada, set out to build a series of lessons that would not only engage her Grade 5 students in the setting and themes of the book, *The Secret Garden* by Frances Hodgson Burnett, but also enable learning relevant to many different school subjects in their curriculum.

The class starts by reading the novel together as a class using the iBooks app to get a sense of the plot. This introductory activity takes place in March, the time of year when the snow begins to melt in Canada and the students' gardens can be seen again. The app allows students to highlight key passages, take notes, look up definitions of unfamiliar words and listen to the text. Sparkes (2016) reports that this enables each student to read and to develop understanding of the, sometimes complex, concepts and characters at their own pace. With the text stored on the iPads for later reference the students then head outside to take photographs using the on-board camera. They study plant growth, focusing on the potential for life in the soil and how that contrasts with the bleak gardens after winter.

Exploring how their own local gardens are coming to life also connects the students directly to the book's themes and characters and they are asked to choose 15 to 20 of their photos to illustrate the concept of 'rebirth', one of the *The Secret Garden*'s key themes. Each student then composes a piece of music to reflect the mood of their garden as it comes to life, using a collection of instruments within the GarageBand app. This will then feature as a score to accompany their photos. To create the final project, students combine their photos, music and a title page, created using the Explain Everything app to visually convey the novel's themes, into an iMovie montage. This final activity enables them to express both their feelings about growth and rebirth and their learning about the relationship between the garden setting, the different moods evoked and the novel's themes. The students are also given the opportunity to show this under-standing using a fourth app, Minecraft – the 3D modelling app – to build a three-dimensional representation of the story's setting. The teacher explains how this enables her to assess their learning:

> In Minecraft, I can actually walk through their understanding of the setting of *The Secret Garden*. I can see the manor house, the garden and all the elements of setting that they have picked up and put in their re-creation of the garden.
>
> *(Sparkes, 2016)*

She also reports that having the variety of apps available enables using the iPad to help make learning accessible to all her students by capitalising on the different modes in which the arte-facts can be created. For example, the use of Minecraft reported above enabled a student with written and verbal language issues to show her that he had clearly understood the novel's theme (Sparkes, 2016).

3.5 Conclusion

The six exemplar case studies presented above show how primary level teachers have employed both generic tools commonly found on mobile devices such as the camera and the word processor to take notes and apps designed for fun and games as well as apps specifically designed to support learning in their teaching. As the following set of case studies of mobile phone use in secondary schools will show, secondary level teachers have also made use of a similar range. In the case of secondary schools though, a much wider range of devices are used. Despite the numbers of early PDA studies, such as those described in Chapter 2, many primary schools remain uncomfortable at the thought of young children bringing expensive devices like smart-phones to school.

Questions

- What are the pros and cons of issuing children at primary or elementary school with their own mobile devices for a lesson or task?
- What features can you find that are common to more than three of the case studies presented above?
- What particular challenges do you think the teachers in the different case studies planned for?

Further reading

Further case studies from primary or elementary school contexts take a bit of hunting out though some can be found in academic texts and handbooks including:

Berge, Z. L. and Muilenburg, L. (2013). *Handbook of Mobile Learning*. New York: Routledge.

Crompton, H. and Traxler, J. (Eds) (2015) *Mobile Learning and Mathematics*. London: Routledge.

Crompton, H. and Traxler, J. (Eds) (2015) *Mobile Learning and STEM: Case Studies in Practice.* London: Routledge.

Galloway, J., John, M. and McTaggart, M. (2014) *Learning with Mobile and Handheld Technologies.* London: Routledge.

Mentor, D. (Ed.) (2016) *Handbook of Research on Mobile Learning in Contemporary Classrooms.* Hershey, PA: IGI Global.

Y. Zhang (Ed.) (2015) *Handbook of Mobile Teaching and Learning,* Springer International Publishing

and on the web:

Apple's 'Teacher Stories' at www.apple.com/uk/education/real-stories/

4 Current and recent mobile learning teaching and learning initiatives in secondary schools

4.1 Introduction

This chapter again presents an overview of recent and ongoing mobile learning and teaching initiatives to set the scene for the reader. The case studies included range from the provision of iPads in classrooms in relatively affluent nations such as the USA or the UK to using SMS texting for literacy and numeracy teaching in developing countries via students using their own phones inside and outside the classroom to support school learning. These examples have been sourced from the many made publicly available through presentation at educational research conferences, on school websites, in blogs and newspaper or journal articles. They have been selected to provide a wide representation of school teaching subjects and a range of countries.

The chapter focuses on the use of mobile devices in secondary (middle and/or high) schools for older children and teenagers. The use of mobile devices in colleges designed for students over the age of 16 is not included; interested readers are directed to the UK Joint Information Systems Committee guide 'Mobile learning: A practical guide for educational organisations planning to implement a mobile learning initiative' and its accompanying case studies currently located at https://www.jisc.ac.uk/guides/mobile-learning. Within each school type, primary or secondary, case study examples of mobile learning activities are further sub-divided into whether they are targeted at work inside or outside the classroom and whether or not they focus on using the devices for collaboration, thus following the dimensions of mobile learning introduced earlier in Chapter 2, Section 2.3.

In secondary schools, the picture with respect to mobile devices is more varied than with the primary schools discussed in Chapter 3. Parents are less reluctant to allow their older children to use mobile phones and, whether the school is supporting or attempting to prevent their use, numbers make their way into school every day. A 2013 Pew Research Centre survey of US Advanced Placement and National Writing Project teachers reports that 73% of them say that they and/or their students use their mobile phones in the classroom or to complete assignments (Purcell et al., 2013). Also many schools are at varying stages of different tablet computer initiatives. Such initiatives follow different models from school or school district provided to BYOD. In the UK the increasingly frequent expectation that parents pay (up front or in instalments) to enable the school to provide an iPad has aroused ire. In August 2016 the *Guardian*, a national newspaper, was reporting 'Textbooks are being dropped in favour of technology, with parents saying they are being lumbered with much of the cost'. However, studies of iPad adoption, such as Chou et al.'s (2012) exploratory case study examining four 9th grade Geography classrooms in a major city in the Midwest US, tend to report that the positives outweigh the negatives. Chou et al. (2012) found the teachers reported a number of benefits to iPad use in class that included the following:

- Active engagement: There are more varieties of apps than on the older computers for student-centred activities.
- Increased time for projects: Students could start a project or task as soon as they entered the classroom without wasting time starting up the equipment.
- Improved information literacy and digital citizenship: Students could conduct an information search at a faster pace using a variety of apps and websites. They also learned about digital citizenship through the process.
- Student-centred activities: Students could learn at their own pace, collaborate with a team and offer advice to each other through various apps.
- Enhanced teaching with updated information: Teachers could use apps with up-to-date Geography information to engage students.

These benefits though were accompanied by the following challenges:

- Distraction: Students could get off track while looking up information on the website or attempt to use apps that were more entertaining and not central to the task.
- Lack of teacher-selected apps: Although there are a number of Geography apps, there could be more apps for word processing, Geography-related topics and challenge-based activities.
- Teachers and students need more time and training: Having iPads posed challenges for both teachers and students who have not used mobile devices.

This mix of pros and cons is similarly reported in other countries. From their large-scale survey of over 6,000 students in 18 secondary schools using iPads in Quebec province, Canada, Karsenti and Fievez (2013) found students divided over key benefits with a quarter to a half of them mentioning ease of portability, access to information, quality of student presentations, creativity and motivation. However, they were largely united in reporting ease of distraction as the major con. One Canadian student noted, '[…] it's hard to concentrate in class […] all my Facebook friends are online at the same time' (Karsenti and Fievez, 2013, p.31).

Cheng and Haagen (2015) report from a high school in Beijing, China where students in two 11th grade classes were given a 7" Android tablet to try out. In the follow-up survey 90% of students stated that the mobile devices had proven useful particularly in learning English. Reasons given by the 10% who had not found mobile devices useful included an inability to prevent themselves listening to music or playing games as well as insufficient opportunities made to use them in class. Other studies of iPad as well as mobile phone use for inside class are discussed in the following section.

4.2 Inside school

Indeed, reports on mobile device use in secondary schools in different countries can be found widely on the web, often in teacher blogs or on school or on the relevant hardware manufacturer's websites. These tend to describe one-off case studies or evaluations comparing the performance of classes using mobile devices with those taught more traditionally, more reflective theory-led analyses are rarer, especially those reporting on learning taking place over a substantial period of time.

However, that said, Parsons and Adhikari (2016) helpfully use a sociocultural framework adapted from the one proposed by Pachler et al. (2010) to frame their analysis of three years of teacher, student and parent feedback on the use of mobile devices by teenage students in New Zealand. These students, in Years 9 and 10 (ages 13–14), attend a large secondary school with approximately 2,000 students on the roll. The school operates a BYOD policy; the response to which has been surveyed by the research team in each of the last three years. The analytical framework they used centres on three aspects (Pachler et al., 2010) namely: structures such as the curriculum and the digital infrastructure; agency including the roles, skills and place of the stakeholder groups and cultural practices such as social interaction and culturally situated meaning making. Of the three groups surveyed, the teachers responded the most positively to the BYOD innovations, and the parents had the most reservations. Students provided a range of views, both positive, citing higher productivity, ease of access to resources and better learning outcomes, and negative, including reduction of handwriting skills and associated potential for off-task behaviour of both themselves and others.

Furthermore, in all three stakeholder group perspectives, the power of agency was clearly observable. As noted above, it was teachers, who have the most agency, who were the most positive about the move towards BYOD, and parents, who have the least agency, who had the most reservations. With respect to cultural practices, one of the most frequently noted BYOD triggered changes reported by both teachers and students was increased levels of peer collaboration amongst students. The students themselves also noted additional communication with adults citing both teachers and parents as examples. However, the parents were less happy about impact on social interaction with one reporting 'Well I am sure they are learning something but they are glued to the damn thing' (Parsons and Adhikari, 2016, p.76). This comment is reinforced by the students' survey responses which show educational activity as the most frequent use made of the technology. Accessing social media came in at second place but with reported frequency of use of only just over half as often. In terms of structures, it appeared that, following the move to BYOD, classrooms were more devolved, collaborative, group based and student centric. Teachers' accounts of this were very similar with the following being typical:

> The focus in the classroom has changed, very student centred. Inquiry learning style is the norm and sharing is an important component of the class environment. Front of the room instruction is less important, in fact there is not really a front of the room. Have been experimenting with different classroom set outs.
>
> *(Parsons and Adhikari, 2016, p.70)*

This impact on classroom structure was also noted on the other side of the world by Tirocchi (2015) reporting on research taking place in an Italian lower secondary school that was included in the national 'Cl@ssi 2.0' programme, based on the 'Digital Classroom of Tomorrow' (DCOT) concept. In such schools students' mobile phones are perceived as a useful teaching tool (although students generally use tablets for learning) and as an additional resource for group work. Students in this particular school could choose to bring their own mobile devices to class, though the school does not provide a free Wi-Fi connection. The result, Tirocchi (2015) observed, is that lessons are increasingly dialogic and participatory, not the least because the technologies used have changed the spatial configuration of the classroom, with desks now arranged in small islands.

The following case study illustrating how the introduction of mobile devices can change formal didactic classroom teaching structures and be used in multiple ways to support learning is taken from another of Apple's classroom stories showcasing the work of their Distinguished Educators.

Using iPads 1:1: 'Heart anatomy with a digital pulse'

In this case study a high school science teacher in Texas teaching a credit-bearing 11th/12th grade anatomy and physiology course reports on how she used a variety of apps on school district supplied iPads to enhance teaching and learning (Deinhammer, 2016). The emphasis throughout on interactivity and visualisation in demonstrating the complexity of the human heart both engages students and scaffolds their understanding.

Deinhammer (2016) introduces the unit on the heart to the students by setting reading from an iBook anatomy textbook which features videos, photo galleries, multi-touch images and illustrations to support students in understanding the complex circulatory system and its interacting structures and organs. Once the students have a foundational understanding of the heart's anatomy, they rotate through a series of stations in the teaching lab where they experiment, observe, and dissect, using the iPad to support each activity. The learning station activities comprise the following:

- Manipulating a life-size model heart, photographing it with the iPad's onboard camera and annotating the images using Photo Editor for later revision study.
- A histology lab where students use the MotiConnect app to connect their iPad to a digital microscope camera to examine slides of various cardiovascular tissues such as healthy and unhealthy arteries and veins. Students then open the photos in the Notability app to label them for later study. They can also review normal blood flow through a healthy artery and vein and view a clogged artery using the BioDigital Human app.
- Logging their heart rate at rest and during exercise. Each student uses a Pasco Passport Hand Grip Heart Rate Sensor to transmit their heart beat over Bluetooth to the SPARKVue app to graph in real time. They also use The Human Body Lite app to see how the organ structures change when blood flows through the heart during physical exertion.
- Dissecting an actual sheep heart and using images from The Human Body Lite app and the Life on Earth iBook used earlier to help them find and identify the parts relevant parts such as the atria, the ventricles, valves, arteries, and veins.

Then once the teacher feels that students have a good understanding of how the heart functions, she gives them a series of final assignments to pick from so they can demonstrate their learning. As she points out:

> You have to reach the individual student in order for them to learn. If you don't find a way to personalize it and make it real for them, they're not going to be successful.
>
> *(Deinhammer, 2016)*

To demonstrate their learning students can choose from making a stop-motion video to show the flow of blood through the heart with iMotion, making an animated children's book about the heart and lungs working together using SketchBook Express, using the iMovie to produce a tutorial for young learners on heart health or using Popplet lite to create a mind map or graphic organiser to show the functions of the heart. This final assignment is targeted at students who might need a review of the basics learned from the original materials and the lab activities. Clearly, as in the earlier primary level case study *Personalising inquiry learning through using HTC Smartphones 1:1* the teacher is capitalising on the wealth of free and inexpensive apps now available to enable student choice of learning tasks. Indeed, the school also allows students to bring their own devices which could have different operating systems so it may well be possible that the teacher is now managing a whole variety of alternative apps.

This wide range of ways in which iPads (not forgetting other smartphones with a similar range of apps) can be used to support classroom-based learning has been recognised in a study of a lower secondary school in the west of Denmark which teaches students in their 7th, 8th and 9th year of schooling (Meyer, 2015). At the beginning of the school year (2012) all students in the 7th form (3 classes) as well as two special needs classes were given iPads to keep for the entire school year. Meyer (2015) was particularly interested in how iPads can enter into and work as part of an ecology of learning resources. She reports that the school found that the iPad acted as a flexible technology in terms of size, form and functionality, allowing students to, for instance, use it as a tape recorder, a jotter, a dictionary, an image bank, an encyclopaedia, a display and so on. In this way the iPad became part of students' emergent and relational uses of different kinds of resources that were relevant for their specific learning needs.

However, there is no requirement to have an iPad with its readily available suite of educational apps for mobile learning to be effective. This next case study focuses on the use of mobile phones and/or MP3 players and teaching via podcasting.

Studying citizenship and intercultural education through collaboratively creating podcasts

This case study arises from the Italian arm of an EC-funded project intended to test innovative and multimodal training approaches to support integration of, and active citizenship for, young immigrants (Ranieri and Bruni, 2013). It was set in the context of a large Chinese immigrant community in Italy and involved citizenship education teachers working with their students aged 13–15 to review and create podcasts. A podcast is a digital recording, usually an audio file though it can include video (a vodcast), which is made available on the internet for downloading to a computer or a mobile device. Most if not all mobile phones can act as MP3 players and replay podcasts. Like the Bike Baron game discussed in the earlier case study *Collaborative group work using iPads: Raising standards in boys' writing using gaming* the mobile device-based activity was used as a stimulus for group work.

The teaching programme conceived for the project comprised four modules, each with four units. For example, for the intercultural education module, the four units were One Country: Many Cultures; Sport; Non-verbal Communication and Culture; and finally, the Internet as a Tool for Intercultural Dialogue. For each teaching unit, students were asked to listen to four podcasts out of school and then, in class, to discuss in pairs or small groups the key issues that had cropped up.

The discussion was prompted by the teacher if necessary and acted as a preliminary step towards content creation for the students' own podcasts. Each group of students was then required to produce their own podcast with the aim of developing their self-expression skills within a collaborative process. This process was conceived as an opportunity to bridge cultural and linguistic differences. The decision to focus on podcasting was supported by earlier research studies with older students such as that reported by Oliver (2005) who argues that podcasting contributes to students' learning by increasing their motivation and engagement, while Khaniya (2006) highlights that it supports access to authentic contexts. The podcasts created lasted between 2 and 4 minutes and followed a radio sketch format, conveying content through the dramatisation of a real-life situation with dialogue and background sounds. These dramas created by the students included both episodes about their daily lives – an oral exam, afternoon break, doing homework, etc. – and imaginary situations, like the original idea of interviewing a personified nation.

Results of a student survey set up to evaluate the initiative showed that more than half (65%) of the students involved found it easy to download and listen to the podcasts and almost 70% of the students declared that the work done helped them to enhance their knowledge in an enjoyable way. For example, by substituting textbooks with new learning instruments and by having the opportunity to successfully experiment with the use of technologies not only for entertainment but also for other aims. For example, one student commented: 'I learnt things in a different way and I learnt something new about technology'. They particularly appreciated the opportunity to create their own podcasts in groups, reporting that this was 'an original method to work with classmates' and to 'understand what they really think'. Indeed, those observing the initiative felt that, through open discussion and exchange of ideas, the students got to know each other better. They clearly felt free to talk into the microphone and record their voices. In the survey 70% of the students pointed out they now had a better understanding of cultures that are different from theirs. Additionally, almost all students stated that the learning activity was truly enriching in so far as it enabled them to successfully experiment with the use of technologies, not only for fun but also to express themselves. For example, one student observed: 'I learnt things in a different way and I had the opportunity to show others what I've learnt'. This learning was endorsed by most of the teachers who appreciated the quality of the communicative format used, highlighting the positive effects on the students' participation and motivation. However, there were a few students such as those with low levels of proficiency in the Italian language or with very low technical skills who found podcast creation too challenging and, as ever, not everyone contributed equally to the task which could be detrimental to the group's work.

As before though, the 'mobile' in mobile learning implies that the extra potential to support learning supplied by cell or mobile phones and tablets through access to apps and/or the internet results from their use to support learning in contexts outside school. The next two case studies illustrate first the use of QR codes (printed barcodes that photographing on a smartphone or tablet triggers web-based content) to augment learning on a school field trip and, second, the ways in which school students in different countries are using their mobile phones to support them with their homework.

4.3 Outside school

Where possible, secondary schools will organise visits outside of school to curriculum-relevant locations such as a nearby river for science, a mountainside for geography and ancient buildings for history with the aim of enhancing student engagement through authentic learning. This next case study illustrates how augmented reality apps can be used to deliver extra background information whether sound, text or pictures to students' mobile devices directly at the point of interest.

BYOD augmented reality (AR) team tours at the Swan River foreshore

This case study describes an exploration of the potential of augmented reality to enhance curriculum-based excursions or field trips to the Swan River area in Perth, Western Australia conducted by the Association of Independent Schools of Western Australia (AISWA) (Clarke, 2013). This area has good educational potential for several curriculum areas because of the examples of cultural artefacts, biodiversity, historical links, commercial activities and current affairs issues found there. Indeed, dozens of authentic links to material for twelve different subject areas were mapped against the curriculum for Years 7–10 addressing cross-curricular priorities as well as subject content. The content (delivered multimodally on the smartphone at the selected location markers) included media such as local news reports, historical images, audio commentaries, quizzes and plain text. The tours were set up using the AR app FreshAiR and each location marker was either a QR code, an image or a set of pre-determined GPS coordinates. The app's interface on the mobile phone displays compass bearings, a 'map view' (to help with location) and pin-like location markers in a 'reality view' (looking through the device's viewfinder). Students could use any FreshAiR compatible 3G smartphone (iPhone or Android) to navigate the tour and any other handheld devices to participate in activities en route (e.g. iPad, camera, audio recorder).

Over a five-month period almost 170 students from Years 7 to 10 and 11 teachers participated in five different versions of the AR tour which was designed to be undertaken in teams and structured to promote genuine collaboration. Each tour included tasks such as collecting images, reading QR codes and Aurasma triggers, recording sounds, making observations, capturing video, reading inscriptions for clues and looking out for the safety of each other. It was arranged that students in each team would need to take different responsibilities and share the learning load to succeed. Their teachers were encouraged to step back, to let the groups manage themselves and take responsibility for their own learning.

Clarke (2013) reports that the results were positive; the students seemed to have genuinely engaged at many levels with the mobile AR activities, the 'outdoor classroom' and the differentiated multimodal delivery of content. The participating teachers were very encouraged by this. They were all surprised though at the range of devices that the students brought along. Not all devices had operating systems or GPS tolerances suitable for the FreshAiR app, but most teams could problem-solve this by reshuffling responsibilities within the group or sharing resources. Most teachers had actively participated earlier in selecting/modifying the tour content to suit their needs and all made suggestions about additional content to better suit their classes. For example, one tour was built for Year 10 'Politics and Law' and another modified for Year 8 'Indigenous Culture of the River'.

Teachers noted that their AR tour (customised for each class) appeared to be very well suited to the learning and personal needs of the age group and reported that they were 'inspired' by the outcomes. They were surprised that the students were able to manage so well by themselves (with the technology and the task management). They were also impressed that: students took responsibility for each other's safety and were supportive of each other; students showed minimal stress about technical difficulties; (difficult) weather conditions didn't seem to distract them and walking distance (3–5 km) wasn't an issue for most.

A final interesting point to note was, though none of the teachers were solely English (subject) teachers, there was a general heightened awareness (articulated in anecdotal comments) about the pedagogical value of multimodal literacies and 'texts' (ways of communicating messages). They had noted increased levels of 'engagement' and/or 'reflection' by various students when the content was delivered through such texts.

The next case study, however, covers several different countries and focuses on a more prosaic, everyday use of mobile phones outside school – for homework.

Using your mobile phone at home for schoolwork 1:1

In 2012, a survey conducted by TRU (Teenage Research Unlimited, a US research company targeting the youth market) commissioned by the Verizon Foundation found that more than 1 in 3 middle school, students, ages 11–14, were using their mobile devices to complete homework (Verizon, 2012). While there are some doubts about this survey, it was online only and funded by a communications technology company, there are interesting results. Whereas 39% of middle school students use smartphones for homework, only 6% report that they can use the smartphone in the classroom for school work. Also, more Hispanic and African American middle school students reported using their smartphones for homework than Caucasian students. Nearly one half of all Hispanic middle school students (49%) said they used smartphones for homework.

More recently, first year students in a class studying Business Management and Economics at a Swedish upper secondary school, were surveyed on how they used their mobile phones for school work at home (Ott et al., 2014). Their results are shown in Table 4.1 below.

Table 4.1 Frequencies of students' use of mobile phones for school work at home (n = 28)

	At least once a month (%)	At least once a week (%)
I use the mobile phone as calculator	11	86
I use the mobile phone for translation	11	78
I browse the internet for information	11	68
I look at images	30	44
I cooperate with my classmates by social media	47	43
I cooperate with my classmates by texting	50	39
I take pictures for school assignments	29	36
I revise lesson notes	21	29
I use the mobile phone to access the LMS	29	28
I cooperate with my classmates by talk or video calls	25	22
I edit audio and video	14	22
I watch material produced by the teacher	30	15
I record audio and video	29	11
I use the mobile phone to tether a computer to the internet	50	11
I write texts for school assignments	11	11
I communicate with my teachers	32	8
I watch films on the internet for information	39	0

More than two-thirds of the students report using the internet on their smartphones at home at least once a week for searching or browsing for information, or to find translations to support their studies and even more use the phone as calculator. Just under half (44%) use their phone to look for images in support of schoolwork and just over a third (36%) use its camera to take pictures for school assignments on a more than weekly basis. There is also frequent communication with peers asking for and giving help on assignments via social media and texting.

Students in developing countries too are turning to their mobile phones to help them out with their homework. Mwapwele and Roodt (2016) emphasise how important Tanzanian students' use of their mobile devices for learning outside school is. They spend more time in the outside school environment where using apps or the internet on mobile devices can assist them in understanding concepts and with content creation. In their survey of around 200 Year 12 students in Dar-es-salaam Mwapwele and Roodt (2016) found that nearly three-quarters of the students (73%) had used Google on their mobile phones for schoolwork with 44% saying that they had used YouTube. Nearly a third (31%) had used the camera or video on their device for learning and a similar number (32%) had used the maps app.

The advantages of using mobile phones for school work pointed out by the Tanzanian students at follow-up interview included finding further information via the internet, access to pictures that "'explain better', greater flexibility than textbooks and communicating with other students about schoolwork. They also had several concerns such as language issues, device compatibility, and possible unreliability of academic content on some internet sites.

The above case study has illustrated ways in which students have personally chosen to use their mobile devices outside of school to support work set by the school to be completed at home. The next two case studies present examples where mobile devices are used to formally link educational activities in the classroom with authentic or real-life contexts in the local surroundings of the school.

4.4 Bringing the outside inside

In these final two case studies, from Denmark and the USA, we read about ways in which teachers have organised learning opportunities that centre on using mobile devices to transport information, captured outside the classroom, into class. Thus the teachers and researchers involved are employing mobile devices to support students 'learning across multiple contexts' (Crompton, 2013, p.4). In this first case study though the emphasis is on how linking learning opportunities into a story that unfolds partly on the students' mobile phones and partly in the real world engages learners.

'Storifying' natural science education: A mobile urban drama played in teams

Hansen et al. (2010) introduce the notion of 'mobile urban drama' and describe how a particular production, an environmental thriller, for 7th to 9th Grade students was implemented in a city nature reserve in Denmark. Mobile urban drama is a general concept that has been adapted for out-of-school learning projects by introducing support for solving assignments and producing multimedia-based documentation for learning purposes. This initiative takes as its starting point Resnick's (1987) views on out-of-school learning reiterated long before mobile phones became widespread. She highlighted the following four issues that make out-of-school learning a necessary complement to classroom learning:

1. Individual cognition in school versus shared cognition outside.
2. Pure mentation in school versus tool manipulation outside.
3. Symbol manipulation in school versus contextualized reasoning outside school.
4. Generalized learning in school versus situation-specific competencies outside.

(Resnick, 1987, pp.13–15)

The story itself is that the class has been chosen to help a scientific research team, faced with the threat of a dangerous invading virus, record various habitats to show how the natural ecosystem could be restored if necessary. The students, working in teams of 2 to 4, navigate through four different habitats (open field, forest, lake and a forest lake) by means of maps on their mobile phones. At these four habitats the students examine the area and take photos and/or video documenting their work. They are supported in this through location-triggered audio, recordings made by Max, a scientific researcher in microbiology and ecology, and Søren, who is a nature guide as well as a historian specialising in myths and superstition. It takes about three hours to complete all the set tasks. For example, at each location trigger the students are asked to conduct different assignments such as drawing what they see, taking pictures of what they find with the mobile phones, and collecting soil tests. In addition, they take turns at role playing an interviewer, an interviewee or a cameraman to create a video commentary. The interviewer asks the questions given on the mobile phone – e.g. 'Which animals live here?', 'What do they eat?' or 'How does the soil smell? And how does it feel?'. The interviewee describes the conditions, and the cameraman makes sure that the process is well documented utilising the video camera on his/her mobile phone. The produced materials are saved as a local copy on the mobile phones and are then tagged with context information and automatically uploaded to a central server. One important point is that the mobile phones can also be used to contact the teacher in case of trouble.

Once back in the classroom the students and teacher can easily retrieve their data from the server. All of the files are named with a date, group number, post number and time of the day. Based on this data, the students then work in their groups to process the collected notes, images and video and to recapitulate the concepts being learned. Each group must work with the material (editing the video commentaries into a documentary, making a PowerPoint presentation and a written report) and present their findings in class. The teacher then discusses these with the whole class reinforcing the key concepts relevant to the subject being taught.

The mobile urban drama was evaluated by four classes and their teachers. All of the teachers reported that they all had good overall experiences with sending the students out independently in their groups. The way the activity enhanced learner autonomy was noted by two of them. Another common point reported was the way a field trip, as a shared experience for the students, could be used to explain and contextualise more theoretical material presented later on in school. With respect to the use of a dramatic story in a lesson plan, all of the teachers said that the narrative contributed in a positive manner as it made the experience more engaging and made natural science theory and concepts more digestible to the students.

In the next case study, two US researchers investigate in detail how students used loaned iPod Touches to capture photos and video outside class for use in maths lessons. Their aim was to enable teachers to build on students' informal digital practices through bringing authentic materials from everyday experience into the classroom to scaffold rich mathematical interactions around these artefacts.

Mathematics and mobile learning 1:1 and in pairs: Capturing, analysing and modelling linear phenomena

White and Martin (2014) present data from their classroom-based design experiment conducted with a mixed-age cohort of sixteen 7th, 8th and 9th Grade students set up to explore the potential of leveraging students' informal digital practices as resources for designing mathematics classrooms activities. It took place at a small urban charter school in the USA with a diverse, predominantly low-income student population and an innovative, inquiry-based curriculum.

During a two-week unit on linear functions and graphs students were tasked with using a loaned iPod Touch for out of class homework assignments that included using the on-board camera to first to capture photos of lines with a variety of slopes and then to record videos of linearly varying phenomena. Examples of photos brought in by the class included tiles on a floor, the edge of a door, a string of lights and the videos planned included people on an escalator or walking in the street. While images and videos were captured individually, once back in class, the students worked in pairs using the iOS apps Group-Graph and VideoPhysics respectively to analyse them.

The Group-Graph app included a tool that allows students to construct and determine the slope of one or more lines in the image in the form of the standard equation for a straight line $y = mx + c$ where m is the line's slope. So, the student activity involved student pairs selecting one of their photos taken on their iPods, uploading it to a public graphing display and determining the slope of the lines shown. White and Martin (2014)'s analysis of the conversation between two students engaged in doing this shows how the activity scaffolded the students in making mathematical sense of the images they had collected.

The second activity using VideoPhysics required students to annotate their videos captured at home with time-sequenced Cartesian coordinate points that can then be exported into data tables and again displayed graphically. The two examples reported by White and Martin (2014) comprise students analysing, first, a short video clip of a student's friend walking and, second, with the friend first breaking into a run. The teacher-researchers note how in the first video example, the student appears to have identified a kind of phenomenon that would produce a linear graph of distance over time, i.e. uniform, unidirectional motion captured from a stationary camera. Additionally, in the second example, she appeared to have taken pains to hold the other elements of the film constant while introducing acceleration thus indicating that she was actively exploring ideas about variation over time as she made her movies and the resulting distance-time graphs.

The amount of mathematical reasoning seen in the classroom triggered by the images and video captured by the students for homework clearly impressed the two teacher-researchers. They conclude that the way students can carry mobile digital devices with them as they move across contexts creates the potential to build bridges between the everyday objects of students' interest, and the mathematics of the classroom.

4.5 Issues in leading school-based mobile learning initiatives

In the twelve case studies presented in this and the preceding chapter I have tried to show a broad range of classroom-relevant mobile learning opportunities. While they represent a rich variety of ways in which teachers across the world are capitalising on the presence of mobile devices in schools, there are many other initiatives, recent and ongoing, and I apologise to all those who are not included here because of limited space.

It is also important to point out that the case studies included here have focused on published examples of effective practice in using mobile devices in schools. It is much harder to find reports of where things go wrong or those where allowing students to use mobile devices in class has not made much difference. An example of the latter was, however, reported by de Oliveira and Maia (2016) in their survey on the ways in which middle school students in Recife, a large city in Brazil, report using mobile devices in lessons. They note that currently schools in Recife are marked by a serious dichotomy in their educational setting. On the one hand, there are public policies supporting the distribution of tablet computers for students in the 2nd and 3rd year of high school, yet on the other, legal documents (laws, decrees, school regulations) prohibit the use of smartphones and the like on school premises. Their aim was to investigate what actually was taking place in the schools by asking the students themselves. They found that overwhelmingly teachers employed school-supplied mobile devices in traditional teacher exposition modes, i.e. mostly presenting slides and showing images or video, displaying a strong holdover from pre-existing pedagogical practice.

In another example, interviews with the science teachers at a secondary school in Turkey conducted for a Masters dissertation (Kaya, 2013) highlighted how a lack of preparation, both technical and pedagogical, affected a 1:1 iPads in-school initiative. Students received the tablets but few subject-relevant apps and the teachers were frustrated by their tendency to download and play games in place of set work, In particular, to be effective, the teachers felt they needed both connectivity between their computer and the iPads so as to be able to view the student activity and professional development to build up teaching with iPad strategies and more productive lesson plans. This finding that students can easily be distracted from school work by chat, games and social media easily accessed via mobile devices seems to underpin Beland and Murphy (2015)'s reported discovery that banning mobile phones in UK schools was linked with small but significant improvements in test scores amongst students, with the lowest-achieving students gaining twice as much as average students.

Indeed, academic colleagues aiming to conduct a systematic literature review on iPad use in schools (Khalid et al., 2015) noted that, while the wider media reports many frustrations with iPads when used as a part of the formal learning environment, most of the articles they found using university library resources, such as bibliographic databases, reflect positive experiences. Khalid et al. (2015) list the following barriers to adopting iPad use in schools that they found were reported:

- Teachers' technological knowledge and skills.
- Cost – including maintenance and insurance as well as any apps.

- Software – it needs to be administered, licensed and updated.
- Distractions.
- Pedagogy – since the iPad is new in an educational context, there is not enough literature available to support teachers' professional learning.

Many of these are explored in more detail in the following chapters of this book, which is intended to remedy the situation regarding the lack of available literature to support teachers noted above. In the meantime, here is some advice from a US head teacher who has led a number of digital initiatives including students bringing their own devices to school (BYOD) (Sheninger, 2016). Eric Sheninger was Principal at New Milford High School where, under his leadership, the school became a globally recognised model for innovative practices. He writes that the key to successfully implementing sustainable change begins with asking the right questions. Below are examples of such questions.

- Is your infrastructure ready?
- Have you developed a shared vision that takes into account staff, student, and community input?
- Have you developed a strategic plan to ensure the initiative will positively impact student learning? How will you evaluate effectiveness?
- Has the curriculum been updated and other resources explored?
- Have you created policies that protect students and staff while promoting creativity?
- Have the staff been trained in digital pedagogy (lesson/project design, assessment, etc.)? Do they possess the confidence to integrate the devices with purpose to support/enhance learning? Have fears and challenges been addressed?
- How will equity be ensured in a BYOD environment? What will you do if students forget their devices, don't have them, or have no access to Wi-Fi outside of school?
- Has a plan been developed to train students? What will be done to educate parents?
- How will you build community support?
- What evidence will be provided for key stakeholders such as the governing body or the Board of Education and community on the progress of the initiative?

This last point addressing the need to think through how and why a mobile learning initiative will be evaluated and the evidence that will need to be collected to record its progress leads us directly to the next two chapters which discuss respectively evaluating mobile learning in schools and the training needed to ensure their effectiveness alongside the challenges involved.

Questions

- What features can you find that are common to more than three of the case studies presented above?
- What particular challenges do you think the teachers in the different case studies planned for?
- As a secondary school teacher, how would you respond to a parent concerned that children in your class are wasting their time using mobile devices?

Further reading

Further case studies can be found in academic texts and handbooks including:

Berge, Z. L. and Muilenburg, L. (2013) *Handbook of Mobile Learning*. New York: Routledge.

Crompton, H. and Traxler, J. (Eds) (2015) *Mobile Learning and Mathematics*. London: Routledge.

Crompton, H. and Traxler, J. (Eds) (2015) *Mobile Learning and STEM: Case Studies in Practice*. London: Routledge.

Galloway, J., John, M. and McTaggart, M. (2014). *Learning with Mobile and Handheld Technologies*. London: Routledge.

Mentor, D. (Ed.) (2016) *Handbook of Research on Mobile Learning in Contemporary Classrooms*. Hershey, PA: IGI Global.

Y. Zhang (Ed.) (2015) *Handbook of Mobile Teaching and Learning*. Springer International Publishing.

and on the web:

Apple's 'Teacher Stories' at www.apple.com/uk/education/real-stories/

5 Evaluating mobile learning, sustainability and underpinning theory

Chapters 2 to 4 have presented a range of initiatives illustrating the range and potential of mobile learning activities that have taken and are still taking place in schools; however, looking back at the examples presented, many are small scale and not all have been sustainable over time. Implementing mobile learning school wide is not quite the same as realising a one-off research project. As Cerrato-Pargman and Milrad (2016) point out, larger, school-based mobile learning initiatives are confronted with complex and dynamic settings where high expectations driven by the motivating outcomes of such earlier, small-scale research projects can create additional pressures. Furthermore, the issues surrounding ensuring sustainability of any initiative are complex. As highlighted by Century and Levy (2004) there are intangible and contextual factors such as the perceptions of those involved, their philosophy behind the initiative and the culture in which it is set in addition to the more obvious tangible factors which include suitable materials, leadership support and professional development for key staff. This leads us to consider the challenges involved in measuring if, when and where a lesson, a unit, or a whole school-based mobile learning initiative is successful. When a dozen US secondary school teachers experienced in teaching with iPads were interviewed for a doctoral research project, they all reported evaluation (of lessons, teaching resources and digital tools) was a key skill that they found was needed to support them in teaching via iPads (Kim, 2014). On a larger scale we need to identify where and why some initiatives have struggled or succeeded and share what lessons have been learned. Thus this chapter discusses evaluating mobile learning in schools, the types of learning opportunities that can be anticipated and the issue of sustainability.

5.1 Evaluating mobile learning

However, before addressing potential methods for evaluating mobile learning environments I should just like to alert the reader to the need first to consider the purpose of a proposed evaluation and, in particular, who it is for. Importantly, Wingkvist and Ericsson (2009) point out, in their review of the lessons learned from three mobile learning initiatives (university as well as school based), that the results of the evaluation of a mobile learning initiative are what can and will be 'judged' by others. More specifically, they alert us to the need to be mindful of the range of potential stakeholders in the outcomes of the evaluation; any mobile learning initiative has more stakeholders than the immediately obvious ones, the teachers and the students themselves. Senior leadership teams whether from the district or the school and the supplying technology manufacturers spring to mind and, furthermore, Merchant (2012) reminds us of how, in the case of mobile phones in schools, stakeholders can even include the national press. Reports on such initiatives are newsworthy for, as he says, 'mobiles sit at the more contentious end of the continuum of opinion about technology in education' (Merchant, 2012 p.775). It is, therefore, important to carefully consider the evaluation process, the full range of interested parties and the evaluation strategies to be used need to be designed before the initiative begins. So, how do you evaluate a mobile learning initiative?

This question was first considered in detail at a workshop conducted at Nottingham University, UK in 2006 on behalf of Kaleidoscope, the EC-funded Network of Excellence on research into technology-enhanced learning. The workshop was set up by researchers belonging to the network's Mobile Learning Initiative in order to address the big issues that were being increasingly found in European research projects involving the use of mobile devices in informal as well as formal educational contexts. Evaluation was then seen as a big issue alongside others that included pinning down the nature of mobile learning itself; designing effectively for mobile learning opportunities that transcend contexts; potential conflicts between personal technologies and classroom-based learning and affective and ethical issues (Sharples, 2006). In the 'Big Issues' workshop report Taylor (2006) notes that, traditionally, evaluators would expect to connect the success of the design for a learning activity involving mobile devices to the success with which the learners achieved the stipulated learning outcomes. However, the workshop participants had pointed out that, in their experience, learning outcomes in mobile learning initiatives are flexible and adaptive. For example, they may appear unexpectedly and relate to the extent to which someone has assimilated information into their own experience or development, rather than the reproduction of knowledge in a pre-post evaluation survey. Other alternative approaches to evaluation that had been successfully used by the workshop participants included: analysis of learner contributions to a joint product; phone or computer log analysis yielding information about ongoing interactions; statistical analysis of activity patterns and giving teachers the means to collect data themselves, particularly when it helped support their role. Taylor (2006, p.26) concluded that 'evaluation needs to respond to the challenges of learning in the Mobile Age' and that an emphasis on activity analysis as well as context would be the way forward. She also notes that the fact that mobile learners are increasingly independent is to be celebrated rather than regretted, though it means that evaluators will need to be more agile and responsive.

Such challenges for the evaluators were outlined helpfully in more detail by Sharples (2009). He highlights the following issues that researchers were finding cropped up repeatedly when they were attempting to evaluate mobile learning interventions. First, there is the obvious fact that the learning itself is likely to be mobile, leading to challenges in tracking the learning activity or activities across locations and, quite possibly, involving informal as well as formal contexts. Then, linked to communication being an underpinning tenet of mobile devices, such learning may involve multiple participants in different locations and who are using a variety of personal and institutional technologies that include home or classroom desktop computers or laptops as well as tablets or phones. Finally, he points out (Sharples, 2009, p.21) that there may be specific ethical problems involved, asking 'how can and should we monitor everyday activity?'. This latter point is of such importance that the entire next chapter of this book is devoted to it. In the meantime, I present two examples to show how the rich range of activities occurring and learning opportunities arising during mobile learning initiatives have been evaluated previously.

In this first example, Smith et al. (2007) report their detailed process evaluation of a trial for an e-Science usability project called My Mobile Mission (M3) which involved multiple data collection streams evaluating children's use of mobile devices during a field trip outside school. The trial was conducted in an attempt to better understand mobile technology as a mediator in e-Science learning activities. Their aim was to capture sufficient data to reveal:

- what learners were doing;
- what they discussed during small group activities;
- what aspects of their environment were attended to and stimulated their thoughts;
- where they were at that time;
- what work products resulted while paying attention to social factors such as adult helpers and interaction with those not connected to the running of the experience;
- how technology mediated the learners' activity.

In the trial, six learners (11 year olds, in three pairs, with one or two adult facilitators to each pair) engaged in an outdoor treasure hunt activity, with each group using two mobile phones and a video camera. On the one phone, learners received clues as text messages leading them to find examples of sustainable energy on a university eco-campus and on the other, learners took photographs of the objects they found. These were uploaded for safe storage and later web-based review, reflection and summary construction into a multimedia story once back at base. It was found that, through reviewing the audio, video and image records captured by the learners alongside the phone and text messages logged during the activity and the final multimedia artefacts produced, the researchers gained a rich picture of the learners' experience. However, in this study, actual learning gains were not assessed though the authors report in a different publication that 'judging by the children's enthusiasm, the M3 trial went very well' (Wyeth et al., 2008, p.30) and they describe how the children constructed meaning as they encountered examples of sustainable energy concepts in practice. Wyeth et al. (2008) also report finding some usability issues linked to the technologies being trialled.

In a more recent example, Turner (2016) constructed a framework to support his evaluation of mobile learning initiatives taking place at an international school in Hong Kong that had over 1,800 students aged from 3 to 18. The evaluation was based around setting the types of opportunities afforded by mobile devices to support learning within the context of the school digital learning objectives. The opportunities themselves were: increased access, both to learning itself and to online information, tools and resources; building personal relationships with learning, involving personalisation of choice and pathways; increased interactivity and connecting across contexts. These opportunities focus on learning as valued, visible, connected and progressive. So, through review of available data in school, which included access to discussions within teaching team groups and departments, including recording their outcomes through collaborative tools such as Google Docs and access to students' personal digital portfolios, Turner (2016) evaluated a number of school projects. Taking, for example, a Grade 8 science project that involved students working collaboratively in groups of 3 to 4 to create the chapters for an e-book on diseases for younger students, Turner (2016) showed that the project supported the following mobile learning affordances:

- Increased access as the students worked via the school's online learning platform even when the group members were not co-located.
- Increased accessibility to content with students drawing on a range of web sources.
- Building personal relationships with new software tools such as iBook author and further developing their digital literacy.
- Personalisation of learning choices and pathways through student groups making individual choices over e-book design and widgets to be used.
- Increased interactivity through employing widgets including quizzes and interactive graphics.
- Connecting across contexts, working through both virtual and real-life activities and with the Grade 6 students as the intended audience.

It is clear that reviewing the students' digital portfolios, used to publish digital schoolwork, to gain peer and teacher feedback, and to chart learning against school curriculum objectives provided both a visible record of each student's digital learning journey and helped to connect findings from the discussions on teacher digital pedagogy. Turner (ibid.) concluded that, in this example, the school digital learning objectives, that learning was valued, visible, connected and progressive, were supported as follows:

- valued through assessing the e-book as a formal subject project for both science and design as subjects together with feedback from the Grade 6 audience;
- visibility through the e-book's publication on the school learning platform;
- connected through support for the group learning and problem-solving approaches involved in collaborative publishing; and
- progressive as the e-book creation formed a basis for deep learning, building knowledge through publishing science work to a different audience.

Readers will notice, however, that neither of the above two evaluation studies addresses 'hard' evaluation techniques such as usability surveys or comparing learning outcome measures with those of a control group. Nevertheless, qualitative evidence of learning is presented in the first example in the form of reported conversations during children's decision making as they tackled the 'treasure hunt' and in the final artefacts created. Similarly, illustrations from the artefacts created are used to evidence learning in the latter example. As Sharples (2007) pointed out, it is hard for researchers to source reliable data on outcome measures assessing the usefulness or effectiveness of mobile learning activities and many tend to rely on participant self-report. In this context the observations and artefact reviews noted in the above examples add considerable weight where evidence is needed. Additionally, direct learning outcome measures will vary with educational aims and context and, with mobile learning being so interwoven with other everyday activities, both inside and outside school, it is challenging to source an accurate control group.

Later Sharples (2009) reminds us that any method of evaluation will depend on what the evaluators want to know, who will then need to know their results and for what purpose are they to be used. For example, evaluation as education research will be concerned with under-standing how fundamental learning processes can be mediated, enhanced and transformed whereas evaluation to inform design will focus on usability issues. He suggests taking three focal areas for evaluating a mobile learning initiative: usability, effectiveness and satisfaction (Sharples, 2009). These were built into the following set of precepts for mobile learning evalu-ation published later that year in the opening volume of the *International Journal of Mobile and Blended Learning* to provide guidance for other mobile learning researchers (Vavoula and Sharples, 2009, p.60). The list includes:

- Capture and analyse learning in context, with consideration of learner privacy.
- Assess the usability of the technology and how it affects the learning experience.
- Look beyond measurable cognitive gains into changes in the learning process and practice.
- Consider organisational issues in the adoption of mobile learning practice and its integration with existing practices and understand how this integration affects attributes of in/formality.
- Span the lifecycle of the mobile learning innovation that is evaluated, from conception to full deployment and beyond.

Vavoula and Sharples (2009) go on to show how these precepts guided their evaluation of MyArtSpace, a structured inquiry learning activity enabled and scaffolded through mobile tech-nology, that connected learning in the classroom with learning in museums and galleries. MyArt-Space itself is an app that enables students to connect learning from a school trip to a museum or art gallery with in-class activities of planning and further study. Students are prompted to create their own interpretations of artefacts and exhibits when at the museum through making notes, taking photos and recording sounds using early smartphones. Then later, when back at school, these are reviewed, reflected on and organised into online galleries by the students to present their findings from the trip to the class and can also be shared with their friends and family (Vavoula et al., 2009). The evaluation of the MyArtSpace initiative was also informed by the lifecycle approach to educational technology evaluation proposed by Meek (2006) and the awareness that evaluation can be conducted at different levels of granularity. In summary, Vavoula and Sharples (2009) created and tested a framework for mobile learning evaluation on the MyArtSpace mobile learning initiative. It was termed the 'M3 framework' as three levels are postulated: micro, which examines the individual activities of technology users and assesses the utility/usability of the app; meso, which investigates the learning experience as a whole, identifying learning breakthroughs and breakdowns; and macro, which examines the impact of the new technology on established learning and educational practices. As a result, they reported that they found valuable insights both into the app, its design and functionality, and into the school and museum contexts and learning cultures. They conclude that the M3 framework provided 'a structured format to assess usability, educational and organisational impact, and their inter-relationships' (Vavoula and Sharples, 2009, p. 65).

Ahmed and Parsons (2013) also used the M3 evaluation framework, this time to evaluate a mobile web-based app, ThinknLearn, for science education that was designed to assist high school students when moving around the science classroom, performing hands-on-activities. The app supports the students in generating hypotheses and in collecting data during science inquiry investigations to test them by providing on-screen prompts and multiple-choice questions. On initial reflection though, they realised that the macro level would involve the establishment of both abductive science inquiry practices and mobile learning in school science education, which was not yet possible in the current educational climate. So, focusing on the micro level, they collected data on the app's usability and quality from 86 (3 classes) 15–16 year old science students in a school in New Zealand via questionnaire and semi-structured group discussions. The questionnaire was used to source quantitative data on the usability and quality of the app and devices used through standard Likert scale measures of attitude or perception and the recordings of the discussions, to source qualitative data providing detailed explanations to underpin the quantitative results. The app itself was found to be usable, with straightforward navigation, and easy to understand. It was also found, from the students' perspective, to be effective and enjoyable and to stimulate their thinking.

Further evaluation then, at the meso level, involved comparing this group of students' performance at a variety of science learning tasks with that of a further three classes who had not experienced the use of the ThinknLearn app and acted as a control. These tasks included pre- and post-tests comprising multiple-choice questions (with a second post-test two months after the original learning activity) and writing hypotheses with explanations while performing further science experiments. Analysis of results showed a small, statistically significant increase in performance on the initial post-test for the experimental group who used ThinknLearn whereas the increase in performance seen in the control group was even smaller and not statistically significant. At the later post-test designed to assess learning retention the difference was less obvious; however, the experimental group maintained their advantage over the control group. Differences between the groups were even clearer though when assessing their ability to formulate and explain hypotheses.

While Ahmed and Parsons (2013) do not themselves reflect on their use of the M3 framework it is clear that it allowed them to frame and construct a thorough evaluation of a school-based science learning initiative. Thus using the framework fulfilled Wingkvist and Ericsson (2009)'s two points that it is important to evaluate any mobile learning initiative in a thorough way, and that the evaluation methods should be designed before the initiative begins. Indeed, Wingkvist and Ericsson (2009) went on to say that one of the lessons they learned from evaluating three mobile learning initiatives is that evaluation should be continuous; designed and planned in the light of the different stakeholders and that the initiative itself should be flexible so that it can be adapted in response to the evaluation outcome. They also recommend co-designing the evaluation with those who may be affected through, for example, workshops with stakeholders, teachers, researchers, and domain experts (with specific knowledge of the intended scenarios).

One of the largest evaluations of mobile device use in schools conducted recently follows this advice. It was an evaluation of iPad adoption by five primary and three secondary schools in Scotland carried out by the Technology Enhanced Learning Research Group at the University of Hull (Burden et al., 2012). Again, a mixed methods research design was used, this time consisting of quantitative data collection through online questionnaire surveys and qualitative approaches comprising interviews, focus groups and analysis of both documents used in school and participants' video diaries. The online survey instrument was used first to collect baseline data from parents and students at the start of the initiative and largely repeated at the end of the pilot phase four months later in order to identify any changes and shifts in attitudes and practices. The baseline survey invited parents and students to describe their existing use of technology in order to establish the frequency of technology use, both at home and at school and to identify attitudes towards technology, particularly mobile technologies. A slightly modified set of questions was included in the endline survey to enable the researchers to identify any patterns such as trends or changes in attitude towards the use of technology, which now included the student's iPad, both in school and at home. Both the parental and student surveys were administered through the individual pilot schools; however, only 62% of the 138 parents repeated the survey. Both baseline and exit surveys were completed, however, by 261 of the 262 students involved in the study. In addition, interviews were conducted with representatives of all the other relevant stakeholder groups: teachers and local and district education managers. This included every 'iPad lead' teacher in each school which, in many cases, included two individuals as many schools paired teachers for the purpose of the pilot. In total 11 class teachers and nearly all the head teachers or relevant senior staff were interviewed. Additionally, education officers from the three local authorities where the schools were sited were interviewed separately to investigate the leadership for and management of the initiative perspective.

The researchers visited each of the eight pilot schools at least once to observe lessons, talk with a focus group of students and interview the key staff. Additionally, a significant amount of documentary data was collected from students and teachers. Each teacher whose class was given iPads was asked to maintain a reflective journal during the course of the pilot and also to identify six students to ask to keep their own video diaries of their mobile learning activities. The teachers were given access to a 'cloud' based storage account where they were asked to post these various artefacts on a regular basis. However, the short duration of the evaluation, which coincided with the busiest school term, made some of these data collection approaches problematic and it was not possible to ensure a complete return from each school. The data available to the research team sourced through this holistic approach was still considerable.

It was found (Burden et al., 2012) that, over the course of the evaluation period, daily technology use during lessons rocketed from being reported by 10% of the students to 80%. The secondary school students appeared to use their iPad slightly more frequently than the primary school students. All the students, teachers and parents reported significantly increased levels of students' motivation about and interest in their work at school leading to greater engagement and autonomy. In the questionnaires, 99% of the students reported using the iPads made lessons more fun, 96% that it led to more interest in learning and 92% that they learned more when using them. Teachers also reported that using the iPads led to more collaboration rather than less. Students from the six schools that allowed them to take the iPad home reported using it there for a wide variety of tasks with homework set by teachers being the most common activity. From their parents' perspective though, there was a need to limit the amount of time their children spent online at home. Their reasons for this varied but, somewhat surprisingly, concerns about online safety and privacy were relatively minor (9 per cent) compared to factors such as health and fitness (37 per cent).

Moving from the meso level of the participants reporting on the learning experience as a whole (Vavoula and Sharples, 2009) to the macro level examining the impact on educational practices, in Burden et al.'s (2012) study, it was clear that leadership and management of change was a key issue faced by the project leaders and stakeholders. Other key issues for stakeholders reported were maintaining and/or building relationships with the local authority and local community, concerns over e-safety and student behaviour with devices (this will be discussed further in Chapter 8) and resourcing the initiative during and beyond the duration of the pilot study (Burden et al., 2012).

As well as employing survey and interview techniques for data collection, Burden et al. (2012) asked a number of students to record video diaries to capture their use of the iPads for the researchers. However, in the end, only a few were provided. A possible alternative method for providing information on actual use of the devices, the analysis of internal computer logs or captured network activity was not considered for, as Wishart (2013) points out, there are ethical questions about recording from a device that crosses public-private boundaries. Nonetheless, this route was successful in the following study reported by Wong (2016) where the class teacher sought to assess and evaluate their students' learning progress during a flipped classroom initiative. In the 'flipped classroom', a term introduced by Bergmann and Sams (2012), students are asked to engage in lesson preparation that focuses on acquiring key information ahead of the lesson, e.g. by watching a video on their mobile phone so that the teacher can spend more time on active learning opportunities reinforcing and applying the new knowledge during the lesson itself. While this study (Wong, 2016) captured data from undergraduates in Hong Kong, the cloud-based resources used are available to and indeed, used in, many thousands of schools.

Just over 100 students on different education programmes were asked to review a short video (of eight minutes maximum) stored on YouTube before their class and, to support the students in accessing them, links to each video were posted to Schoology, a free, mobile-friendly, cloud-based Learning Management System. Course notes and reference materials were also made available on Schoology along with discussion threads in the built-in discussion forums for students to discuss and submit their pre-lesson preparation work. Schoology also includes attendance records, an online gradebook, tests and quizzes and homework dropboxes. Its interface, familiar from other social media such as Facebook, facilitates collaboration amongst a class, a group, or a school. Additionally, in class, the lecturer used Socrative, a cloud-based student response system, to enable the students to engage in interactive, formative assessment by using their mobile devices to answer quizzes and spot tests. Both Socrative and Schoology enable teachers to access detailed classroom and student data on their own devices. YouTube also monitors video watching activity. Thus both students' activities both in-class and out-of-class could be logged and analysed either by Schoology, YouTube studio or by the mobile instant feedback system being used (e.g. Socrative).

Visualisation tools produced by Schoology such as the number of 'hits' on a resource or the number of posts in a discussion over time showed how active students were at participating in the learning process. This was backed up by YouTube statistics which can even inform the teacher of how much of each video was watched and on which device as well as the number of views each day. Socrative, too, provides visualisation tools so that the teacher can monitor the class scores on different assessments over time. Thus learning analytics data can provide a rich picture forming a third data stream with which to triangulate observation and participant self-report in evaluating a mobile learning initiative. However, while students in Wong's (2016) study recognised the potential of learning analytics in enabling teachers to personalise learning opportunities, we should note that some raised concerns about being aware that the teacher was monitoring the analytics data, which added pressure and could become threatening.

From the above examples we can see that evaluating a mobile learning initiative is challenging; mobile learning opportunities do not stay still to be measured and have the potential to become messy at times. In addition, at one of the early conferences of the International Association for Mobile Learning, Traxler and Kukulska-Hulme (2005) reported that many of the evaluations of mobile learning trials and pilots they had reviewed rested only on a 'common sense' view of learning. Thus, in the case of evaluation, as they pointed out, this means that there is not always much theoretical justification or coherence to support the selection and use of any given evaluation techniques or methods. This view was repeated in Cheung and Hew's (2009) findings from their review of published research on mobile learning initiatives in both schools and universities. Cheung and Hew (2009) found that the researchers tended to place greater emphasis on the features of mobile devices and procedures for their use, rather than on the theoretical rationale or justification for using them. If we are to evaluate future mobile learning initiatives more effectively, we need first to establish a clear view of the underpinning learning principles, as originally advocated by Traxler and Kukulska-Hulme (2005). This argument is reinforced by Sharples's (2009) point that evaluation as education research is concerned with understanding how *fundamental* learning processes can be mediated, enhanced and transformed. Taking this more theoretical stance also helps address Traxler's (2007) concern that evaluation should be consistent, a recognised challenge in any mobile learning context, through centring on the principle rather than the device. Thus the next section of this chapter introduces several relevant key concepts, taken from established learning theory, which can be used to underpin explanations of mobile learning opportunities.

5.2 Theoretical principles underpinning mobile learning opportunities

In many of the examples cited so far in this book, mobile learning opportunities have been reported as productive, both engaging and enlightening for the students involved. Understanding the theoretical principles on which such productive learning is based is central to evaluating any of these or similar learning opportunities. We, therefore, turn now to considering, from first principles, why learning supported through the use of mobile devices can be particularly engaging or effective.

For example, taking a cognitive perspective on learning, that is to say focusing on learning as a change in an individual's internal, mental processes that enables new knowledge, attitudes and/or new behaviour, we can see that the theoretical approaches that appear to be most relevant to mobile learning are those that stem from the constructivist approach. In this approach, the learner is seen as an active constructor building new knowledge through reflection on novel experiences and new information. It stems from Piaget's (1952) original descriptions of how a child constructs their own understanding of their world, building on previous knowledge and understanding, in his theories of cognitive development. In the case of mobile learning, opportunities arise to build on information captured in one context in another and that information may encompass multiple modes: visual (still and moving images), text and sound (music and voice) thus making for more opportunities for the learner to encode and memorise it (Mayer, 1997). Many of the examples presented in Chapters 3 and 4 (Looi et al., 2011; Nordmark and Milrad, 2012; Ekanayake, 2011; Sparkes, 2016; Clarke, 2013; Hansen et al., 2010; White and Martin, 2014) involve students building information across contexts into new knowledge informed by the authentic, situated nature of those mobile learning opportunities. These contexts range from inside to outside the classroom, from home to school, from formal to informal learning opportunities and from the virtual to the real and vice versa. Indeed, as constructivism is often associated with pedagogic approaches that promote active learning, or learning by doing, even fixed location, i.e. in-class mobile learning (enabling learners to work interactively using mobile devices) can be included.

Seymour Papert (1980) himself built further on these ideas when he applied Piagetian theories to children's learning with computers to create the concept of constructionism. This emphasises 'learning by making' as opposed to 'learning by doing' and Papert believed that learning was most effective when it was part and parcel of an activity the learner experiences as constructing a meaningful product. Constructionist learning involves the learner making their thinking explicit by, for example, designing a computer program in LOGO. This also allows the learner to see the results of their thought processes, making it easier to revise or 'debug' them and, hopefully, building metacognitive skills. A good example of mobile device apps being able to scaffold students constructing their own understanding by making their thinking explicit is the use of Sketchy, the simple animation tool used in the Singaporean primary science class reported in Chapter 3 (Looi et al., 2011). Whyley (2006), director of the Learning2Go Project, one of the first large-scale mobile learning initiatives where more than a thousand school students in the UK were using personal digital assistants (PDAs, i.e. early smartphones) to support their learning lists Sketchy as a 'killer' application for PDA use. He considers it to be 'a superb "Flickbook" animation tool, which learners enjoy using to illustrate their understanding of science concepts and other ideas' (Whyley, 2006). Indeed, constructing an animation is particularly helpful in building understanding of dynamic concepts in science with the external representation (video) not only enabling learners but also their teachers to see the results of their thought processes. In a study of making simple animations using mobile phone and digital cameras in schools reported by Wishart (2016) all the teachers involved found that the way making animations exposed their students' understanding gave them the opportunity to see and promptly address any misconceptions. This was seen as clearly beneficial to student learning.

As with the primary school case studies presented under Section 3.4 'Bringing the outside inside' the animation example described above centres on the use of the mobile phone camera. It is, of course, quite possible to use handheld digital cameras instead for mobile learning activities that enable bringing authentic contexts from outside into the classroom. For example, Wishart and Triggs (2010) report from the EC-funded 'MuseumScouts' project that the teachers involved overwhelmingly (88% of those surveyed) agreed with the notion that their students learned from engaging with authentic museum artefacts. In this project, conducted in five European countries, secondary school students used information about and images of artefacts they captured during museum visits and field trips to design short interactive multimedia teaching presentations with collaborative authoring tools. Thus the project aimed to engender deep learning through technology supported knowledge acquisition, communication and, in particular, transformation for teaching others. This aim arose from the aforementioned active learning concept that, to embed learning, learners need to actively manipulate and use the information they acquire. Not only that, but also project partners reported that most learners welcomed the increased autonomy that came with the MuseumScouts approach. Nearly 90% of the 25 teachers involved agreed that participating in the project encouraged the students to take more responsibility for their work than they would have done normally. This was a gateway to students' more active involvement in learning and to thinking about learning processes.

Thus it appears that having access to their own mobile device on school visits and in school enables learners to control, or at least feel more in control of, their learning opportunities. Indeed, Jones (2006) in Mike Sharples' report on the Kaleidoscope Big Issues in Mobile Learning workshop described the importance of learner autonomy or control as a feature of the relationship of users with their mobile devices. In particular, she noted the relationship between control and the strength of association between the use of mobile devices and informal learning. Learners often find their informal learning activities more motivating than learning in formal settings such as schools because they have the freedom to define tasks and relate activities to their own goals and have control over their goals.

Furthermore, mobile devices enable both context aware or situated learning and collaborative learning, which offer opportunities for further engaging students and enhancing their learning. The former is supported by the authenticity principle already noted above and enables students to access 'on the spot' contextually relevant supporting information (Sharples, 2010) which promotes learning; however, this applies more out of than inside school. The latter, engaging in learning involving and/or supported by others, aligns more with the principles of learning as social constructivism, i.e. building understanding through interactions with others. Social constructivism theory stems from Vygotsky's original rejection of Piagetian constructivism as it did not include the social context in which learning takes place. Vygotsky (1978) argued that all cognitive functions including thought and language originate in and are products of social interactions. With mobile devices enabling both collaboration around the device as seen in the Bike Baron game example of a primary school-based mobile learning initiative (Williams, 2012) and collaboration via the device as seen in students' self-report in Ott et al.'s (2014) study into how they use mobile phones for school work at home, social interactions are key in many instances of mobile learning. Both of these examples were presented earlier in Chapter 3. Furthermore, Parsons and Adhikari (2016) noted that in their longitudinal study of a New Zealand school running a BYOD policy that use of mobile devices can enable collaborative learning to extend in real time beyond the school gates. They highlight that students were seen to use apps like iMessage to 'help kids connect with sick members of their group in group projects' (p.76).

Thus constructivist learning principles, including social constructivism, can be seen to underpin all mobile learning activities. The ease with which handheld mobile devices can be carried to different locations enables mobile learning opportunities in authentic locations or contexts or for information to be captured there to be built on later in school. These contexts can include the virtual enabling mobile learning activities to take place within the classroom. Such activities tend also to involve potential opportunities for learner autonomy or control in active learning situations and consequently can be seen by many as disruptive to traditional classroom-based learning (Sharples, 2002). The associated opportunities that can indeed impact on classroom behaviour will be discussed later in Chapter 8. Last, but not least though, these devices are above all communication tools and they can enable collaboration via voice, text and social media within and between classes as well as providing links to authentic settings for group work.

5.3 Pedagogical principles underpinning teaching via mobile learning opportunities

Learning theory discussed in the preceding section can clearly inform teachers' planning for teaching approaches and strategies to be used for school-based mobile learning opportunities. Indeed, an exploration of over 380 US preservice teachers' intentions as to whether or not to use mobile devices for teaching conducted by Hur et al. (2015) found that holding constructivist beliefs and perceived ease of use indirectly influenced preservice teachers' plans for classroom mobile technology adoption. Two factors that more directly influenced intention to use mobile devices for teaching though were perceived usefulness of the devices and perception about one's own self-efficacy for technology integration, with perceived usefulness being the stronger predictor. Unpicking these findings using structural equation modelling showed that holding constructivist beliefs had a positive influence on perceived usefulness of mobile devices.

Other researchers have focused more on identifying the pedagogical principles behind teaching for mobile learning. For example, the science teacher educators Ekanayake and Wishart (2014a) showed how mobile phones can support science teaching, in particular with communication during planning lessons and through visualisation. For capturing images enables teachers to relate subject knowledge to be taught to authentic locations and activities and to support assessment and post-lesson evaluation and reflection. Other teacher educators such as Kearney et al. (2012) also set out to explore how educators are using the distinctive pedagogical features of mobile learning. They describe how they developed a pedagogical framework for mobile learning through scrutinising the teaching activities taking place in mobile learning projects located in two teacher education communities. One project took place in England and the other in Australia. Kearney et al.'s (2012) framework was then refined by using it to work through six published mobile learning scenarios to ensure it effectively identified the underpinning pedagogical principles. The resulting framework is shown in Figure 5.1 and centres on three key principles: collaboration, personalisation and authenticity that Kearney et al. (2012) term 'feature pedagogies'.

As described later by Kearney et al. (2015) the collaboration feature pedagogy picks up on the collaborative learning principles introduced above in Section 5.2 and captures the frequently reported conversational, connected aspects of mobile learning (Sharples et al., 2007). It comprises two sub-themes: conversation and data sharing; conversation as learners engage in negotiating meaning, potentially forging rich networked connections with other people and data sharing as collaborating over information and resources across time and space. The personalisation feature pedagogy has strong implications for ownership, agency and autonomous learning as well as customisation through tailoring learning opportunities to individual learners via apps such as Nearpod and Classkick. Lastly, the authenticity feature pedagogy, which also appeared amongst the learning principles presented in the previous section, highlights opportunities for contextualised, participatory, situated learning. Its sub-themes of contextualisation and situatedness bring to bear the significance of learners' involvement in rich, contextualised

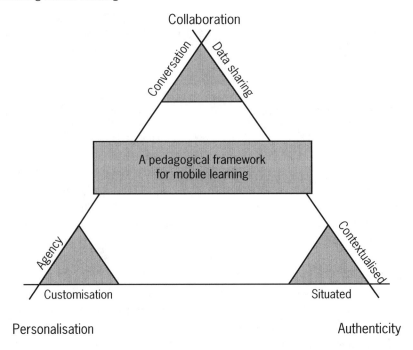

Figure 5.1 A framework for mobile learning adapted from Kearney et al. (2012)

tasks (e.g. realistic setting and use of tools), involving participation in real-life, in-situ practices. Learners can generate their own rich contexts (Pachler et al., 2010) with or through their mobile devices. The deeper contextualisation of teacher-set tasks in these physical or virtual spaces can be supported by geo-location and data capture facilities (Brown, 2010).

Kearney et al. (2015) further explored these three feature, or signature, pedagogies for mobile learning through a survey of over 100 practising Australian and European school teachers – 38% of their participants taught at the primary or elementary level whereas 62% taught in secondary school contexts and just under half (45%) perceived themselves as experienced users of mobile devices in their teaching. The survey results reinforced collaboration as a signature mobile pedagogy with most of the mobile learning activities described by teachers being highly social and collaborative in nature, albeit within a traditional face-to-face classroom context rather than a remote virtual one. Furthermore, authenticity as signature mobile pedagogy of a mobile learning task was rated significantly higher by the teachers than both collaboration and personalisation. This was despite the lack of genuinely situated scenarios reported, for example, where students used their mobile device in authentic contexts such as museums or on a field trip outside of the classroom. However, Kearney et al. (2015) suggest teachers must be conceptualising the construct of authenticity through a more nuanced lens which centres around the authenticity of the tool and the task, not only the setting. Though, that said, as Ekanayake and Wishart (2014b) point out, mobile device images and video can be deployed in learning activities to add authenticity. However, the personalisation signature mobile pedagogy was not rated highly by teachers, which, while it may be partially explained by the low level of device ownership seen amongst the students in this particular sample, Kearney et al. (2015) found surprising. They note that the lack of opportunities for students to demonstrate their own autonomy and agency seen in their survey runs contrary to the growing body of evidence high-lighting agency and student autonomy as amongst the most important features of mobile learn-ing. It certainly appears that these results support the perception that aspects of mobile learning are in conflict with traditional classroom-based learning (Mifsud, 2014).

5.4 Sustainability of classroom-based mobile learning opportunities

This conflict impacts, as Ng and Nicholas (2013) point out, on the sustainability of classroom-based mobile learning initiatives. Unless the teachers fully involve themselves with facilitating learning using the mobile devices to support achieving the goals of a mobile learning pro-gramme it will always falter and quite possibly fail. Based on their three-year study of the actions of a secondary school in Australia in its attempt to introduce and sustain a whole school mobile learning initiative using PDAs, Ng and Nicholas (2013) consider that pedagogical sustainability is possible with PDAs. However, it is very dependent on the classroom teachers' knowledge of the capabilities and limitations of the devices themselves, and the available applications, as well as knowing how to integrate them effectively into their teaching. Whether the integration of the mobile learning device's affordances is effective (hence sustainable) depends on the pedagogy adopted. As the Australian programme coordinator in the observed school commented, 'if the teachers maintain a "teach from the front" approach while using mobile devices, there will be a conflict' (Ng and Nicholas, 2013, p.713). In another Australian study of mobile learning initiatives in ten independent schools (Pegrum et al., 2013) staff issues were flagged up as crucial across the board with one interviewee reporting 'the staff is the biggest blocker'. Issues identified in these schools included teachers' lack of enthusiasm as well as uncertainty over how to integrate mobile devices with their teaching or doing so in pedagogically limited ways.

Ng and Nicholas (2013) concluded that effective integration of mobile devices into school-based teaching and learning is complex. Many studies focus on the technology but it is the fundamental issues that are human related that need to be addressed as sustainability is dependent on successful interactions between the leadership team, the community, the techni-cal support team and the key users, the teachers and students themselves. Sustainability means developing positive attitudes in students and teachers towards the programme and ensuring effective communication between everyone involved. This means ensuring the availa-bility of the devices and other supporting technologies, e.g. wireless, printers, smartboards, data projector and software for pedagogical practices. It also means providing the necessary support for the maintenance of the programmes, e.g. time release for scaffolded professional development and fixing technical issues. Ng and Nicholas (2013) add that trust between the key players and 'buy in' are important so that everyone involved has some form of ownership of the programme. Trust also opens up communication that is not undermining and increases the willingness to share ideas.

Therefore, in the current climate where rapidly evolving devices and time-poor teachers mean the introduction of mobile learning into the classroom inevitably produces tensions

(Pegrum et al., 2013) and these tensions reach beyond the classroom itself to include national policy (Cerrato-Pargman and Milrad, 2016), effective professional development to support those involved is clearly essential. This is nothing new: in an overview of their studies on PDA use in classrooms in the UK in the early 2000s, McFarlane et al. (2009) point out that the positive impact of mobile device use is limited if teachers have only had limited professional development in pedagogy and in the incorporation of devices in learning. I therefore turn, in the next chapter, to considering research on the impact of professional development and teacher education in mobile learning.

Questions

- When evaluating a mobile learning initiative what data will you be aiming to collect from each of the different stakeholder groups – students, teachers, parents, other school staff, and district officials – and how can you obtain it?
- Does Kearney et al.'s (2012) framework of three distinctive pedagogical features – collaboration, authenticity and personalisation – suffice to cover the underpinning rationale for using mobile learning in the classroom? If not, what is missing?
- What three factors will you need to prioritise to ensure a mobile learning initiative is sustained once the novelty wears off?

Annotated further reading

- Methods for evaluating mobile learning

Sharples, M. (2009) Methods for Evaluating Mobile Learning. In G.N. Vavoula, N. Pachler, and A. Kukulska-Hulme (Eds) *Researching Mobile Learning: Frameworks, Tools and Research Designs*. Oxford: Peter Lang Publishing Group, pp. 17–39.

In this chapter Mike Sharples, a pioneer of mobile learning, discusses issues related to evaluation of mobile learning projects for usability, effectiveness and satisfaction. These issues include: that mobile learning may be mobile (but not necessarily); it certainly may well occur in non-formal settings; it may be extended and interleaved with other learning opportunities; it may involve a variety of personal and/or institutional technologies and it can present particular ethical problems. These issues are illustrated through case studies of the evaluations for three major mobile learning projects. The Mobile Learning Organiser project used diary and interview methods to investigate students' appropriation of mobile technology over a year. The MyArtSpace project developed a multi-level analysis of a service to support learning on school museum visits and the Personal Inquiry project employed critical incident analysis to reveal breakthroughs and breakdowns in the use of mobile technology for inquiry science learning. It also addressed the particular ethical problems of collecting data in the home.

6 Teacher professional development and initial teacher education in mobile learning

This chapter discusses the professional development needed for teachers so as to ensure their effectiveness in view of the new technologies being introduced to a school together with any associated challenges. So many research studies include the conclusion that further and often better training would have made a big difference in how a mobile learning initiative was received and implemented. Teachers, of course, are central to the success of any and all of the initiatives described in this book and teaching via mobile devices is indeed complex. Kim (2014) identified four different pedagogical skills in teaching by using iPads that are needed in addition to having the necessary teaching subject knowledge and technological know-how to operate the devices. The four pedagogical skills were: (1) skill to evaluate lessons, teaching resources and tools; (2) skill to individualise instruction; (3) skill to manage the classroom; and (4) skill to relinquish parts of their role as sole authority and knowledge resource.

Some researchers and practitioners have exploited opportunities to introduce mobile learning into teacher professional development at different stages in teachers' careers. For example, Baran (2014) reviewed a number of research studies on exploring the inclusion of mobile learning in preservice, initial teacher education. However, most other reports, such as those presented in the next section, focus on continuing professional development for experienced teachers. That said though, some other notable studies actually investigate the outcomes of implementing teacher education via mobile devices and these will be discussed in Section 6.2.

6.1 Professional development for mobile learning

In the first instance, focusing on continuing professional development (CPD), Pegrum et al. (2013) make four main recommendations regarding professional development. First, protected time is necessary. Staff need time to attend formal training sessions; to engage in informal collaborations with colleagues; to play with the mobile devices in order to build familiarity; to research apps relevant to their teaching plans and to explore wider pedagogical possibilities. Second, a focus on pedagogy ahead of technology in the professional development sessions is essential. Pegrum et al.'s (2013) interviewees (principals, vice-principals, technology co-ordinators and teachers) reported that teachers needed help integrating new tools in a pedagogically sound manner and to explore truly innovative uses of the devices. Third, targeted and contextualised professional development is most effective for time-poor teachers, standardised training sessions are likely to be less effective than individualised professional development delivered at the point of need. Last, building a professional community of practice or a professional development network as a platform for ongoing professional development is a sustainable model which could encourage collaboration, save time and energy, and avoid schools and teachers 'reinventing the wheel'. McFarlane et al. (2009) endorse the need for building a supportive network and making time available in which to do it. They make the point that allocating teachers time to think, and facilitating contact with other teachers working with mobile devices, in-school and in a wider network, would encourage the 'viral' effect with effective learning opportunities spreading within a school and be beneficial in sustaining development. Specific to their early project McFarlane et al. (2009) add that they found that initial teacher professional development for mobile learning must include the basic operation of the device both on its own and in a network, and offer clear examples of effective use within the classroom. One or two examples of powerful 'killer' applications for teaching and learning were enough to seed uptake across the school but this use needed to be monitored, nourished and sustained. We should note that such encouragement can come from students as well as colleagues. For example, Beauchamp et al. (2015) noted how primary teachers in both Scotland and Wales adopted a diverse range of experiential, informal and playful strategies where they learned at their own pace, in a largely experiential fashion, alongside their students.

Others have advocated schools working in partnership with higher education institutions to support professional development and input, not only on how new technologies may support their existing practices but also how new goals for student learning, teaching practice, school policies and its infrastructure may be aligned in the context of mobile learning opportunities (Anthony and Gimbert, 2015). Anthony and Gimbert (2015) propose that higher education and school-based K-12 partners work together on mobile learning initiative design (including the development of both apps and learning environments that integrate new technologies) as well as on implementation of the mobile learning initiative in order to fully implement and sustain new technologies and practices. They add that implementing a mobile learning initiative is more complex than simply convincing students and teachers to adopt a new app. Schools may need to make adjustments to their goals for student learning and teaching practice, as well as considering what needs to happen throughout an organisation to support these new goals and practices. This includes creating new job titles and positions for technology integration support, professional development offerings, instructional materials, and means of obtaining information from and communicating with teachers.

However, not all schools have local higher education institutions to hand; this is particularly true of under-resourced, developing countries such as those in Africa. Yet, as Botha et al. (2012) point out, while the challenges of connectivity, infrastructure, hardware availability and support constitute the realities of Africa and are well documented in the literature, it also records an enormous growth in cell phone use. Thus, with support from the South African Department of Science and Technology, Botha worked with international colleagues to develop a curricular framework for mobile learning (Botha et al., 2012). This Mobile Learning Curriculum Framework was intended to be a living document hosted online that could support teachers nationally with, for example:

- Training. To facilitate the need for teachers, lecturers, NGO practitioners, etc. to meaningfully engage with instances of professional development in order to become knowledgeable about and/or be qualified in the field of mobile learning.

- Assisting teachers, lecturers and trainers who are, or will soon be, tasked with teaching a module or set of modules focused on mobile learning to a specific audience. Modules could suggest available resources, mobile-enabled pedagogy and possible means of assessment.
- Guiding teachers, lecturers, trainers and other practitioners in mobile-enabled pedagogical practices for their subject teaching. Concerns on how best to design and organise learning instances; addressing concerns such as governance, planning, practicalities, mobile safety and options for developing basic literacy through the use of mobile devices would be significant.

Additionally, the curriculum framework was deliberately non-specific in terms of the target audience and level to accommodate the dynamic nature of the domain as well as the possible implementation intentions of such a curriculum. It can be found on Wikispaces[1] (Botha, 2012) and underpins the development of mobiMOOC[2], the first example of massive open, online courses (MOOCs) developed to support practitioners worldwide with understanding and implementing mobile learning (de Waard et al., 2011). This globally available mobiMOOC initiative was set up in the light of UNESCO's then new support for mobile learning initiatives.

The UNESCO team had recognised that mobile phones had become ubiquitous in the vast majority of countries across the world and offered a unique opportunity to extend educational access to isolated and underprivileged learners (West, 2012). Indeed, the projects reviewed by West (2012) for UNESCO demonstrated that mobile phones offered significant opportunities in that they could support administration and professional development as well instruction. However, UNESCO also recognises that the teacher's role is crucial in ensuring success in any mobile learning initiative (West, 2012) and has already published work intended to provide policy-makers on the different continents with clear ideas for how to improve the ICT skills of their teacher workforces. In 2011 the organisation released the 'ICT Competency Framework for Teachers' toward this end. West (2012) goes on to point out that training teachers to use the mobile devices themselves is a necessary first step for preparing them to help students leverage mobile technologies for learning and that UNESCO surveys suggest that experienced teachers are 'hungry for this type of professional development' (p.15).

One more recent teacher education for mobile learning initiative involving the UK, Greece, Italy and the Netherlands, funded by the EC under its Lifelong Learning Programme and reported by Passey and Zozimo (2016), developed CPD for in-service teachers across primary, secondary and special schools. This focused on mobile learning through appropriate pedagogic uses of mobile or handheld technologies that had been earlier identified through a needs analysis in the four different countries. This needs analysis identified that, while many teachers know of benefits of using handheld devices for teaching and learning, such as their attraction for learners, potential for increasing learner engagement and improving the management of courses, fewer teachers know of issues arising (Passey and Zozimo, 2014). Most frequently, issues reported in this initial analysis were technological. Correspondingly, the main forms of support requested from training sessions were technological and content knowledge. The main teaching practices for mobile learning requested from training sessions were capturing and using imagery and video, research, and having students creating their own notes and books in multimedia formats.

Going on to reflect on the outcomes of the CPD course once implemented, Passey and Zozimo (2016) report that the training and the uses of devices that followed in school can be considered an overall success. In particular it was found that certain forms of activities now being undertaken in classrooms across the four countries involved were reported to be of particular benefit to student learning. They were:

- 'Review and reflect', where students capture audio, imagery and/or video during the lesson and use these in plenary sessions to reflect on what has been covered, consider the key elements learned, how these fit into wider subject or topic pictures, or how ideas might be used;
- 'Think forward', where students access future topic material via the internet and capture relevant thoughts or ideas to contribute to discussions or presentations in class or through online discussions. Students can be encouraged to use the mobile devices at home to research topics for themselves;
- 'Listen to my explanations', where students record audio when they are completing homework assignments and these verbal explanations are listened to and marked by teachers;
- 'Snap and show', where students capture imagery, which is downloaded to a server and accessed through a computer or interactive whiteboard screen, for wider student discussion, perhaps made accessible to parents so that they can see and discuss events that have happened in school;
- 'This is what I've done and how I've done it', where students create presentations of how they have used mobile technologies to tackle particular activities, which are recorded and made accessible on appropriate web-sites for teachers and parents to see and
- 'Tell me how I could improve this', where students can share their work in multimedia formats with peers, mentors, teachers or trusted adults in order to seek comments, evaluative feedback, assessments of their work, and ideas to improve their work.

(Passey and Zozimo, 2016. p.5)

Another European project, still ongoing at the time of writing, MTTEP (Mobilising and Transforming Teacher Education Pedagogies) funded under the Erasmus+ scheme is focusing on the needs of staff employed in teacher education in three schools (in Germany, the Netherlands and Norway) and five universities (in Australia, Germany (2), Norway and the UK). It is developing a bespoke mobile learning toolkit[3] for teacher educators and allied professionals including academics and teachers. The toolkit will comprise a set of instruments, exemplar case studies, guidance and training materials intended to enable teacher educators, teachers and other lecturers outside of teacher education to evaluate their current practice with mobile technologies in order to implement effective new pedagogies which exploit the unique characteristics of mobile technologies. It is based upon the trio of pedagogical affordances of mobile devices: Personalisation (P), Authenticity (A) and Collaboration (C) originally identified by Kearney et al. (2012) and described earlier in Chapter Five, Section 5.3.

An alternative approach would be to train new teachers in designing and implementing mobile learning opportunities as part of their initial teacher education (ITE). Indeed, Baran (2014) found, in her review of 37 studies researching the use of mobile learning that there is an increasing trend in integrating mobile learning in teacher education contexts generating an increasing amount of research into its outcomes; however, theoretical and conceptual perspectives are rarely reported. Engagement with mobile learning and mobile devices is primarily reported as being beneficial though variations exist in the perceptions, attitudes and usage patterns noted and the underpinning challenges informing them were scarcely reported. Baran (2014) also found these mobile learning studies repeatedly reported several key learning opportunities for preservice teachers that supported integration of mobile learning into teacher education settings. These included tasks that involved connectivity and/or collaboration, flipped classroom models, mobility within the physical space of the classroom, backchannel conversations, engaging with task-specific content on mobile devices, mobile learning in school student teaching, performance evaluation and participation in professional learning communities. Indeed, some of these studies have focused on exploring the delivery of initial teacher education or continuing professional development on mobile learning actually via the mobile devices themselves.

6.2 Delivering ITE/CPD by means of mobile learning

In this penultimate section of the chapter I consider instances where teacher education and/or professional development has actually been delivered via the mobile devices themselves. This was my original introduction to mobile learning. With funding from the Teacher Training Agency I issued PDAs to 14 science teacher trainees on a one year PGCE initial teacher education (ITE) programme to explore how the mobile devices could support both trainees' learning and their teaching (Wishart et al., 2007). The fact that mobile devices such as PDAs (the forerunners of today's smartphones) are both highly portable and offer learning and teaching support (Naismith et al., 2004) is particularly relevant to ITE where students regularly move between university and placement in school. They are expected to acquire, decipher and understand a wealth of information, both pedagogical and practical, in the process. The use of mobile devices was thought to be particularly relevant to the student teacher, who is expected to teach as well as learn, for previous work with teachers using PDAs in schools (Perry, 2003) had shown that PDAs can be supportive of teaching. In particular they offer considerable potential to make teachers' management and presentation of information more efficient. One science teacher had reported to Perry that he 'would never willingly go without one now; it is my instantly accessible encyclopaedia, thesaurus, periodic table, diary, register/mark book, world map and even star chart!' (Perry, 2003, p. 4). Learning and teaching support for an ITE student via a PDA is grounded in the ability to access information exactly when and where it is needed to support teaching or learning. This information may come from an electronic book, dedicated science software or the web, especially via the course's linked virtual learning environment (VLE), or from previously recorded student data or via communications with peers and tutors. Thus the communications capability is a key feature of the PDA in this context for, as first proposed by Pea (2002), the PDA is acting as a communication channel enabling highly interactive conversations and access to archives of information, knowledge and representations of past activities that can be read, drawn upon and extended as needed.

During initial training the students were shown how the PDAs have the potential to support them in:

- collaborating via the VLE (Blackboard) discussion groups and email;
- accessing course documentation (on PDA or via Blackboard or via synchronisation (synching) with a PC);
- just in time acquisition of knowledge from the web;

- acquisition of science information from e-books and encyclopaedias;
- delivering accurate figures for scientific constants and formulae;
- organising commitments, lesson plans and timetables;
- recording and analysing laboratory results;
- recording student attendance and grades;
- photographing experiments for display and reinforcing student knowledge;
- maintaining a reflective web log (blog) that could allow them to record lesson evaluations and other reflections on their teaching.

They were then loaned the PDAs for the rest of academic year. The student teachers were participant action researchers in the project acting on their teaching and learning by means of the PDA and then reflecting on and amending their practice (Wadsworth, 1998). They reported in twice termly surveys and two focus groups, one halfway through and one at the end of their course. Results showed that only three student teachers used the PDA to its full potential as outlined in the training. Another eight students used theirs intermittently during the year and three gave theirs up. As in Gado et al.'s (2006) study exploring preservice teachers' decisions to use handheld computers in scientific investigations, the school culture and context clearly impacted upon the student teachers' use of the PDAs. The eight students, who used theirs intermittently throughout the year, were the most affected by the sociocultural context of being a student in a school. While recognising that having internet access on the PDA extended their capability to answer questions and plan lessons and having Word enhanced their recording of their observations for later assignments, they tended to feel uncomfortable about the attention gained by using the PDA in class or about asking the school to resolve hardware issues. However, it was of considerable benefit to these students that the small size of the PDA meant it could be returned to a pocket or bag when it was not wanted.

Much more recently Mac Mahon et al. (2016) reported on their study to examine how the professional learning and pedagogical knowledge development of student teachers could be supported following 1:1 roll out of iPads on a one-year, postgraduate, secondary level initial teacher education (ITE) programme in Ireland. They analysed reports from 38 student teachers on their iPad use made via questionnaire and focus group. Mac Mahon et al. (2016) found that the findings could be grouped by five themes. The first and strongest was the effectiveness of the iPad, when used in association with cloud-based storage of files and selected apps, as a tool for enhancing student teachers' personal organisation. Others included the iPad's utility as a tool both for creating and accessing new spaces where learning could occur; the effectiveness of the iPad as a pedagogical tool (when connected to a data projector) for motivating school students' interest and engagement; the use of the iPad with its data, audio and image capture tools as a means of reflection which clearly benefited pedagogical knowledge and the associated impact (both positive and negative) on the placement schools. Challenges to the use of iPads still encountered though included infrastructural and attitudinal factors amongst teachers in schools. In another study with similar findings, this time of preservice teachers in the North of England, Burden and Hopkins (2016) use Ertmer's (1999) distinction between institutional and personal barriers to technology integration helpfully to categorise such factors into first and second order barriers. First order, institutional barriers to using iPads in ITE include: integration with school infrastructures and interoperability issues; available time; concerns about disapproving school cultures; lack of support from university mentors and lack of training. Whereas second order, more personal barriers or challenges include: inability to perceive a pedagogical purpose for the iPad; seeing it more as a tool to make traditional practices more efficient; confidence in one's self and in the devices themselves and distrust of students' ability to manage such devices in school.

However, where initiatives exploring the potential of mobile devices for supporting initial teacher education go ahead, one particular recurrent finding is that the use of images and, in particular, video features strongly throughout. Even in an early study that took place in Finland with home economics teacher trainees, Seppälä and Alamäki (2003) found that their student teachers particularly appreciated the immediacy with which they were able to use their mobile device to capture and share information and to give and gain feedback. The most noticeable thing reported though, was the number of digital pictures taken and uploaded for discussion with peers and tutors. Seppälä and Alamäki (2003) reported that the students considered that using digital pictures in this way grew their professional identity as a teacher of home economics. They could see how they looked in front of their class and how they taught the students. Additionally, the use of still pictures helped students and supervisors to see things that they did not notice in the actual teaching situations.

When I loaned a set of PDAs to modern foreign language (MFL) teacher trainees (Wishart, 2008) we found that the student teachers were tentative about using the mobile devices in school, especially where the school students would be reprimanded if caught using mobile phones. However, where the PDAs did really come into their own was for capturing on-the-spot events spontaneously when pre-booked equipment such as audio or video recorders was not available. One student noted how surprised they were after using the PDA to record students role-playing a situation at a one-off event for those identified as gifted and talented that the sound wasn't at all bad. Another student praised how using the PDA to record was more informal than booking the tape recorder, inserting the tape and pressing play and therefore less intimidating for students practising a new language.

In a more recent example, Ayres et al. (2013) from the University of East London, UK examined the impact of supplying school placement tutors overseeing the initial teacher trainee with iPads. They found that having the iPad facilitated the provision of visual and audio feedback to students as well as the sharing of files through cloud storage, with the student teachers reporting that having the audio/visual feedback was both popular and effective. Ayres et al. (2013) do point out, though, that careful note needs also to be taken of ethical considerations, particularly around storage and sharing of data, as will be discussed in more detail in Chapter 7. For it does appear that the potential of mobile devices in ITE to collect rich data to support student teachers' progress is currently dogged by concerns about their potential to share this information inappropriately or about the view that mobile devices are playthings that should not be seen in school. However, that said, to finish on a positive note Naylor and Gibbs (2015) show how preservice teachers studying English and science could use iPads creatively to collaborate on a cross-curricular field trip that resulted in an e-book of the seashore with images and poems. Results of the participants' survey following the field trip showed that the perceptions of the preservice teachers towards using mobile devices in 'authentic situations' changed positively and there was also a positive impact upon interpersonal skills and confidence of those taking part.

As for delivering continuing professional development for teachers via mobile devices, in addition to the use of mobile devices for capturing evidence and sharing reflections as described with teacher trainees above, there has been notable success with the use of video and audio to support English language teaching. 'English in Action' is a large-scale professional development programme for teachers of English in both primary and secondary schools in Bangladesh. Teachers are provided with iPods (Nano and/or Touch) containing both age-appropriate recordings of classroom language (textbook dialogues, readings, poems and songs) to use and videos of classroom practice illustrating teaching strategies (filmed by local teachers in their schools) for their use. Outcomes following the pilot, with around 700 teachers, reported by Power et al. (2012) showed not only that both primary and secondary school teachers and students were talking more during their English lessons but also that most of this talk time was in English. The teachers were now spending more time asking questions, and giving feedback, which indicates that they are making efforts to involve students in interactive and communicative activities rather than just reading and presenting to the class from the textbook.

West (2012) also makes the point that teachers' use of mobile phones can make professional learning communities effective. He uses the Teaching Biology Project in South Africa as an example. It runs three in-service teacher training workshops each year and in between meetings the group send to each other and receive motivational, administrative and content-specific texts. The project had also established a Facebook page, a Twitter account and a profile on MXit, a popular social media platform in South Africa. The local teachers regularly access the resources and post messages to these sites using their mobile phones. Indeed, teachers worldwide are increasingly using Twitter to support their professional learning (Visser et al., 2014). Following interviews with teachers, teacher advisors and teacher educators in Australia and England, Aubusson et al. (2009) argue that mobile devices are ideally suited to capture the spontaneity of learning moments and to communicate with others about them. The devices can, therefore, enable both reflection-in-action and collaboration, themselves important actions for effective professional learning

6.3 Conclusion

This chapter has considered professional development, quite possibly the foremost issue relevant to ensuring the success of any mobile learning initiative in a school, for sustainability is a known issue in a climate where both curricula and mobile devices change regularly. Not only that but, as implied above, there likely needs to be changes in teachers' pedagogical practices to accommodate the different balance in agency where students have access to digital tools that empower their own learning. Already psychologists in Canada are reporting that children can learn facts equally effectively from iPads as from face-to-face instruction with a teacher (Kwok et al., 2016). Thus ensuring that appropriate continuing professional development is made available for the teachers involved, that the teachers understand the underpinning learning theory and prepare for teaching strategies that involve mobile learning tools is essential. In addition, ensuring appropriate monitoring and evaluation is in place will support the new initiative. Questions have, however, been raised above about how schools receive teachers wishing to use mobile learning. With the view that smartphones are entertainment devices that have no place in school being commonly held, or even mobile phone bans in place, it appears that strong sociocultural pressures militate against the use of personal mobile devices to support teaching and learning in UK schools. Indeed, Hodkinson and Hodkinson (2005) identify the practices and cultures of the different subject departments in schools as one of three dimensions that influence teacher learning. The other two are the dispositions of the individual teacher and the management and regulatory frameworks, at school and national policy levels. If we are to see students making the most of the wide range of learning opportunities offered via mobile devices as described earlier in Chapters 3 and 4 we need to address this sometimes unwelcoming, sometimes hostile, culture. Thus the next two chapters discuss first the ethical questions that arise when teaching via mobile learning and then, in Chapter 8, the behavioural issues commonly concerning teachers about allowing mobile devices in class.

Questions

- You are a full-time teacher and your school is planning on purchasing a set of iPod Touches for Year 8. When would you like training for teaching with the mobile devices and what form should it take?
- What are the pros and cons of using social media such as Facebook, Twitter and/or WeChat on mobile devices for professional development via messaging, audio and video?

Annotated further reading

- Guidelines for mobile learning

UNESCO (2013) Policy Guidelines for Mobile Learning. Available at: http://unesdoc.unesco.org/images/0021/002196/219641E.pdf

Written by Mark West and Steven Vosloo of UNESCO, these guidelines seek to help policy-makers and teachers better understand what mobile learning is and how its unique benefits can be leveraged to advance progress towards Education for All. Their work was informed by a dedicated advisory committee comprising UNESCO staff members from the Education Sector, the Communications and Information Sector, UNESCO Institutes and Field Offices, as well as external specialists from at least 14 different countries. After introducing the unique benefits of mobile learning and illustrating them with case study vignettes, the guidelines outline the following recommendations:

- prioritise the professional development of teachers for success of mobile learning hinges on the ability of teachers to maximise the educational advantages of mobile devices;
- provide necessary technical and well as pedagogical training to teachers when introducing mobile learning solutions and opportunities for, while many teachers know how to use mobile devices, many do not;
- encourage teacher training institutes to incorporate mobile learning into their programmes and curricula; and
- provide opportunities for educators to share strategies for effectively integrating technology in institutions with similar resources and needs.

The guidelines then go on to discuss policy initiatives to highlight how mobile technology can improve teaching, learning and administration in educational institutions.

Notes

1 http://mobilelearningcurriculumframework.wikispaces.com/Home
2 http://mobimooc.wikispaces.com/a+MobiMOOC+hello%21
3 www.mobilelearningtoolkit.com/

7 Ethical considerations arising in school-based mobile learning

In earlier chapters I have alluded to teachers' and researchers' concerns over how allowing children and teenagers access to personal, portable, connected mobile devices in school can foreground ethical questions linked to the devices' capacity to transcend what were once fixed information boundaries. These boundaries range from home to school, from private to public, from the formal to informal, from inside school to outside class and from virtual to real. In this chapter I address these concerns, which are clearly impacting on the potential use of mobile devices in schools and any associated educational innovation (Vosloo, 2012). This can be seen in how uncomfortable the teacher trainees felt in using devices forbidden to their students in the two studies I conducted exploring how ITE students could use PDAs to support them in learning to teach (Wishart et al., 2007; Wishart, 2008) as well as in more recent studies addressing ITE students' use of iPads (Burden and Hopkins, 2016; Mac Mahon et al., 2016).

Vosloo himself, reporting on UNESCO's global review of mobile learning initiatives across dozens of countries, sees the main challenges to incorporating mobile learning in schools as including limited opportunities for teachers to learn how to incorporate mobile technologies into their classroom practices as well as ethical 'concerns about privacy and online safety; negative perceptions regarding the use of mobile phones in education by some teachers and parents; and inequity of device ownership, which still exists despite the fact that mobile phones are the most ubiquitous ICT in history' (Vosloo, 2012, p.8). But what do the teachers and other involved themselves report? This chapter starts by discussing the ethical concerns reported by teachers and mobile learning researchers, illustrating the evidence where found; however, it should be noted that most published reports do not dwell on concerns. Sometimes an issue gains media attention though and is widely shared, impacting on those negative perceptions noted by Vosloo (2012). The chapter goes on to discuss support for teachers; first, in the form of developing policy guidelines and second, in the form of involving them in using ethics frameworks to generate their own scenario-based professional development.

7.1 Ethical concerns reported by teachers and mobile learning researchers

Aubusson et al. (2009) conclude, from interviews with eight educators, comprising teachers, teacher advisors and teacher developers from Australia and the UK, that there are five key ethical concerns relevant to classroom-based mobile learning that teachers should bear in mind. The eight research participants were selected because they are stakeholders in influencing professional learning and/or engagement with digital technology amongst teachers in schools. The issues they identified were: cyberbullying; potential public access to events and materials intended for a limited, school-based audience; sharing of digital materials that include student data for professional purposes; archiving and keeping records of student performance; and ensuring informed parental and student consent. It is interesting to note that three of these issues address data or information sharing which, in the UK, is clearly within the remit of the Data Protection Act (1998)[1]. Burden et al. (2012) helpfully group the types of data whose access they say can be 'an ethical minefield' (p.20) for mobile learning researchers into four. They are:

- text-based data such as SMS texts, tweets and other social media posts plus usernames and status bars;
- visual and audio data whether saved on the device or uploaded or perhaps illegally downloaded;
- location-based data such as GPS data identifying the user's location, their route there and places visited previously; plus
- meta-data such as the information stored about internet search habits by search engines, cookies and browser histories.

The UK Data Protection Act (1998) itself specifies that such data should, amongst other things, be used for limited, specifically stated purposes in a way that is adequate, relevant and not excessive and kept safe and secure. However, as pointed out by Wishart (2009), people using mobile devices and the associated cloud-based storage are not always aware of where the information they are sharing is stored and who can view it. Indeed, Stern (2004) notes the irony in that many adolescents consider online spaces as private, for they do not want parents and family to be aware of their activities, but at the same time much of their activity on the web is public to networks ranging from friends through to anyone with internet access.

One of the issues from Aubusson et al.'s original list (2009), cyberbullying, will be discussed in the next chapter under behavioural concerns associated with enabling mobile phone use in schools, and the last, ensuring informed parental and student consent, is well established within the field of mobile learning research. It was one of the major ethical issues inherent in mobile learning noted by Traxler and Bridges (2004) at MLearn 2004 in Rome, the first truly international conference on mobile learning. The others were anonymity and confidentiality for participants in mobile learning initiatives and obeying professional guidance on participant risk, payment to participants and cultural differences. However, as Traxler and Bridges (2004) themselves note, taking the example of informed consent, that in 'pure' mobile learning, following formal guidance is potentially problematic for a number of reasons. These reasons centre on the unpredictability of research that follows the learner using a mobile device across different contexts, both virtual and real and where there may be insufficient means for would-be participants to check their understanding of the mobile learning initiative and their part in it, or even of the way the different functions of their mobile device operate. Andrews et al. (2015) later point out that research in these environments can take many forms as educational researchers, including teachers researching their own practice, use data collected on students' mobile devices in, and across, private and semi-public domains that include the classroom, the field, during workplace training, informal learning and private study in students' homes. Pachler (2010) adds that mobile learning practices are also personal, intimately bound up with the individuals concerned as well as the formation and reformation of their identity and their relationship with members of their peer group. In their original paper Traxler and Bridges (2004) went on to highlight that mobile learning could even take place across several different countries and consequently across different legal jurisdictions, which begs the question of whose ethical guidelines should a researcher be following in the first place.

Fortunately Lally et al. (2012) remind us of the role iterative and participatory research ethics can play in educational research and go on to show how they can be used to address the unpredictability of context and activity inherent in mobile and ubiquitous learning. Indeed, Carmichael and Youdell (2007) had already proposed moving away from a 'permission seeking' approach to an iterative, fluid cycle of ethical practice when reporting on their research into the use of online, virtual collaboration environments for educational research. Lally et al. (2012) went on to add another seven major ethical considerations generated from a thematic review of the published ethical guidelines of twelve major international organisations relevant to research into mobile, ubiquitous and immersive technology enhanced learning (MUITEL). These included informed consent, access to the technology (with associated potential for discrimination, even abuse), user generated, personal content or data, potential for attachment to loaned devices, the introduction of unsuitable materials, intrusion into privacy and the blurring of boundaries. They conclude that ethical review processes are most valuable in MUITEL research if they are understood not as 'approval' or 'clearance' by an ethics committee or professional body but as contributing to, or even initiating, formative and dialogic practice. However, they point out that questions remain over exactly how you construct such a more comprehensive ethical process, particularly in boundary-crossing areas like mobile and ubiquitous learning research.

Returning to the practitioners' perspectives, similarly to Aubusson et al. (2009), Wishart (2009) also noted five key areas of potential ethical concern relevant to both teachers and educational researchers though the list differs slightly. This list, derived from discussions with teachers, teacher advisors and teacher educators (n=17) in the UK, includes informed consent, the ownership of the mobile device and of the information on it and the data collected, images (the ease of taking, sharing and publishing them), sharing user-generated content and personal data and data protection, storage and loss. However, she also further questions the role of available ethical guidance from mobile learning researchers and other professional associations and points out a number of situations commonly occurring in mobile learning research where change and complexity impact upon its usefulness. Aubusson et al. (2009) add teachers' concerns that ensuring all guidance is complied with conflicts with the potential usefulness of mobile devices when used in their teaching to capture aspects of their practice spontaneously. One of their participants complained 'It has to be a pre-arranged and agreed activity' (p. 242).

In the USA, Thomas et al. (2013) asked teachers at the annual district conference on Imagining the Future of Learning (IFL) to identify what they perceived as the main barriers to using cell phones in the classroom. The majority of teachers (48 or 61.5%) responded that access and cost were the major barriers. Other barriers included disruption of class (40 or 51%), access of inappropriate content (37 or 47.4%), cheating (29 or 37.2%), cyberbullying (26 or 33.3%), negative impact of texting on student writing (20 or 25.6%) and sexting (19 or 24.4%). While cheating, disruption, cyberbullying and sexting are clearly issues of student behaviour and so will be discussed in Chapter 8, access and cost remain an ethical question for schools. Whose responsibility is it to ensure students have access to mobile devices? The school's? The students' families?

What about ensuring that they are brought to school, fully charged each day or that there are spares available in case of accidental damage?

While schools' policies for managing students bringing their own device to school are discussed in the next section we should note that schools in both New Zealand and the UK have made national newspaper headlines in their respective countries by requiring parents to supply children with iPads. According to Maas (2011) a secondary school in Auckland drew criticism from national budget and education advisors who believed its plans would cause a two-tier education system as many families would struggle to afford an iPad. Similarly, Helm (2013) reports in the *Guardian* about parents' and teaching union representatives' concerns over schools' plans in the south of England. Even the US high school in the case study '*Using iPads 1:1: Heart anatomy with a digital pulse*' reported in Chapter 4 that managed supply and maintenance of the iPads expected parents to pay for annual insurance or make good any damage that occurred. It seems likely that, given social inequalities present in schools across the globe, equity of access is liable to remain a contentious issue. However, that said, Dyson et al. (*in press*) note that mobile learning is already being used across the Asia Pacific region to overcome major educational inequities in access to and resourcing for schools.

The design of the mobile devices themselves is an obvious contributor to many of the teachers' concerns noted above. Highly portable, they are an ideal tool to support learning across contexts and boundaries. Also the multiple functions of mobile phones and tablets, particularly their use for taking photographs and videos and the ease with which these images can be uploaded to file-sharing and social media websites, create huge risks of privacy infringements (Wishart and Green, 2010). One particular concern for teachers is that the much smaller size of mobile devices compared to traditional cameras and video cameras makes them 'infinitely more portable and unobtrusive', allowing surreptitious recording to be much more likely than was possible with the older technology (Aubusson et al., 2009, p. 243). Again, because of their size, theft and loss of mobile phones are quite common, compromising data security (Wishart, 2009). Lastly, mobile devices are not just physical tools, they are gateways to cyberspace and virtual worlds. This has been a longstanding issue for teachers concerned about the ease with which students can share and publish inappropriately or unintentionally and also for mobile learning researchers questioning how to gain informed consent from all parties potentially involved in a task via a participant's internet-connected mobile device (Traxler and Bridges, 2004). Zimmer (2010) suggests that the increasing integration of the internet and of web 2.0 environments is creating not just challenges in relation to research in the digital era, but conceptual gaps. As well as notions about what constitutes consent, these gaps include understandings around privacy and effective strategies for anonymising data, and the inexperience of ethics committees in relation to research in these new environments (Zimmer, 2010). Given all the above challenges schools have occasionally struggled; however, early adopters are now experienced and the next section discusses the policies that these schools have put in place to support their teachers in managing classroom-based mobile learning initiatives.

7.2 Policy guidance for teachers

This will be illustrated initially via the current UK national picture of school policy guidance over ethical concerns associated with implementing mobile learning opportunities for secondary school students. A small, opportunity sample of school policy is presented below. We need to be mindful though that, in the case of schools, RM Education (a leading educational technology provider)'s annual survey indicates that currently only 29% of secondary schools in the UK have opted for some form of BYOD (Forbes, 2016). This level, though, has already triggered concerns about equity of access as discussed in the preceding section. The UK National Association of Head Teachers has reported that lack of government funding is forcing schools to ask parents to pay for their children's mobile devices (Hobby, 2016). Clearly, not all parents can afford to do so.

One of the earliest UK schools to put a BYOD policy in place was the Thomas Hardye School in the south west of the country, in Dorset. This school is an academy, i.e. a state-funded community school which is directly funded by the UK Department for Education and independent of local authority control. It is a larger than average-sized secondary school with over 2,000 students from Years 9–13 (those aged 13–19) and has catered for students bringing their own mobile devices for over five years now. Its policy clearly includes all devices used to access the school's IT resources and communications systems whether smartphones, PDAs, tablets, and laptop or notebook computers. Its advertised purpose is to protect school systems while enabling students to freely access them and it sets out the way in which the school may monitor such use. It is closely coupled to the school's student ICT Acceptable Use Policy, which reminds students that while use of the latest technology is actively encouraged at the school it comes with a responsibility to protect students, staff and the school from abuse of the system and highlights responsible use solely under the class teacher's direction and e-safety issues. Lee and Levins (2016), who included Thomas Hardye in their analysis of eleven BYOD pathfinder schools in the UK, USA, Australia and New Zealand, report that, at Thomas Hardye, there has been scant abuse of the trust accorded to the many thousands of students.

Another school that was an early adopter of BYOD is Saltash.net Community School, also in the south west of England. Similarly a larger-than-average secondary school, Saltash.net is also now a stand-alone academy. Interestingly, its approach is to cover BYOD within the school's e-safety policy, thus prioritising the safe and responsible use of mobile devices. The school points out that it recognises that there is a wide range of rapidly developing communications technologies which have the potential to enhance learning and expressly allows both students and staff to use mobile phones both in lessons and for social networking in breaks.

On the opposite side of the country, Maidstone Grammar in Kent, a smaller yet still larger than average selective boys' school under Local Authority control with just over 1,200 students, again prioritises the use of mobile devices in school for educational purposes. Indeed, its BYOD policy opens with the emphasis that the use of personal devices at school is to be 'exclusively educational'. Other opening emphases are that, similarly to the Thomas Hardye school, the use of personal ICT devices falls under the school's Internet Acceptable Use Policy and that students are not permitted to connect to any external wireless or networking service while using a personal ICT device in school. The latter allows the school to monitor student use of its Wi-Fi network.

However, the picture in schools in England is divided and these case studies are not representative of the whole country. A survey conducted by Canvas (the VLE provider) found that more than one-third of teachers (34 percent) in the UK have banned personal devices such as mobile phones and tablets from their classroom, significantly more than in US schools (23%) (Canvas, 2016). The survey also found that the majority of the teachers (62%) believe such technology distracts students from learning. But then, even more of the teachers, 74%, believed these mobile technologies can make their job easier, if integrated effectively and used as an educational tool rather than a leisure device.

Other countries have different emphases. For instance, the example of a cell phone policy provided for the use of schools in Gauteng province, South Africa, developed by the region's elearning Directorate (GDE, 2011) emphasises, in addition to the concerns already discussed above, that learners who carry or use cell phones in public, particularly when travelling to and from school, have become the targets of criminals. Also that theft of cell phones at school can be a persistent problem. This can likely lead to private and personal material, including photos, video clips, voice messages and personal details, becoming accessible by undesirable individuals and groups when cell phones are lost, borrowed or stolen. Another early adopting school district in Ohio in the USA highlights that only the internet gateway provided by the school may be accessed by students' mobile devices while on campus[2]. Students are required to acknowledge that the school's network filters will be applied to their connection to the internet and attempts will not be made to bypass them.

Thus school acceptable use policies tend to be driven by local behavioural concerns rather than a comprehensive understanding of the ethical questions teachers may be faced with such as when spotting inappropriate or overly personal material on a student's device or online. However, following their in-depth investigation of UK schools adopting mobile learning for Becta, the then national agency supporting the use of digital technology in schools, Hartnell-Young and Heym (2008, p. 24) point out: 'we do not recommend that schools rush into wholesale policy change at the outset, but rather a gradual adoption as attitudes and behaviours align with purposeful learning, until the school reaches the tipping point, and using mobile phones is as natural as using any other technology'. This fits well with the role of iterative and participatory research ethics mentioned in the preceding section with schools being ready to change and adapt in the light of circumstance.

Thus I am proposing moving away from a pre-ordained, rule-based approach to dealing with ethical questions to a more participatory approach with all parties concerned engaging with an underpinning ethic of responsibility for safe and sensible practice. For, as Andrews et al. (2011) point out, any consideration of the ethics of mobile learning must acknowledge the need for a positive ethic of inclusion and personal responsibility, not just harm minimisation. However, for that to be the case in practice all stakeholders and any associated researchers need to be well trained and confident in how to deal with any ethical questions they are challenged with. The next section, therefore, introduces a way forward for professional development recommended by Andrews et al. (2015) that has resulted from several workshops with mobile learning researchers and school-based practitioners.

7.3 Advancing ethical frameworks and scenario-based training

In this section I consider first the role of ethics frameworks, the possibilities for which were made clear to me during a discussion workshop with teachers, teacher educators and researchers for the Institute for Advanced Studies Workshop Series 'Adding a Mobile Dimension to Teaching and Learning' in 2008. During our discussions it became evident that, in the ever-changing contexts inherent to mobile learning, where students adopt new digital practices to support their learning, our usual experience of focusing on our relevant professional codes of conduct was unhelpful. For, like Hammersley and Traianou (2012), we were finding that research ethics framing tends to be prescriptive with the expectation that researchers will be fully informed by their relevant educational association's codes of conduct. Examples of these include the British and American Educational Research Associations' ethical guidelines. Additionally, if the researchers are working with teachers of young people and children then this expectation includes the teachers' 'Duty of Care' statement as outlined in their relevant national teaching standards. This was leading to a multiplicity of 'rules' that were dutifully reviewed in the initial stages of designing a research project, yet were liable to be promptly overtaken within the project's lifetime by students using new devices whose data capturing, storing and sharing capabilities not even they are fully aware of. Additionally, Davies (2013) notes how, when reflecting on ethical challenges involving research into pervasive computing, first gaining that appropriate ethical approval is a significant challenge in itself. He goes on to make the point that questions of how to adopt an ethical approach to pervasive computing extend beyond the research domain, affecting practitioners as well. This, too, is clearly relevant in the field of mobile learning research where teaching colleagues are the key actors. Batchelor et al. (2012) go so far as to describe this context as 'innovative teachers being ensnared within the everyday prosaic, unstructured and utopian perspective' of mobile learning. Here they believe there is an onslaught of technologies bringing with it a range of ethical concerns. More simply, yet aptly, Clark et al. (2009) use the term 'digital dissonance' to describe the teachers' tension with respect to learners' appropriation of Web 2.0 technologies in formal educational contexts.

In this early discussion workshop the following five aspects were suggested as key ethical concerns (Wishart, 2009):

- relevant professional codes of conduct;
- informed consent and whose;
- ownership of device, information on it and data collected;
- images, the ease of taking, sharing and publishing;
- user-generated content and children's personal information; and
- data protection, storage and loss of children's work.

Then, in line with Batchelor and Botha's (2009) proposal that a move from a rules-based system of addressing ethical concerns (the aforementioned codes of conduct) to a value-based system could accommodate new technology developments in mobile learning, I considered these concerns in the light of a simpler, value-based way forward. One such approach, introduced thousands of years ago by Greek philosophers, is widely accepted in medical practice (Beauchamp and Childress, 1983) with its four ethical principles: do good, avoid harm, autonomy and justice. It is now also regularly found in ethics primers. The first two principles are fairly self-explanatory. The principle of autonomy requires that people have the right to be treated as autonomous agents, with their own self-directed goals and rights to choice, self-determination, privacy and control over personal information. Persons with diminished autonomy, for example, students, must have their autonomy protected by responsible others (Howard et al., 2004). We can consider the principle of justice as implying equity of access to mobile learning opportunities and to the mobile devices as tools to support learning. This approach was used to develop the

Table 7.1   Original ethics framework for mobile learning research

	Do good	*Avoid harm*	*Autonomy*	*Justice/Equal access*
Personal information				
Images				
Informed consent				
Ownership				
Data storage and protection				
User-generated content				

framework shown in Table 7.1 above as reported by Wishart (2009). The matrix shown arises from the combination of the four accepted ethical principles as described above with what were deemed, at the discussion workshops, to be the key, most pressing ethical concerns that teachers and other educators come across in their everyday work. It was believed that these would also be of high priority in research into mobile learning.

Each cell in the table, where a key ethical concern intersects with an underpinning ethical principle, becomes an opportunity for reflection as to what is current practice and what is good practice. Not all intersections will give rise to relevant concerns, depending on the situation under consideration, and in some instances it will be hard to balance principles. For example, with researching the use of mobile devices to capture and share images, 'avoid harm' may conflict with the concept of 'respect user choice' embodied in the more general principle of 'autonomy'. Indeed, what constitutes doing good, avoiding harm, autonomy or justice can itself be controversial and is likely to vary across situations and cultures. However, the act of considering the range of ethical concerns involved will alert the researchers to the need to come to an agreement with the students and teachers participating in the research with respect to that key concern. Also one particular benefit noted by a practitioner at a workshop for the STELLAR European research Network of Excellence in technology enhanced learning where the framework was tested (Wishart, 2010) was that including the principle of beneficence stimulated thinking through how to develop a proposed opportunity to 'do good'.

Interestingly, Farrow (2011) adopted a similar structural approach in his work to develop an analytical tool to support mobile learning researchers in understanding the nature of ethical issues beyond the more customary strategic focus on gaining research approval. Taking the concepts of deontological ethics (based on moral responsibilities, codes or duties), consequentialist ethics (based on the outcomes of an action) and virtue ethics (based on developing as a good person) from moral philosophy, he first develops them in the context of mobile learning to create a second level taxonomy. This taxonomy comprises three concepts: responsibilities, outcomes and personal development, plus three further spaces that overlap the boundaries between each pair of concepts. Farrow (2011) then cross-tabulates this taxonomy with the ethical issues highlighted by the EC-funded, MOTILL Project (Arrigo et al., 2010) which was set up to identify best practices in using mobile technologies to support lifelong learning in four countries. The MOTILL team had found that the ethical issues of most concern to them could be categorised into three key areas: accessibility, privacy/security and copyright. It is noticeable though, that issues such as cyberbullying and accessing age-inappropriate information do not appear in either of these two thoughtfully considered frameworks yet regularly crop up when teachers discuss concerns over adopting mobile learning. They will be discussed alongside other behavioural concerns commonly associated with young people's use of mobile phones such as distraction and cheating.

There were two further discussion workshops with teachers, researchers and teacher educators dealing with ethics and mobile learning held in 2012. The first workshop took place at the mLearn 2012 conference in Helsinki, which attracted researchers and practitioners from around the world. The second was conducted in Sydney as the focus of the annual Mobile Learning Research Workshop, conducted by anzMLearn (the Australian and New Zealand Mobile Learning Group) with attendees from Australasia. At these, Andrews et al. (2015) put forward their workshop-based approach of engaging educational practitioners in developing their own ethical frameworks. Each workshop began by examining the principles and frameworks that inform the codes of conduct and policies which guide technology use in educational institutions generally. The limitations of classic rules-based (deontological) approaches were noted by participants and the need identified for a more flexible method of dealing with ethical issues in the shifting contexts that characterise mobile learning. In open discussion participants brainstormed their own concerns about teaching with and researching mobile learning and from this list the issues felt to be most important were prioritised. Then, in order to prepare teachers, student teachers, lecturers and researchers in managing young people's use of mobile devices with all the issues just discussed, the different frameworks created were used to generate scenarios to prompt further discussions.

Scenarios, or simulated case studies, are a means of articulating issues from real-world experiences and exploring ways forward for the future (Kamtsiou et al., 2007). They are often used in teaching ethical issues for such an approach supports contextualisation of issues, exploration of multiple perspectives, reflection, and opportunities to develop collaborative solutions (Herrington et al., 2003). Ethical scenarios themselves are usually complex and not clear cut, presenting the varied viewpoints and conflicting priorities of the stakeholders, thus avoiding glib solutions (Spinello, 2003). The aim is not to teach people right from wrong but to equip them with the ability to reason about ethics. They represent a participant-centred learning process since those working through them are actively engaged in finding a solution. Scenarios have the advantage of making ethical issues concrete, moving 'from abstractions to realities' (Costanzo and Handelsman, 1998). Their embedding within a specific context assists professionals to prepare for the ethical challenges they will face in their own practice. Thus, for researchers into mobile learning, scenarios can provide a way of considering the complexities of dynamic and unpredictable mobile learning situations and develop a personal ethical response.

In summary, the aim was, therefore, to work alongside the participants to devise exemplar scenarios to support mobile learning researchers and teachers engaged in researching their practice with mobile learning. The approach taken followed a participatory design methodology (Spinuzzi, 2005) and involved having experienced researchers collaboratively design scenarios, having first discussed and agreed the underpinning ethics framework to be used. Thus the workshop participants engage with the production of three elements:

1. an ethics framework or ethical decision-making strategy in the context of which the scenario is to be considered. The framework, principles or strategy form a tool for assisting participants to consider the ethical dimensions of the scenario;

2. the scenario itself; and
3. a set of questions to stimulate ethical discussion of the scenario.

This triad neatly meets with the advice of Howard et al. (2004) for professional development in ethics. The exemplar scenarios presented later in this chapter are derived from those that were developed by participants at these two further discussion workshops. As described above, the scenarios grew out of key ethical concerns surrounding mobile learning research raised by participants at the two events. The following key concerns related to ethical issues surrounding mobile learning opportunities and the challenges of teaching via or researching into them were put forward at the two workshops:

- Boundaries such as those between formal-informal, public-private, home-school, real-virtual contexts. Mobile devices are 'boundary objects' (Pimmer and Gröhbiel, 2013) easily carried between contexts enabling information more usually restricted to one context to be accessed in another.
- Privacy – as boundaries are crossed there are opportunities for teachers or researchers observing students using their personal mobile devices to infringe privacy. There is also the need to obtain permissions by third parties, for example, when students are on work experience, and the possibility of accidental inclusion of outsiders in student-generated content on say, a field trip.
- Anonymity versus respecting the desire to self-publish. This is a particular challenge when a teacher is also the researcher, the accepted practice of ensuring that participants in a research project remain anonymous conflicts with their students' desire to celebrate their work via the social media apps on their mobile phones.
- Ownership of data – whose data is on the mobile device or on the server and who owns it. This is a particular concern in respect of ownership of images where perception varies along with the context where the images were captured, in school or in a park, for example.
- Participants' awareness of device capabilities such as what data is being logged by the different apps and who can view it.
- Accessibility – students who are differently able or who may come from different cultures or home environments and what this means regarding both the range of mobile devices available to the proposed participants and costs, e.g., for devices to access the internet and usage charges incurred.
- Risk analysis – the unexpected consequences of complexity, boundary crossing and changing circumstances as a teaching opportunity or research project set up in one space is impacted by information and sociocultural expectations from others.

Cross-tabulating these with the four key ethical principles introduced above resulted in the new framework shown in Table 7.2. The framework was then used as a starter to generate initial discussion about ethical issues and then formed the base for production of scenarios to use to practise debate and generate the skills of ethical analysis. This table is followed by two examples of the scenarios for mobile learning practice selected from the wider range of scenarios that were developed from this framework at the two workshops. Further scenarios can be seen at the website of the International Association for Mobile Learning[3].

Table 7.2 New framework outlining potential ethical concerns in mobile learning

	Do good	*Avoid harm*	*Autonomy*	*Justice/ Equal access*
Boundaries				
Privacy				
Anonymity				
Accessibility				
Ownership				
Awareness				
Risk analysis				

Scenario 1: Whose story is it?

Key issues highlighted: Maintaining anonymity versus respecting a participant's desire to keep up a digital identity.

Research question: How can learners be protected as producers of student-generated online content?

Description: It is common to see people on the spot when a major event happens using their mobile phones to upload images and comments to the web whether to formal news sites or via social networking sites such as Twitter. Sometimes these citizen journalists are anonymous through the use of pseudonyms and sometimes the profile associated with their comments provides full details of their job and location. Could creating an online newspaper in school using handheld mobile devices with cameras to capture and upload stories effectively boost children's literacy? In which case, to what extent should anonymity be enforced?

Questions to be considered:

- Will the online presence of the newspaper be publicised? By the school? By the researcher? By inspectors of education sharing good practice? Does sharing at a conference count as publicising?
- How will the issue of inclusion of images or video of interviewees or bystanders be dealt with? Is this an ethical or legal issue, or both? Should third parties captured in multimedia files be asked for their consent to stories being written about them and the posting of these to the school website?
- Who would the school and children want to show their work to? Parents, friends, family, relatives living overseas, other schools?
- To what extent should anonymity be enforced? What is the children's opinion as article authors as to whether the researcher should protect their anonymity? Who else should be asked, parents, teacher, the head teacher?

Other issues that may arise:

Use of pseudonyms online – identifying the actors in this situation.

Other similar situations:

Researching mobile learning opportunities in the study of nature may mean discussing whether a participant's discovery of, for example, an invasive species, a visiting migrant bird or the location of a rare breed should be anonymised or publicised. In this case there are the possible consequences for the species itself as well as the participant to be considered.

Scenario 2: Who pays?

Key issues highlighted: Accessibility and equity of mobile learning opportunities based on the BYOD model and involving learners who come potentially from varying economic backgrounds.

Research question: How can teaching using the BYOD approach be made equitable for all student participants?

Description: A teacher is planning research for their doctorate investigating developing learning activities bridging inside and outside school contexts for teenagers using their own mobile devices and expecting them to text or post online from the locations of interest such as museums and art galleries.

Questions to be considered:

- What types of devices are available to the class and will it be possible to provide devices to students who don't have them? What is it that the devices are needed to do? Will a student reliant, say, on BBM messaging want to use a loaned smartphone rather than their own?
- How will the learners be connected? They will have access via different cell phone networks. There will be differences in coverage, data plans, number of texts included, etc. If using up texts on a school project, does that impact on social text count, i.e. affect their social life? How aware are the learners of different connectivity routes and their associated cost, e.g. 3G vs Wi-Fi and what about unintended costs associated with exceeding data limits, e.g. with photos or video? If choosing Wi-Fi, there will be a loss of immediacy if the learners need to go elsewhere to upload their data.
- What about access for dyslexic or disabled students? Will they need extra functionality such as screen readers and who will purchase this? Though the BYOD model might overcome some of that as students may well have already acquired aids such as magnifiers.
- How will parents feel? There may be a pressure on them to ensure their children can access learning – displaced cost from school to parents. Also, what about the parents' support for the learning activity: will they consider the use of mobile phones at school work?

Other issues that may arise:

- If there are instructions or information that need to be downloaded by the students to their devices to support them while on location there may well be a cost of putting it into a suitable universally accessible form such as EPub.
- There is also the chance that students may engage in off-task activities using their own mobile phones.

Other similar situations:

Any activity which relies on access to a service paid for by the participants or where participants may, through different abilities or needs, be more or less able to access the service.

It was found that, by enabling participating researchers to focus discussion on ethical issues, the realistic scenarios generated could assist them to work through potential issues and develop strategies to deal with and, if possible, avoid ethical breaches before they happen. The use of such frameworks in discussions to develop scenarios enables teachers and lecturers to be better informed and more confident in dealing with breaches of privacy, inappropriate access or data loss, i.e. those ethical rather than legal challenges that may occur when students bring their own devices to class.

7.4 Conclusion

As Andrews et al. (2015) point out, by exploring mobile technology-based teaching and learning activities inside and outside school using multimedia content created or captured with mobile devices, teachers are promoting the means for students to become lifelong learners outside formal educational contexts. Employing mobile devices can extend opportunities for formal learning way beyond traditional boundaries, into the home, into cyberspace, into unforeseen futures. This chapter has, therefore, considered the wide range of ethical challenges associated with this boundary crossing that can arise when children use their personal, internet-connected mobile devices in schools.

In the face of these challenges schools work hard to keep their 'acceptable use' or 'responsible use' policies up to date; however, the apparently constantly evolving digital devices and children's creative thinking about the uses to which they can be put can make this a thankless task. Along with my colleagues Laurel Dyson and Trish Andrews, I recommend instead finding a path to develop 'personal responsibility' and addressing the hard issues in ways that promote good practice in the use of mobile technology in teaching and learning contexts. To enable this, teachers need to be aware of both opportunities and issues and to have planned strategies for dealing with any potential concerns. We, therefore, proposed scenario development, combined with an active discussion of an ongoing ethics framework, as a way to secure ethical professional development of educational practitioners.

Scenario generation workshops were found to be an effective method of stimulating discussion and raising awareness of potential ethical concerns. In particular, first engaging the participants in discussion and planning the underpinning ethical framework to be used enabled both participants' voices to be heard and the subsequent discussions tailored to their needs and interests. Thus we concluded that collaboratively creating scenarios and ethical frameworks could provide a way of understanding the issues associated with mobile learning opportunities in formal educational contexts and their potential consequences, and a means to develop appropriate solutions. In addition, these scenarios provide a resource that other teachers and educational researchers can work through to explore the issues and plan possible solutions.

However, even when the ethical questions outlined above are planned for and managed well, the all too frequent perception that mobile devices are in themselves distracting and disruptive is sadly not unfounded (Vosloo, 2012). UNESCO's global reviews of mobile learning initiatives and their policy implications found that across a range of countries 'learners have used them [mobile phones] for cheating, cyberbullying, 'sexting' – sending sexually explicit messages or photographs via SMS/MMS texts – and accessing inappropriate content or dangerous people online' (Vosloo, 2012, p. 40). The next chapter, therefore, focuses on these behavioural concerns that are regularly associated with young people's mobile phone use.

Questions

- Have a look at the apps you regularly use on a mobile device, what data are they storing or sharing about you? What terms and conditions did you agree to and did you understand or even read them?
- How would you follow up the discovery of inappropriate personal information or images that a parent had left on your student's mobile device?

Annotated further reading

- Discussing ethics frameworks and scenario-based learning

Andrews, T., Dyson, L. and Wishart, J. (2015) Advancing ethics frameworks and scenario-based learning to support educational research into mobile learning. *International Journal of Research & Method in Education*, 38(3), 320–34.

This paper, part of a special issue on e-research in educational contexts, reports on the ethical challenges arising from researching in the wide range of mobile learning situations and contexts. Such challenges tend to result from the immediacy with which mobile devices connect to social media, heightened privacy concerns and uncertainty about informed consent. The paper proposes that engaging in the creation of ethics frameworks and scenario-based learning can assist educational researchers to better understand the ethical complexities of research using mobile devices and social media. The authors go on to make the case for this approach to be used for professional development for mobile learning researchers, which, of course, will also include teachers researching their own mobile learning practice.

Activities

- Create your own ethics framework

Work with colleagues or your peers to create your own ethics framework in the form of a table with your concerns placed as rows and the four principles – doing good, avoiding harm, autonomy and justice – as columns. Can you develop any scenarios to illustrate the juxtapositions of these rows and columns to help others understand the issues you have included?

Notes

1 www.legislation.gov.uk/ukpga/1998/29/contents
2 http://sm.k12.oh.us/assets/pdf/BYOT-AUPv2.pdf
3 http://iamlearn.org/?page_id=285

8 Behaviour matters in mobile learning

As Vosloo (2012) points out, in his summary of key policy issues for stakeholders put together following the largest ever international review of mobile learning by UNESCO, negative social attitudes towards mobile phones are the biggest barrier to their adoption in schools. Vosloo (2012) considers that these attitudes, held by some policy-makers, administrators, teachers and parents, generally stem from a lack of knowledge about the educational uses of phones and an overgeneralised perception that mobile devices are distracting and disruptive. Additionally, mobile phones are often regarded as undesirable or harmful because educators have heard about learners using them for cheating, cyberbullying, 'sexting' (sending sexually explicit messages or images via SMS) and accessing inappropriate content or dangerous people online. Sadly, these concerns are not entirely unfounded. Vosloo (2012) notes that, according to earlier media polls of teenagers in the USA:

- One-third of teens with mobile phones have admitted to using their phones to cheat, and two-thirds of all teens have reported that others in their school cheat with mobile phones (CommonSense Media, 2009);
- Twenty-six per cent of teenagers have reported receiving bullying or harassing text messages or phone calls (Lenhart et al., 2010); and
- Four per cent of teens have reported sending a sexually suggestive image via text message with fifteen per cent reporting receiving a text of that nature (Lenhart et al., 2010).

However, as Vosloo (2012) notes, the moral 'panics' over these issues often stem from or are influenced by popular media discourses that are emotive and fraught with distortions (Chigona and Chigona, 2008). In short, the extent to which safety risks and problem behaviour are associated with mobile phones is often exaggerated. Or is it? This chapter will review recent research into behavioural issues cropping up in schools that can be squarely attributed to students' use of mobile phones. It will conclude by addressing measures taken by teachers and other school personnel to minimise effectively these kinds of disruption.

8.1 Disruptive devices

Describing one of the first mobile learning projects, evaluating HandLeR (a personal device that combined a pen-operated tablet computer, digital camera and Wi-Fi communication) with a group of 11-year-old primary school children, Mike Sharples was first to highlight the associated potential of mobile devices for class disruption (Sharples, 2002). However, he was thinking of the potential challenge that classroom-based connected mobile device use could create for teacher-led instruction rather than malicious behaviour. He notes that when using mobile devices 'the students create links to the outside world, to a world of activities and conversations that they control, and that match neither the teacher's agenda nor the curriculum' (Sharples, 2002, p.510).

On a more mundane note, teachers in a number of countries are reporting that they are frequently frustrated by students bringing their mobile devices into school and forgetting to silence them. For example Porter et al. (2016) found during visits to 24 schools across Ghana, Malawi and South Africa that significant numbers of students reported negative impacts of mobile phones on their schoolwork in the last year. Around 13% in Ghana, 42% in Malawi and a surprising 69% in South Africa said that this included disruption by their own or by other students' phones. Class disruption associated with mobile phone use at one time principally involved students', or even the teachers', phones ringing out (in each country over 60% of students also reported their teachers as having used a phone in lesson time). Similarly, in the USA, a survey of over 1,000 teachers from Tennessee and Kentucky reported by Thomas et al. (2014) found nearly four-fifths (78.9%) reported concerns over mobile phones disrupting class. Evidence from US students supplied in one of the regular large-scale internet and technology use surveys conducted by the Pew Research Center (Lenhart et al., 2010) supports this concern; 58% of cell-phone owning teens at schools that ban phones reported they had sent a text message during class. There is further evidence from the USA that the teachers are being distracted too. Obringer and Coffey (2007) report that 31% of the 112 high school principals who responded to a survey mailed out randomly to 200 high schools representing all 50 states agree that cell phone use by teachers adversely affects their sustained focus on the classroom/students.

However, with smartphones and increasing numbers of social media apps, the number of potential routes for distraction has escalated. One 16-year-old student in Porter et al.'s (2016) study reports 'At times you find that you are in class but friends are busy sending you messages on WhatsApp and you are not concentrating' (p.28). This disruption also eats into work outside school; a 17 year old told the researchers 'We spend our crucial time in MXit [a South African chat app] instead of doing our homework. I am unable to control myself and refrain from social networks' (p.30).

Porter et al. (2016) also note that, where mobile phone operators offer cheap night call rates, this appears to contribute to reductions in concentration in class, as a result of disrupted sleep patterns. In their survey of African countries only 11.2% of enrolled young people in Ghana said they had had their sleep disrupted by cell phone use, but 27.2% in Malawi and 57.5% in South Africa were affected. This finding is global; a study of over 90,000 adolescents in Japan (Munezawa et al., 2011) found that nearly 5% of junior high school students and nearly 11% of senior high school students reported using their mobile phones every day after 'lights out'. In another survey of over 1,000 Australian adolescents, Gamble et al. (2014) found that nearly 30% said they used cell phones in bed almost every, or every, night and that this was associated with delayed sleep onset. However, we must be mindful that mobile phone use is only one of multiple sociocultural factors disrupting today's adolescents' sleep (Carskadon, 2011) and that they may be being used to support schoolwork.

Disruption is not confined to mobile phones, Kaya (2013) found, in her small-scale study in a high school in a Turkish city, that science teachers in Turkey struggled following the distribution of tablet personal computers (TPCs) to their classes. Without science-specific software or a means of linking the tablets to the Interactive Whiteboard being used by the teacher the students quickly capitalised on using them for off-task opportunities such as gaming. Five of the eight teachers in the study reported class management issues associated with having the TPCs. One of teachers in her study reported how immersive students found the devices.

> 'A student who was actively participating to the class before having TPC had sat in the backmost seat [...] holding the TPC below the desk. [...] He was deeply concentrated on it that he seemed like isolated from the world even though his desk-mate was warning him about me. As I said, he did not hear anything. I arrived to his desk. He said "Pardon!".'

However, in this study the TPCs had been delivered without accompanying in-service training, the importance of which is noted and discussed in Chapter 6 of this book. That said, studies in other countries where teachers have been offered training have also noted the potential of mobile devices for off-task behaviour. For example, 13.8% of students in Parsons and Adhikari's (2016) longitudinal study of the first two years of a Bring Your Own Device (BYOD) initiative in a New Zealand secondary school, reported concerns over the way mobile devices were being used in class for off-task behaviour, both by themselves and their classmates. Thomas et al. (2014) found that this potential for use for off-task behaviour provided insight into the, apparently contradictory, findings of their survey of 1,121 teachers in Kentucky and Tennessee intended to determine their support for the use of mobile phones in the classroom. Their results showed that, whereas only 39% of teachers reported supporting the use of cell phones in the classroom, 59.4% said that they do, or would, allow students to use them for school-related work. A large majority of the teachers had also reported concerns about the ability of phones to be used for disrupting class (78.9%) as well as about the possibility of their use for cheating (82.4%) or cyberbullying (79.9%). However, Thomas et al. (2014) suggest another explanation for the contradiction. It could be that a perception by teachers that banning mobile phones outright provides them with a degree of control over the integration of mobile phones into their lessons that would be absent otherwise. For example, teachers may feel the school-wide ban gives them the opportunity to select the classes in which they quietly allow students to use their phones, thus enabling them to select the more advanced classes that they may believe more capable of using their phones responsibly.

Interestingly the biggest concern of teachers in Thomas et al.'s (2014) US survey was that mobile phones could be used by students for cheating though they were also very concerned about potential use for cyberbullying. These two issues result from malicious use by the owner or user of the mobile device rather than the sort of unthinking use that results in disruption and all three are problems stemming from individual students' behaviour rather than the device itself. However, they are deemed a serious challenge to open use of mobile devices in schools and are therefore discussed in the following two sections

8.2 Plagiarism and cheating

As mentioned in the opening lines of this chapter, in the poll conducted for CommonSense Media, a California-based non-profit organisation dedicated to improving the impact of media and entertainment on kids and families, 35% of teenagers asked admitted to using their cell phones to cheat in school (CommonSense Media, 2009). The students disclosed that they text each other answers and refer to notes stored on their cell phones during tests and have also downloaded papers from the internet to turn in as their own work. The CommonSense Media team feel that because the digital world is distant, hard to track, and mostly anonymous, the students are less likely to see the consequences of their online actions, especially when they feel they won't get caught. Indeed, while Lenhart et al. (2010) did not include questions on cheating with mobile phones in the Pew Research Center large-scale survey of teenagers, they report that most of the teens in the associated nine focus groups held in Michigan said that they have heard that other students have used cell phones to cheat. Some even admitted to doing it themselves. Thematic analysis of the focus group discussions showed that this cheating is carried out by texting answers to others, sharing photos of exam questions, taking photos of textbook pages to bring into an exam and sourcing question answers online, especially through websites that claim they will answer any question. A high school girl commented about taking photos of the book in:

> It's kind of like a sheet of notes, but it is on your phone. It's not like you have to pull out a piece of paper and unfold it and make a lot of noise. It is easier.
>
> (*Lenhart et al., p.85*)

In addition, several of the teenage students mentioned that they use their phone as their calculator, which can also be a method for cheating when calculators are not allowed during maths exams.

Worryingly, as the CommonSense Media team (2009) point out, many students don't recognise much of this activity as cheating. Other key findings from their poll included the discoveries that while 41% of teenage students say that storing notes on a cell phone to access during a test is a serious cheating offence, another 23% don't think it's cheating at all. Similarly, 45% of the students say that texting friends about answers during tests is a serious cheating offence, while 20% said it's not cheating at all. They hide this activity from their parents; a survey of 200 Irish teenagers by McAfee, the antivirus software provider, showed that 33% have unofficially looked up answers to a test or an assignment online and over half wipe their browser history to conceal this alongside other illegal activities (McAfee, 2013). However, while Thomas and Muñoz (2016) report in another survey of 628 high school students in the Midwest United States that 40% of them reported concerns about use of mobile phones for cheating, it has been hard to find other international, peer reviewed, corroborative evidence of school age children cheating via mobile phones. Except that is, in the media; the CommonSense Media (2009) study reported above made newspaper headlines around the world and the trend continues with headlines such as 'Mobile phones drive increase in exam cheating' (the *Guardian*, 2010), 'Report reveals how teachers, students used phones to cheat in KCSE' (*AllAfrica*, 2016), 'Nineteen students get score of '0' for cheating' (*Phnom Penh Post*, 2016). In New Zealand, the Stuff news website reports that, in 2015, ninety-five national exam-sitters were caught with mobile phones, and seven were caught actually using their phones during exams (Dooney, 2016). Thus while the practice clearly exists there is little academic research on whether having access to mobile phones is actually a driver or whether these students would have cheated anyway. There is plenty of published academic research though on college and university students' underhand class activities; Campbell (2006) provides a useful introduction. He makes the useful point though that while the internet opens a world of opportunity for students to cheat or plagiarise, it also can be used to detect and hinder the practice with programs such as turnitin.com.

With respect to plagiarism, McFarlane (2015) questions whether students using mobile devices or other digital tools are deliberately cheating or simply guilty of poor citation practice. She describes a 'cut and paste culture' (p.57) and cites a teaching union (ATL) survey conducted in 2008 which suggests over 50% of teachers consider plagiarism to be a major problem; however, yet again, this raises the question as to whether teachers are being effectively trained to help students deploy mobile devices to support their schoolwork. At least, though, dealing with cheating and plagiarism takes place within school and dealing with them is firmly within the teachers' gift. Another complex and worrying issue for teachers is the increased use of mobile phones for cyberbullying, which, while it mostly happens outside school hours, can affect students badly. For, as Keengwe et al. (2014) note, mobile phones turned on during a break between lessons can quickly result in a flurry of upsets as students receive hurtful messages from the morning or night before and teachers end up dealing with issues generated by behaviours that took place outside school.

8.3 Cyberbullying

So what is cyberbullying? Willard (2007) describes it as 'being cruel to others by sending or posting harmful material or engaging in other forms of social aggression using the internet or other digital technologies' (pp.5–10). She lists eight different forms of cyberbullying, which include:

- Flaming, that is online attacks in Twitter for example or via comments on a website that use strong, rude and/or angry language;
- Harassment, that is repeatedly sending abusive and insulting messages;
- Denigration, which is putting someone down online through sending or posting gossip about them with the aim of damaging their reputation or friendships;
- Impersonation, that is pretending to be another person online and sending or posting material to get that person in trouble, to damage their reputation or to access their resources;
- Outing, that is sharing someone's secrets including embarrassing information and/or images online;
- Trickery, which is talking someone into outing themselves through deception;
- Exclusion, which is intentionally and cruelly excluding someone from an online group;
- Cyberstalking, that is sending continuously obsessive messages through digital technology including threats or posting upsetting material online and creates significant fear.

Sadly, this appears to be a worldwide phenomenon. In their 'Net Children Go Mobile' report of an extensive survey of 3,500 children aged 9–16 across seven European countries for the EC's Safer Internet programme, Mascheroni and Cuman (2014) note the level of online bullying, reported by 12% of the children, now exceeds face-to-face bullying, reported by 10%. In all the countries surveyed reported levels of being bullied online or via mobile communication had risen since an earlier survey in 2010. Indeed, Mascheroni and Cuman (2014) report that 'some children believe that mobile devices facilitate online bullying because these devices allow them to be constantly online and available' (p. 28). In another European study, in Spain, Cerezo et al. (2016) found a significant association between bullying behaviours and level of use of digital technology through a survey of over 1,300 secondary and high school adolescents. However, their results indicated more involvement in traditional bullying (12%) than in cyberbullying (7.7%). Changing continents, during their visits to schools in three African countries, Porter et al. (2016) asked young people who had used a phone in the last 12 months whether they had ever experienced unwanted, unpleasant or upsetting calls or texts. They found that this was occurring quite often with 2.8% in Ghana, 6.6% in Malawi and 16.5% in South Africa indicating that it was a substantial problem. Similar levels of cyberbullying are reported by Lin and Lai (2016) who discuss three large-scale surveys carried out in Hong Kong in 2009–2010 where all three reported between 11% and 22% of children as having had experience of cyberbullying with between a third and a half of the cyberbullying happening amongst schoolmates. The link with level of technology use also appeared in Utsumi's (2010) study of middle school students in Japan where results indicated that, while 67% of regular internet users were not involved in cyberbullying, 8% reported that they were bullies, 7% that they were victims, and 18% that they were both bullies and victims. Those who were bullies and/or victims also reported longer use of the internet than the students who were not involved in cyberbullying at all. In Australia, Sakelliariou and Carroll (2012) report that victimisation via the internet was the most common form of cyberbullying found in schools in the two large cities they surveyed. They found 11.5% of students (Years 6 to 12; 9–18 years old) reporting at least one experience of it during the school year with junior secondary school students (Years 8 to 10) the most likely to be victimised in this way. In the USA, Patchin (2013) of the Cyberbullying Research Center reports an even higher figure, about 24% of the students in the regular surveys the Center has conducted since 2006 have told them that they have been cyberbullied at some point in their lifetimes. They don't report information as to whether this was at school or at home.

An even larger figure was reported in a recent large-scale survey of over 600 Nigerian secondary school students by Olumide et al. (2016). They found 26% of male students and 22% of females said they had perpetrated electronic aggression, while 42.7% of females reported they had been victims compared to 36.8% of males. Interestingly, more females (58.1%) than males (40.3%) perpetrated electronic aggression via phone calls and more males (33.8%) than females (22.6%) perpetrated electronic aggression via chatrooms. That said though, the researchers found that the frequency of internet use was significantly higher amongst male than female students. We should also bear in mind that, as Livingstone and Smith (2014) point out in a research review selected for the annual special issue of the *Journal of Child Psychology and Psychiatry*, the term 'cyberbullying' is sometimes used too loosely, without reference to either repetition or power imbalance. Nevertheless, teachers everywhere are clearly worried by the practice. In another recent survey, members of the UK Association of School and College Leaders (NCB/ASCL, 2016) reported that incidence of cyberbullying was increasing to the extent that a small number of schools reported it affecting 40% or more of their students. Worryingly it's not just affecting older children, Monks et al. (2012) surveyed 220 children aged from 7 to 11 from primary schools in England and found that cyberbullying was both used and experienced by some children in this age group. This was largely in the form of nasty texts with 31% admitting to having sent them. While these children were not posting publicly about each other, clearly many others are and McFarlane (2015) notes how the public posting of unpleasant messages adds to discomfort and humiliation of victims. She also suggests an association with this reported increase in levels of cyberbullying and anonymity with websites that do not support the ability to post anonymously being less likely to host cyberbullying. It's not just the students either: while it's much rarer, Kyriacou and Zuin (2016) report on the cyberbullying of teachers by students posting videos of them taken during class on YouTube.

One final point, from Porter et al.'s (2016) study, described above, is that, at interview, the researchers heard reports of bullying and harassment amongst school students that were often related to girls being pestered by schoolboys or older men, including teachers. Of particular concern were the occasional reports they received of sexting (sending and receiving sexually explicit photographs and/or messages via cell phone), including amongst primary-level students in Ghana and South Africa. This new practice is discussed alongside reports of pornography linked to smartphone use in the next section.

8.4 Pornography and sexting

One of the first major surveys on teenagers and sexting was conducted in the USA by the Pew Research Center for its Internet & American Life Project (Lenhart, 2009). This telephone survey of 800 US teenagers aged from 12 to 17 conducted via landline and cell phones found that 4% of cell phone owning teenagers say they have sent sexually suggestive images of themselves to someone else via text messaging whereas 15% have received them. Follow up through focus groups revealed that there are three main scenarios for sexting: 1) the exchange of images solely between two romantic partners; 2) exchanges between partners that are shared with others outside the relationship; and 3) exchanges between people who are not yet in a relationship, but where at least one person hopes to be. Another, a pan-European project, the EU Kids Online survey funded by the EC's Better Internet for Kids programme reported by Livingstone et al. (2011) found, through interview of over 25,000 9–16 year olds across 25 European countries, that 15% of the 11–16 year olds have received sexual messages or images from their peers and 3% say that they have sent or posted such messages. Additionally, one-eighth of those who received such messages, or nearly 2% of all this group, report they were fairly or very upset by this. While a good number of the children who had been bothered (60%) sought support from others about this they rarely (only 2%) spoke to a teacher, more commonly they spoke to friends (38%) or a parent (30%). Such upset can be exacerbated when things go wrong. In a US-based survey of black and Hispanic youth exploring the prevalence of sexting amongst ethnic minority students, Fleschler Peskin et al. (2013) found that 18.2% of over 1,000 tenth graders had had a nude or semi-nude picture or video that was originally meant to be private shared with them.

Phippen (2016) makes the point that, even if upset, students are very unlikely to share this information with adults such as teachers for fear of getting into trouble. In earlier research with students in schools in the south west of England he had found widespread knowledge of sexting amongst 13–14 year olds. The students even at Year 7 (11 years old) were asking for more information on the practice and how to deal with it, whereas by and large the teachers' perspective was that Year 7 was too young and it should be left until Year 10. One important point, picked up by Albury (2016), is that adults, such as teachers, who adopt an abstinence approach to their students' use of mobile and online media are not likely to be seen as a source of support by those young people who are at risk.

Figures in the different international studies on the prevalence of sexting vary widely. In their national survey of Australian secondary students and sexual health, Mitchell et al. (2014) report it to be as high as over 50% of students reporting having received a sexually explicit text message with 43% having sent one. Whereas in Vanden Abeele et al.'s (2014) study only 6% of Flemish teens (11–20 years of age) reported having sent a 'sext'. However, as Cooper et al. (2016) point out, such surveys are dogged by inconsistencies in the way that research in this area has defined the content of messages as 'sexting' as well as in the relationship contexts within which the messages have been sent. They add that many of the definitions of sexting are dependent on a subjective evaluation, for example 'nearly nude' or 'sexually explicit' which makes comparison difficult. For these reasons, estimates as to the prevalence of sexting behaviours will continue to vary. In addition, in the report of the above Australian study its authors acknowledge several limitations on its validity; with its focus it was extremely difficult to obtain sufficient schools willing to participate and even then students willing to complete the survey (Mitchell et al., 2014). There were also a number of limitations unique to their online recruitment methodology.

Mascheroni and Cuman (2014) report that European children are in two minds as to whether having a mobile device with internet access is actually associated with inappropriate behaviour. Their research for the Net Children Go Mobile project found that, although some children believed that new devices are not necessarily linked to access to unwanted sexual content, some think the new devices and platforms offer new options for young people to share and access sexual content. For example, some girls from Romania and Spain complained about boys bringing and sharing sexual material at school.

Indeed, the earlier EU Kids Online survey found that children of all ages have seen sexual images online, i.e. those showing people naked or people having sex (Livingstone et al., 2011). The frequency varied though with both age and device used from 5% of 9 year olds to 25% of 15 year olds seeing such images on websites and similarly from 1% to 6% via their mobile phone. In Ringrose et al.'s (2012) in-depth exploration of children's perceptions of sexting and mobile porn on behalf of the UK national children's charity, the NSPCC, several boys talked about having porn on their mobile phone. The researchers report that porn appeared to be an ordinary part of daily life for boys and was sometimes viewed in school. Vanden Abeele et al. (2014) also note that mobile porn use is a male-dominated practice. In addition, they highlight the role of the peer group; boys who perceived more peer pressure were also more likely to report having pornographic content on their mobile phones. Somewhat worryingly though, in their research review undertaken on behalf of the UK children's commissioner, Horvath et al. (2013) note emerging evidence that indicates young people are increasingly drawing on such pornography as a result of dissatisfaction with the sex education they are receiving. They are expecting it to educate and give information regarding sexual practices and norms.

Hinduja and Patchin (2012) emphasise though that, despite teachers' concerns, technology isn't the problem, it's just that teen behaviour with technology can be. Allen (2015) though considers that the issue needs unpacking more thoughtfully. She points out that, whether for good or for bad, mobile phones or young people can't be anything on their own, they only exist intra-relationally with each other in an entanglement that blurs the human-technology divide. Similar consideration leads Albury (2016) to conclude that access to online media via mobile devices in school enables a doubling (or multiplication) of space and place that facilitates ongoing parallel engagements with friends yet within the classroom. This enables students to evade classroom discipline yet leaves an online footprint that makes their desires and bodies visible to their peers and open adult surveillance. Albury (2016) goes on to propose that, rather than attempting to police these practices, teachers need to engage with students and parents to produce a whole school approach that acknowledges current mobile media practices. This would support teachers through formal recognition of this merger of on- and offline intimacies and in overtly engaging with their impact in the classroom. However, others have very different ideas on and, approaches to, the prevention of disruptive or inappropriate use of mobile devices in schools. These are discussed in the next section.

8.5 Strategies for prevention of behavioural issues

A number of approaches to developing strategies and set ups that actively prevent or at least minimise inappropriate use of mobile devices have been trialled and evaluated by schools. These target both technical solutions and students' behaviour and are outlined below alongside reflections on their effectiveness.

Filters

Vosloo (2012) points out that in many countries the safeguarding of learners is a legal responsibility when learners are under a certain age. Safety mandates include controlling access to potentially harmful content, such as violent, pornographic or age-inappropriate material, and preventing bullying communications. Nearly all schools that provide internet access via Wi-Fi for students whether they are using their own or the school's mobile devices will ensure that internet provision is filtered, preventing access to material deemed inappropriate by the school or school district's ICT manager. However, many teachers find such systems frustrating when they themselves cannot access say YouTube for a teaching resource. Biology teachers in particular have good reason to moan about porn filtering systems that work on the amount of flesh tone in an image and prevent access to Human Biology teaching materials. As teachers we are aware that we can get specific websites approved, it just adds more time to advance lesson planning. From the ICT team's perspective, it is time consuming to keep the filters updated and to defend their systems from students trying to get around the restrictions.

There is also a more important argument that by filtering out inappropriate material we don't get to teach students how to respond when they come across it outside school. Nor does it filter internet provision via mobile phone networks which can be accessed in school by those willing to pay for their data. So what should children know?

Teaching children about responsible online behaviour

In the first instance, children (and teachers) should know how to seek help for a cyberbehaviour issue that is causing a problem. Many service providers have recognised this and it is common today to be able to report a post in a chatroom or on website to a moderator. How quickly this report gets acted on can be questionable though. However, a number of groups, both national government-funded educational organisations and third sector charitable organisations, provide specific educational resources to support children and protect them from internet-based or mobile phone harm.

In the UK these currently include www.thinkuknow.co.uk, run by the National Crime Agency and http://www.childnet.com/resources, provided by the charity Childnet International, as well as resources on what to do about cyberbullying from the national charity for prevention of cruelty to children, the NSPCC. The two sites mentioned each comprise a suite of resources including videos targeted at different age groups, their teachers and their parents or carers. Another support system run by the National Crime Agency is CEOP, its Child Exploitation and Online Protection Command, which focuses on tackling threats to children. It provides code for children's website developers that enables a one-click button for children to alert them to any concerns.

Similarly in the USA, www.webwisekids.org/, part of the Federal government's Project Safe Childhood initiative, provides educational resources including computer programs and games for schools on online safety. Also in the USA, WiredSafety, a New Jersey charity, resources teaching about online safety via websites such as http://teenangels.org/, http://tweenangels.org/ and http://StopCyberbullying.org. As does NetSmartz Workshop at www.netsmartzkids.org/ which is an interactive, educational programme of the National Center for Missing and Exploited Children (NCMEC) funded by the US Department of Justice that provides age-appropriate resources to help teach children how to be safer on- and offline. In Africa the mission of the African Children Cyber Safety Initiative (ACCSI), www.jidaw.com/childrencybersafety/ is to advance the cause of safe internet culture for African children and youth.

There isn't space here to list more of these abundant resources; many countries provide similar support in their own national languages that are designed to be interesting and relevant to their young people, e.g. with popular media characters, cartoons and games. Online safety also forms part of the National Curriculum in many countries; in just one example Singapore's Cyber-Wellness Curriculum includes both set lessons for teachers to use in the formal curriculum and school-wide programmes (assembly talks, activities) to reinforce the importance of safe and responsible internet use. However, while plenty of material is available internationally to support children in safe and responsible internet use and in cases of cyberbullying, there is little targeted directly at safe and responsible mobile phone use. That said, as seen in the section on School BYOD policies in Chapter 7 (Section 7.2), schools that allow children to bring mobile devices to classes provide clear guidance on what is and what isn't acceptable use.

Acceptable use policies

Vosloo (2012) recognises that the use of mobile devices and other ICTs does pose certain risks, and points out that it is critical that policies are in place to protect learners and teachers. In his UNESCO report he adds that protective policies for online and mobile usage should exist on the national level – such as the USA's federal Children's Internet Protection Act (CIPA) regulations – as well as the district or institutional level. For guidance on e-safety, policy-makers can refer to the different national bodies such as ThinkUKnow and Project Safe Childhood and non-profit organisations like Childnet International and WiredSafety, all mentioned in the above section. However, through reviewing a number of BYOD school policies on use of mobile devices in and outside class, it was concluded that school acceptable use policies tend to be driven mostly by local behavioural concerns.

Both Hinduja and Patchin (2012) and Hartnell-Young and Heym (2008) agree that the focus of such policies should address behaviour rather than a particular technology or device. Hartnell-Young and Heym (2008) believe that moving the focus of schools' acceptable use of technology policies from the devices themselves to the activities they are used for would be a useful step forward in engendering a more open climate in which to enable both teachers and students to explore the potential of mobile phones to support learning. Similarly, Kyriacou and Zuin (2016) endorse a more open, whole school approach when they conclude that teachers, head teachers, students, parents and welfare professionals all need to work together to consider how best to deal with the cyberbullying of teachers by students. Hartnell-Young and Heym (2008) add that such policies will need to address:

- ownership of digital equipment and devices and access to network connections;
- tools to support curriculum and its personalisation;
- appropriate behaviour in school and other contexts;
- privacy and security of data, including photographs and video clips.

However, as Cramer and Hayes (2010) note, these policies are often more like 'unacceptable use' policies, focusing on how students shouldn't use mobile phones and the consequences for breaking the rules. Their concern is that such stringent guidelines can leave little room or desire for innovation in teaching or learning. Mine is more that such rule-based approaches don't always function well in the shifting contexts that characterise mobile learning and the digital landscape and that we should look more to resourcing 'responsible' rather than simply 'acceptable' use. This would involve ensuring that individual teachers are able to support students learning about their responsibility to 'navigate and stay safe in their media world' (Kolb, 2008, p.8) rather than assigning that responsibility away to following a standard set of rules. As Cramer and Hayes (2010) say, policies should remind students and parents of the ongoing negotiation between the desire to use technologies and school objectives, as well as perceived versus actual risks. Dyson et al. (2013) helpfully suggest four principles with which to underpin such a responsible use policy: enhanced learner agency, personal responsibility, involvement of all stakeholders and a focus on ethical behaviour. They also note the need to include aspects of mobile phone etiquette to avoid disrupting others.

8.6 Conclusion

It is clear that integrating mobile devices into teaching and learning throws up the potential for disruption. That disruption can take a number of forms, some more worrying than others, and all need to be planned for. Katz (2005) classifies problems generated by mobile phone use by students in educational settings into four groups: disruption of class, delinquency (theft and cyberbullying), chicanery (cheating and plagiarism) and erosion of teacher autonomy. Yet these groupings clearly result from student behaviour and not the technology *per se*. West (2012) points out that while many educators and parents cite online safety concerns as yet another reason to ban mobile devices from schools, mobile learning actually provides an opportunity to promote student safety. This could be through teaching students to navigate online environments responsibly or by using the communication features on mobile phones in an emergency to pro-vide learners with safety-related information quickly. However, schools are likely to ban things they believe a) encourage students to adopt improper moral values or b) enable students to waste time that should be spent pursuing the school's learning goals (Thomas, 2008) and, as seen above, both of these can be applied to the case of mobile phones. However, that does no one a service; it prevents students from benefiting from mobile learning opportunities, which Dyson et al. (2013) go so far as to describe in itself as unethical and does not enable teachers to demonstrate responsible use. Indeed, the development of educational research into how to effectively employ handheld mobile devices in class is currently being held back by local and, in some cases, state or national regulatory frameworks that target the tool and not the operator. Should we hold mobile phones responsible for the way they are treated by some uninformed young people? I agree with Kolb (2008) who concludes that, instead of spending time, energy and money creating policies to fight cell phone use in schools, we would be better served by directing our resources towards finding useful ways to integrate these devices as knowledge construction, data collection and collaborative communication tools. And, of course, supporting the professional development of teachers, as discussed in Chapter 6, to enable this to happen.

Questions

- What 'classroom rules' would you put in place for students' use of mobile devices in your classroom and how could you ensure students felt a sense of ownership over or responsibility for making certain they were kept to?
- Last year, two girls from a secondary school in Northern Ireland created a two-minute video[1] on the impact of cyberbullying as part of their personal, social and health education. What are the pros and cons of using freely available apps such as iMovie on mobile devices to teach about responsible ways to use the devices themselves?

Annotated further reading

- EU Kids Online: Findings, Methods, Recommendations

Link to project overview report available at: www.lse.ac.uk/media@lse/research/EUKidsOnline/

This interactive report, created by the project team, updates and analyses the original 25-country, pan-European EU Kids Online survey on children's online access and behaviour and contains a wealth of material. In addition to the project findings it includes an open access, searchable database of the evidence collected and a research toolkit based on the team's data collection methods to guide researchers. Clearly, children's online opportunities, behaviours and risks encountered were different in the different countries involved and the report contains video contributions from 32 different countries in nearly as many languages (with English translation). The interactive report also links to the different national publications and reports that resulted from the study, often with video and examples of the tools used.

- Mobile learning and policies

Vosloo, S. (2012) Mobile learning and policies: Key issues to consider. UNESCO Working Series on Mobile Learning. Paris: UNESCO. Available at: http://unesdoc.unesco.org/images/0021/002176/217638E.pdf

This report by Steve Vosloo is informed from the first twelve papers of the UNESCO Working Paper Series on Mobile Learning where mobile learning initiatives in five different global regions – Europe, Asia, North America, Latin America, Africa and the Middle East – were reviewed by UNESCO national representatives. It raises key issues and questions that need to be considered when formulating policies related to mobile learning access and behaviour. It seeks to equip policy stakeholders with a better understanding of mobile learning and its contexts. The two chapters that are most directly relevant to readers of this book are the one on teaching, learning and education planning and management and the subsequent one on inclusive and safe education. The former addresses educational content that could and should be available for mobile devices, the learning contexts that are likely to arise and associated planning and professional development. The latter considers change management as well as safe mobile learning, digital citizenship and literacy and inclusion and accessibility.

Note

1 https://www.youtube.com/watch?v=2BNB5Z8qBuc

9 Assessing mobile learning

This chapter discusses the challenges in capturing, recording and assessing mobile learning including how mobile devices can be used for assessment of creative work and work outside the classroom. There are multiple examples; indeed, Nikou and Economides (2013) identify eight different categories of 'm-assessment practices' (p.347) in Greece that largely capitalise on the range of the different situations in which mobile devices have been trialled. From Australia Hartnell-Young (2016) points out that this is often teacher led with teachers taking the initiative to use technology tools to better know their learners. In the Australian Council for Educational Research (ACER)'s annual 'rolling summit' on assessment reform and innovation teachers are reporting on their use of tablets and cameras for coaching purposes and to record obvious progress for self, peer and teacher assessment. They have established class community web-sites, and cloud-based platforms and quizzes where teachers can give timely feedback. Some used adaptive testing and on demand assessments provided by education departments. Others provided continuous reporting to parents through a learning management system or through digital portfolios. Furthermore, in many countries, there has been a big increase in the number of teachers using classroom response system apps such as Socrative or Poll Everywhere both to engage students and to see what they know.

Nikou and Economides (2013) go on to highlight the ability of mobile devices to offer context aware, personalised, adaptive and/or collaborative learning opportunities with immediate feed-back as key to their use for assessment in both schools and universities. The presence of mobile devices in national assessments though is more questionable and, as described in the previous chapter, until now more often associated with plagiarism and cheating than a valued source of information. One particularly influential study demonstrating positive outcomes of the use of mobile devices in summative assessment was Project e-Scape, a UK Qualifications and Curriculum Agency commissioned study into the use of PDAs and other digital tools to support portfolio-based assessment for the national Design Technology examinations. Indeed, an entire issue of the *International Journal of Technology and Design Education* (Williams and Kimbell, 2012) was devoted to reporting on the project. Furthermore, many educators, especially those that subscribe to the ethos presented in the 21st Century Skills Framework (Trilling and Fadel, 2009) are beginning to question whether our current assessment strategies, that are still cen-tred around individual pen and paper examinations developed early in the last century, are fit for purpose in the twenty-first. This chapter, therefore, comprises four sections, the first address-ing the classroom-based use of mobile devices in formative assessment to support student learning and the second piloting the use of mobile devices in summative assessments for formal awards. The third questions whether there is a need to develop new assessment mechanisms for today's students equipped with smartphones and/or tablet computers and the fourth addresses possible implications for the use of mobile devices in assessment.

9.1 Using mobile devices in formative assessment for learning

Several of the case studies described in Chapters 3 and 4 include teacher reflections on how their use of mobile phones or iPads in class enables them to see what their students have learnt. This information can then be used as feedback to modify future teaching and learning activities and, as stated in Black and Wiliam's (1998) definition of formative assessment, 'enables them to adapt the teaching to meet student needs' (p.140). Interestingly, these are all examples from primary school teachers that centre on the use of images and video and I have reflected on this importance of imagery and visualisation to mobile learning pedagogy elsewhere (Ekanayake and Wishart, 2014b). In *Personalising inquiry learning through using HTC Smartphones 1:1*, a primary science class mobile learning initiative (Looi et al., 2011), the students used both an animation app to visualise their understanding of how the digestive system works and recorded video of them 'teaching' this to their parents. This helped both them and their teacher assess the quality of their work. In *Using camera phones in small groups: 'The diversity of leaves'*, another primary science class (Ekanayake, 2011), the teacher reported that having the images children had taken in the school garden using their mobile phone cameras available enabled her to assess on the fly. She also found she could correct the students' misconceptions about the leaf structures through re-viewing or replaying the images when it was required. In *Using iPads 1:1 'The Secret Garden grows into an immersive experience'* Sparkes (2016) described how using Minecraft, the 3D modelling app, enabled her to assess students' learning by 'walking through' their 3D visualisations that showed all the elements of the novel's setting that they had picked up on and put into their re-creation of the garden. Indeed, in Beauchamp and Hillier's (2014) study exploring how iPads were introduced and implemented in several Welsh primary school classrooms their support for assessment for learning opportunities was singled out for its perceived, positive impact.

In his detailed exploration of teachers' beliefs about assessment and their use of the screencasting app Explain Everything on iPads with their students, Richards (2014) showed how screencasting provided outlets for the formative assessment approaches that the teachers wanted to achieve. He describes three teachers, their beliefs, their classes and the outcomes of these initiatives. Explain Everything itself is a simple design tool that enables screencasting, which is recording a video of your mobile device or computer screen for teaching or sharing ideas. It enables the user to annotate, animate, narrate, import and/or export almost any digital media such as slides, images and drawings. The first teacher, Shannon, working with Grade 2 students, planned to use the iPad app to take a picture of a book page and ask the students to record themselves reading the passage and then retelling it in order to practise summarising or retelling information from the books. Danica wanted her Grade 5 students to work at their mathematical understanding. She posted a document with three differentiated maths problems about fractions for the students to open in Explain Everything, pick one of the three problems and solve it using any method they prefer and at the same time recording an explanation of the steps they were using. Jeff's end-of-year English project for his Grade 7 students was more flexible; he introduced it as a video reflection where students picked a meaningful moment from the year's teaching and described and analysed it in a screencast.

Richards (2014) reports that by using this screencasting technology on iPads the teachers could view and capture their students' ability in, and understanding of, the different subjects quickly and easily. He adds that, in addition to this enabling formative assessment by the teacher, using Explain Everything resulted in unprompted self-assessment by the students. In all three classes, students created screencast recordings and, without the teacher asking them to do so, played back and listened to what they had created. Some students even went back and adjusted their screencast based on what they heard. There were also many times that dialogue and sharing between students took place without the teacher having prompted it. The teachers also noted the value of how this tool enabled them to access the process of student learning rather than being confined to viewing the final product. Similarly, when studying the use of smartphones and digital cameras in making stop-motion animations to reinforce science learning of dynamic processes such as enzyme action, life cycles or changes of state by teacher trainees, I found that this visualisation enables teachers to both see and discuss what their students know (Wishart, 2017). The Scottish teachers using class sets of iPads observed by Burden et al. (2012) believed that their use for this kind of formative feedback is more meaningful for students than traditional written annotations. It was reported to be particularly effective when students and their peers are encouraged to use apps and the iPad themselves to critique their own work. Indeed, Microsoft now provides free software for both Android and iOS that enables just that. The OneNote Class Notebook app lets a teacher set up a personal workspace for each student in the class, a content library for handouts and a collaboration space for lessons and creative activities. Students go to the content library to get their assignments and can then critique, annotate, sketch or take notes and submit their work. The teacher provides individualised support using their own device to type in each student's private notebook or to write directly on their work. Alternatively, in the collaboration space, they can provide real-time feedback on students' work and encourage them to work together.

In each of the above examples, three or more of the five 'key strategies' of formative assessment endorsed by Wiliam and Thompson (2008) are capitalised on. These are:

- clarifying, understanding and sharing learning intentions and criteria for success;
- engineering effective classroom discussions, activities and tasks that elicit evidence of learning;
- activating learners as instructional resources for one another;
- activating learners as the owners of their own learning; and
- providing feedback that moves learners forward.

In the above examples the teacher' role in supplying feedback is key; however, Hwang and Chang (2011) describe the evaluation of a formative assessment-based mobile learning app aimed at improving the learning attitudes and achievements of students where feedback is automated. The mobile learning activity was designed for a Taiwanese elementary school's local culture course. The objective of the app was to guide the students to understand the historical background of a local temple, its relationship with local culture and learn about the ancient customs via observing the artworks and the cultural relics within it. The app was evaluated by two classes with around 30 Grade 5 students in each. One class acted as a control group and were guided by the standard tour-based mobile learning system, which directed them to visit the same set of target learning objects and asked them the same questions. However, when the students in the control group failed to correctly answer a question, the learning system showed them the correct answer along with the supplementary materials. Therefore, the control group students spent most of the learning time on browsing and reading the learning materials. In contrast, the formative assessment-based mobile learning system only gave hints to the students in the experimental group when they failed to correctly answer a question, provoking them into finding the answers by themselves. Thus the experimental group students spent most of their learning time observing and finding the answers from the target learning objects. The two groups took a pre-test to ensure that they had equal abilities in this subject before the learning activity; there was no significant difference and, if anything, the control group performed better. However, from the experimental results, it was found that the students in the experimental group, who learned with the formative assessment-based mobile learning approach, showed greater learning motivation, especially amongst the lower achieving students, and significantly better learning achievement.

Additionally, the above example demonstrates that specially designed mobile phone apps can support assessment opportunities when outside school at the target learning locations. In several of the case studies reported in Chapters 3 and 4 visits to a location are used to generate products that can be used by teachers to assess what the students learned. In *Collaborative digital story creation using iPods during a school visit* (Nordmark and Milrad, 2012) the products were historical stories, in *'Storifying' natural science education: A mobile urban drama played in teams* (Hansen et al., 2010) the products were short dramas, and cameras on mobile phones feature again in *Mathematics and mobile learning: Capturing, analysing and modelling linear phenomena with photos and video* (White and Martin, 2014). Apps can also be designed to specifically guide and manage peer assessment. Lai and Chen (2013) report on a trial with 276 Grade 6 students in Taiwan tasked with using such an app to grade each other's video projects for creativity, cooperation, content, presentation and flow. The trial was a success with students reporting that using the app on their own smartphones for peer assessment activities enabled them to grasp the defects and advantages of other group projects.

Interestingly, in an earlier study investigating the potential roles for formative assessment support apps designed for the Palm Pilot, a PDA, Yarnall et al. (2006) found their use heightened teachers' attention towards monitoring student thinking in addition to student task completion. Project Whirl comprised a suite of handheld software applications that could be used to support classroom assessment in science inquiry. They included the aforementioned animation creation app, Sketchy, and a multiple-choice quiz design app, Quizzler, and were deployed during science investigations at both elementary and middle school levels. During the project, teachers reported paying significantly more attention than usual to monitoring both student thinking and accountability. Teachers also used the tools to involve students in self and peer assessment. For example, it was found that using Quizzler can make feedback more immediate to students promoting independent assessment skills. It was used by several teachers at the start of taught units both to assess their students' prior knowledge and to encourage them in independently tracking its development as the unit progressed. Using mobile devices running class teacher-designed quizzes to support self-assessment was also trialled by de-Marcos et al. (2010) in a Spanish secondary school, with third year students (14–15 year olds) following a Technology course in secondary education and with sixth formers in the sixth (and final) year (17–18 year olds). The researchers report noticeable improvement in student performance, especially amongst younger learners, accompanied by a relatively low impact on the current teaching activities and methodology.

9.2 Classroom response systems

Indeed, the use of such multiple-choice quizzes for low stakes, formative assessment is the key feature underpinning the current trend in increased use of classroom response systems. These are networks connecting students' handheld mobile devices (via Wi-Fi or cellular technology) with the teacher or lecturer's desktop PC running software that can display the class's answers to simple multiple-choice questions. Results are usually shown as anonymised total frequencies for the different answer choices though some systems allow contributors to identify themselves. The mobile devices needed range from 'clickers' that function only with the system purchased through a class set of tablet PCs to students' own mobile phones. Using them takes preparation ahead of time; some like Socrative are web based and the teacher needs to set up their class register and upload their questions, others like TurningPoint and Poll Everywhere can also be set up to interact with the teacher's presentation slides. Making sure that all the devices to be used are sufficiently charged to last the lesson is also necessary.

Research into the largely 'clicker'-based early classroom response systems in both schools and universities was extensively reviewed by Fies and Marshall (2006), who concluded that there is widespread agreement that they can promote learning when coupled with appropriate pedagogical methodologies. Many of these findings remain applicable to today's more flexible web-based tools using the students' mobile phones as the 'clickers'. Increased engagement through interactivity was often seen though studies tended to focus on individual use in individual student response modes and for conditions where instructors could trace who responded in what way to a given question. There was comment too about the extra work needed to implement this. At that time, learning opportunities arising through small group discussion before making a choice using the classroom response tool were rarely discussed or investigated despite their potential for peer instruction and assessment. The literature also gave clear indication that using classroom response system supported environments led to greater learning gains than traditional learning environments. However, Fies and Marshall (2006) make the point that since the comparison is actually between traditional and interactive engagement models, it is impossible to assess the effectiveness of the technology itself. Indeed, a more recent meta-analysis (Liu et al., 2016) showed that using classroom response systems was not more effective in itself than low-technology methods such as hand raising or response cards in terms of learning performance. Liu et al. (2016) conclude that the positive impacts so frequently reported may be due to the associated greater opportunities for peer discussion now increasingly being seen; however, they had difficulty sourcing school as opposed to college-based studies.

Interestingly though, the studies of the different types of classroom response systems that have taken place in schools tend to be set in science learning contexts. For example, Irving et al. (2009) report on the use of handheld graphing calculators connected via a classroom Wi-Fi network as clickers in teaching physical science at junior high school in the USA. Teachers in their study noted increased engagement with students being interested in seeing both their own and others' results on the quizzes. Indeed, the public display of anonymised quiz answers was reported both to promote class discussion and reveal patterns in the students' wrong answers. Students asked more questions than usual and received more feedback about their learning soon after completing these short assessments. Similarly, Kay and Knaack (2009) report on a study that took place in secondary school science classrooms in Canada. Their students indicated that they were more involved in their science class when a TurningPoint classroom response system was used; however, this was not the case if the associated assessment was intended for summative rather than formative purposes. If that was the case some students, especially girls, became decidedly stressed which Kay (2009) linked to the extra time that was needed to work the novel technology and that, on occasions, it did not work. Batteries needed to be changed, for example. Additionally, one girl pointed out 'I didn't like how we couldn't go back and change the answers' (p.734). In another science classroom-based study from the UK, Moss and Crowley (2011) make the important point that classroom response systems enable information being used to assess student learning to be presented to them in different modes including graphics. This is useful for science diagrams and models and also supports learners who have difficulty with reading and assimilating the text-based questions and answers so often seen in traditional multiple-choice format. In their example Moss and Crowley (2011) show how images can be used to test students' knowledge of the reactivity series of metals by asking them to rank pictures of different chemical reactions starting with the fastest. They add that using such questions and exploring the feedback anonymously with the class allows the teacher to explore and address any misconceptions held by the group.

However, creating questions like these or even simple text-based ones takes time and, as noted earlier by Fies and Marshall (2006), can result in complaints about extra work. Spending the time on designing effective questions is essential though; Beatty et al. (2006) point out that the efficacy of classroom response systems for teaching physics depends strongly on the quality of the questions used. They put forward four complementary mechanisms underlying the purposes for designing classroom response system questions. These are: directing students' attention; stimulating specific cognitive processes; communicating information to the instructor and students via tabulated answer counts; and facilitating the articulation and confrontation of ideas. The effort put into question design is rewarded, as Kang et al. (2014) noted in a study of the use of classroom response systems in Korean high school life science classes. They found that, while sophisticated diagnostic questions for students of a range of ability levels need to be prepared in advance, their use for diagnostic or formative assessment heightened students' levels of concentration in class and resulted in their acquisition of relevant science concepts.

Maeng (2016), in her case study of a US High School Biology teacher who used clickers for some form of formative assessment almost daily, also notes the value of using them to support differentiation. She reports the class teacher's approach in detail:

Once all of the students complete the warm up, Diane finalizes the session which allows each student to see their score on their clicker and Diane to view class data. She quickly looks over the class data, pulls it up for the class to see, and tells them, "Wow. You guys are doing well. Let's look at these quickly and see what ones we need to review." She noticed that most students missed question 5 but few students missed any others—one or two students out of the entire class missed each question. She tells the class, "Question 5 we need to look at. The correct answer is A. The light microscope came first. We can't see cells, cell theory, or DNA before we have the light microscope." She continues, "You guys seem to be just fine on microscopes, so I'm not going to spend time reviewing that. Wow, you guys got 100% on the experimental design question. You guys are doing really well with independent and dependent variables. I'm not going to spend a lot of time on independent and dependent variables."

(Maeng, 2016, p.10)

Diane also used unit pre-assessment data to modify both instruction for small groups of students and planning further lessons within the unit. While Diane attributed her capacity to use formative assessment to the integration of technology, specifically the classroom response system, using such tools does not always go smoothly. Lee et al. (2012) report a number of issues from their classroom observations of 38 American and high school teachers that included broken clickers, invalid answer formats, the software freezing, students' inappropriate attitudes, e.g. turning a quiz into a race and problems when particular mathematical notations were needed. Though again, teachers reported most difficulty with developing the necessary questions and integrating them into a specific curriculum. This was a serious concern for most, resulting in issues with the amount of time that needed to be spent on planning as well as time required in class to include peer discussions.

Outside science Bonaiuti et al. (2015) investigated the role of clickers in five different classes (two grammar and three history) in an Italian secondary school. Their results showed unexpected differences in learning outcomes based on the lesson subjects. It was observed that, while all students were more engaged when using the clickers, it was only in the grammar lessons that this was associated with increased test scores. Bonaiuti et al. (2015) attribute this finding to arguments in grammar being more clearly defined and therefore easier to rehearse and test via multiple-choice questioning. In another study with a similar focus but with younger children, Sheard et al. (2012) found that, on the subsequent grammar test, students who had been using the classroom response systems for formative learning tasks performed significantly better than a control group. This was especially noticeable for average and lower achieving students; however, these effects did not generalise to a more extended, writing task. This again suggests that the use of mobile devices as classroom response systems for formative learning will be particularly effective in subjects where subject knowledge can be tightly framed and thus why their use in science has been so popular.

Teachers can also employ more powerful tools designed for interaction with the audience via their mobile phones during business presentations for classroom-based formative assessment. Many, such as Zeetings, are free to educators or have special price plans that enable restricted, educational use. Such tools also run more extensive, open-ended text-based interactions enabling them to display individual student questions or use an activity (text) wall to display comments as a live feed as well as the more common multiple-choice question formats. Other apps such as Kahoot are designed for interactive quiz-based gameplay; Kahoot itself encourages the 'game' creator to design in opportunities to interact with the teacher or prompt peer discussion. Hu and Huang (2013) report that Adobe Presenter, another business app, was used very effectively on a class set of iPads by the teacher of a large science class in China. The learners were 58 Grade 3 (10 year old) students from Beijing who were studying the different types of plant seeds and their properties. Thus there seems to be plenty of activity in schools surrounding the use of mobile devices for formative assessment but what about using them summatively?

9.3 Using mobile devices for summative assessment for qualifications

While there is ongoing international research into the use of digital tools for summative assessment – for example, the Centre for Schooling and Learning Technologies (CSaLT) at Edith Cowan University and the Assessment Research Centre (ARC) at the Education University of Hong Kong, this has not yet considered potential roles for mobile phones. Instead, mentioning mobile phones and examinations today tends to bring stories of cheating to mind, as described in Chapter 8, Section 8.2. However, there were two much earlier studies into the use of PDAs and mobile phones funded by the then UK Qualifications and Curriculum Authority for portfolio-based summative assessment in ICT and in Design and Technology, projects eVIVA and e-Scape.

In Project eVIVA (McGuire et al., 2004) students created online portfolios of their ICT work to evidence what they knew and could do, the processes they used and the decisions they made. They used curriculum-linked competency statements to set their own targets for the final work. Parents, teachers and other students then gave them feedback on the result either online or by using a mobile phone for text or voice recordings. Once students had completed the final version of their portfolio, they went through an automated oral assessment, the eVIVA, on their mobile phone. Results from this small-scale project, piloted with ICT co-ordinators in five schools and their Key Stage 3 (KS3) classes (11–14 years old), showed that the system provided evidence of both students' work *and* their thought processes, enabling their teachers to make a fairer assessment of ICT capability. Also exhibiting their work in an online portfolio appeared to give students a sense of audience, lifting their expectations and boosting their confidence. Interestingly, the children tended to set higher targets for themselves than their schools would have set for them; they mostly met these targets too. Finally, the teachers reported that engaging with Project eVIVA didn't obviously add to their workload as the KS3 ICT assessments needed to be done anyway.

Project e-Scape (Kimbell, 2012a) was similarly portfolio based; learners (15–16 years old) taking General Certificate of Secondary Education (GCSE) in Design and Technology developed their coursework portfolios in real-time using PDAs to upload text and images directly from school or off-site settings (including studios or workshops and their homes). Kimbell (2008) reports that the strength of using PDAs was in their multi-tasking, enabling learners to use them like digital sketchbooks, digital notebooks, digital cameras and/or digital voice-recorders. The project was trialled in 14 schools in Cornwall in England, over two 3-hour sessions learners were presented with a design task that was to be taken through to a prototype. Teachers were impressed with both the system's functionality and their students' levels of engagement.

- I was amazed how quickly the children grasped the technology and were in no way over-awed by it (I shouldn't have been!)

- I was particularly impressed with how they used the voice recordings and took them so seriously. I feel this has tremendous potential for capturing their thoughts and feelings about their work as they are doing it.
- They found the novelty and ease of use of the PDA's a positive motivator.

(Kimbell, 2012b, p.148)

Kimbell (2008) adds that everything the researchers did for the purposes of collecting evidence for assessment was also found to help scaffold both the progress of the activity and the performance of learners. In the normal course of events, once the students' portfolios are completed, they are graded by their teachers against the examination boards' set criteria and the grades submitted. However, Kimbell (2008) also points out that this system is dogged by issues stemming from different teachers interpreting the different criteria differently. He also notes the inevitability that assessment requires the comparison of work from one learner with work from another. As a result, Project e-Scape also trialled using their 350 portfolios of submitted work, now available online at a single location, to trial an innovative assessment tool. This system, using a judgement mechanism that enabled multiple comparisons of different pairs of portfolios, was found to radically improve summative assessment reliability.

These early successes have echoes in Burden et al.'s (2012) findings from the Scotland iPad evaluation where it was reported that the students themselves discovered how they could use the various notation tools in the iPad, including the camera and audio recording, to keep records of their own progress. As it had already been shown from the parental data that students were more willing to share their school work at home when they were using the iPads, Burden et al. (2012) suggest that setting up mPortfolios could form a more naturalistic way of reporting to and informing parents about their children's progress at school. This would reduce the current need for additional and time-consuming paperwork. Indeed, Turner (2016) describes exactly that, trialling the use of iFolio on iPads with young students (Grade 1) to

- build up a portfolio of learning through media (audio and visual) constructions;
- develop confidence and competence through structured play and inquiry;
- better engage in personalised literacy development;
- better communicate to teachers and parents and
- obtain more timely and focused feedback from a wider range of people.

(Turner, 2016, p.234)

Already in the school, an international school in Hong Kong, all Grade 5 and 6 students manage their own digital portfolio using iFolio which records and displays their learning progress. For example, for digital literacy, students' mPortfolio work was found to support increased access from and interaction with teachers, peers and parents, personal relationships with learning and increased accessibility to content.

It is not just students who need to evidence their work taking place in school but often teachers too. For example, many countries have national set standards against which student teachers' work is assessed before they are permitted to qualify. In one study (Wishart, 2008) I tried getting our Modern Foreign Language (MFL) student teachers to use PDAs to take photographs and videos to evidence the activities they had participated in when on placement in school to show their progress towards the UK national teachers' standards. However, the students were very reluctant to do so, their students assumed the PDA was a phone and they felt very uncomfortable using it in the light of the schools' bans on students' use of mobile phones. Ferrer and Martí (2012) had a bit more success with teacher trainees in Spain. They describe a student teacher taking photos of mushrooms in the forest to illustrate a text-based assignment on teaching natural sciences. Drama trainees used cameras on their mobile phones and Glogster, a poster creation app, to evidence the process of creating a theatre play and then used the phones again to blog reflections on their learning. As Ferrer and Martí (2012) point out, using mobile devices like this, essentially to create multimedia mPortfolios, allows students to present evidence from informal, outside class settings such as field or concert trips as well as from the more usual classroom-based teaching and learning experiences. Participation from their student teachers though was limited, while Ferrer and Martí (2012) describe this in terms of only them just starting out, it seems likely to me that the current sociocultural climate in schools in Spain also militates against trainees' everyday use of mobile devices.

Thus, with the mobile phone bans and the rigid assessment structures seen in schools today, the promise shown in the early studies described above for using mobile or smartphones to support summative assessments has not yet been capitalised on. McFarlane (2015) attributes the lack of schools developing more 1:1 handheld computing initiatives to the mismatch between mobile device use and current assessment practice with high stakes assessments, such as national school leaving and university entrance examinations, that rely on handwriting skills. Indeed, Dede (2010) makes the point that we are more likely to ban the use of technological applications and representations from high stakes testing, rather than aim to measure students' abilities to use these tools, applications and media effectively. Is there, therefore, a need to develop new assessment mechanisms relevant to twenty-first century students that allows them to make the most of the potential of the mobile phone or tablet PC so often found in their purse or pocket?

academics and researchers in Europe.
how 21st-century assessment strategies need to
pture the less tangible themes underlying all key
amentary Recommendation on Key Competences
2006). They go on to highlight how practical tasks
omprehensive assessment in a variety of authentic
lysis, interpretation and reflection (Redecker and
s (2013) recognises the transformational potentia'
nperatives, principles and challenges in reforr
Council for Educational Research. He belie'
gies will include enabling assessments t
with an understanding of learning
ne creation of enhanced assess
vity and increased personali
the potential of using di
isunderstandings acr
ther action, Hart

ever-changing world of work and find fulfilment in their lives are the so-called 21st century skills (Hill and Barber, 2014).

The international response to the 21st century skills concept has been strong. Dede (2010) identifies four bodies from Europe and the USA each presenting slightly different conceptual frameworks for 21st century skills. The P21 Partnership for 21st Century Learning[1] that comprises a number of US states and companies including Ford, Lego, Pearson, Walt Disney, Intel, plus education, play and elearning businesses is one of the largest. In addition to these four there is also the Assessment and Teaching of 21st Century Skills (ATC21S) group in Australia. Each of these bodies represents different combinations of respected academic, government funded, third sector and industrial organisations. This multiplicity of initiatives led Oldfield et al. (2012) to conclude that exactly what constitutes '21st century skills' depended on who you asked; however, some themes are clearly common to all proposed frameworks. These include skills in digital literacy, communication, collaboration, critical thinking and problem solving, creativity and innovation. Listed like this, as Oldfield et al. (2012, p. 22) noted, 'these "21st century skills" often appear to align with the "higher-order" thinking skills identified in Bloom's Taxonomy of Educational Objectives'. We, therefore, need to be looking to assessments that can capture these skills.

This is where digital technology and mobile devices can help. As one 21st-century elementary school teacher put it:

> *Time to move forward and leave standardized testing in the past where it belongs and encourage students to use their phones productively. They have the world at their fingertips and a tool in their pocket that allows them to explore, create and communicate. If we want students to be capable, forward thinking leaders we must teach them to be so.*
>
> *(Dyck, 2015)*

Dyck (2015) adds that her school in Canada is abandoning traditional report cards in favour of continuous reporting through student online portfolios, parental emails, and daily snapshots into learning. Her views above are supported by numerous ac   s in Europe Redecker and Johannessen (2013) point out
go beyond testing factual knowledge to ca
competences outlined in the European Parl
for Lifelong Learning (European Parliament,
using mobile devices can be developed for
contexts, particularly scientific inquiry, and
Johannessen, 2013). From Australia, Master
of new technologies in his report on the i
educational assessment for the Australian
future impact of new and emerging technolo
anywhere, anytime and in ways consistent
lifelong process. This would be alongside t
through use of multimedia, greater interacti
While Masters (2013) also calls attention to
more automated diagnosis of individuals' m
to the learners in a form that guides fu

important role that the teachers have to play in implementing and taking forward any innovation. It is only where teachers and stakeholders work together, as in the 'rolling summit' on assessment reform and innovation organised by the Australian Council for Educational Research, that real, transformative progress can be made. However, in acknowledging the potential for mobile devices to support new ways of collecting data to support assessment of valued skills we need to take care, for, as Masters (2013) noted, advances in technology also have far-reaching implications for the collection, storage, analysis, interpretation and reporting of assessment information. The implications of using mobile devices for assessment anytime in authentic contexts are discussed in the next section.

9.5 Possible implications of using mobile devices for assessment

Many of the ethical questions arising over using mobile devices for school-based assessment such as the merging of formal and informal contexts and access to personal information have already been discussed in detail in Chapter 7. So here I will focus only on the associated collection and storage of data that has been uploaded either via mobile devices or desktop PCs for assessment purposes together with how that data is used.

Indeed, as Timmis et al. (2015) point out, data flow within the education sector, at classroom, institution and national levels, is already prolific. It is likely to increase further: the Open University, UK have identified learning analytics, the application of data and its analysis, not just to monitor progress but also to improve learners' results as one of the key trends in learning that appeared during the last year (Institute of Educational Technology, 2016). However, not only does this raise ethical issues about the degree of consent students may have over the collection and use of such data, equally important are the issues of how they can access, own and/or control their own personal data (Timmis et al., 2015). Timmis et al. (2015) add further concerns over the current rate of development of learning analytic technologies that outpaces that of technologies that share control with students through, for example, the use of portfolios and social software. This could potentially result in over-controlled, impersonal educational environments.

Furthermore, taking things to extremes, we should note My LifeSpace, one of several future mobile learning scenarios generated at discussion workshops sponsored by the UK Joint Information Systems Committee. MyLifeSpace envisages a 'whole of life' assessment strategy supported by data capture using mobile devices and associated cloud-based data storage (Wishart and Green, 2010). It describes the wholesale collection of life experiences, school and work experiences accompanied by prompts to generate learning and reflection from these experiences. It is much bigger than an ePortfolio and incorporates all of the things that a student generates throughout their learning and life journeys, inside and outside school. In the life space, there are virtual stores for different types of information, split into separate areas, such as: qualifications, work experience, assignments and a personal area. However, these areas are not completely separate and are likely to be cross-linked. Documentary evidence, text, audio and video, will be transferred to and from the life store silo store by mobile devices. Apps on the mobile device will help students remember that they are learning all the time, at school or college, at work, touring or at home and to prompt them to record that learning. The process will be multi input, through voice, camera or touch. The app will help learning as it responds to the way that a student organises their work. With appropriate viewing permissions set, a tutor, assessor or employer will visit a student's life store and gain a more rounded picture of their skills and abilities than is currently available.

While such a scenario fulfils Whitelock and Watt's (2008) call for a pedagogically driven model for e-assessment that can allow students to take more control of their own learning and become more reflective, storing such a wealth of data is obviously questionable practice. Also, how would we ensure students rose to such a huge challenge? Yet another, equally unwelcome, alternative is the automated scenario which Masters (2013) envisaged where learning analytics tools use uploaded data to drive teachers' feedback. Timmis et al. (2015) also note the risk that developments in digital technologies will drive assessment methods that will, in turn, drive teaching and learning practices. They propose that one way to mitigate the risk of technology driven assessment practices is for interdisciplinary teams to work together, to foreground the inherent tensions in their different beliefs with respect to technology enhanced learning.

9.6 Conclusion

As Sahin and Mentor (2016) note, using mobile devices, assessment can now take place at any location; a contemporary classroom could be contexts that are not bounded by physical class-room walls, such as when commuting, in kitchens or museums. Indeed, the exploratory studies into school-based assessment using mobile devices described above show the potential value in using them to record student progress. This progress can be captured in different places, outside as well as inside the classroom, and in different modes providing a rich picture of the development of a student's knowledge and skills. This information can, and is, being used by teachers to assess their students' learning formatively. However, by and large, summative assessments tend to rely on more traditional methods such as completing a test paper in the school exam hall. Such one-off assessments capture a student's knowledge at one point in time and several bodies, especially those responsible for developing 21st century skills, are now questioning their use. In an educational climate where skills such as creativity, collaboration, communication and critical thinking are prized, with evidence of ability in their use being sought for entry into employment, there is an exciting future for mobile device-based assessments. These would focus on evaluating and recording the process of learning instead of merely on the product. Additionally, if we were indeed able to change modes of assessment to those more suitable for assessing 21st century skills, education professionals' concerns such as the issues of plagiarism and cheating described in Chapter 8 would not be such a barrier to implementing mobile learning in schools. However, that said, we must remain mindful of the potential to over-collect assessment data and be careful to ensure its ethical and responsible use.

Questions

- Thinking of your specialist subject, design an assessment task that uses a student's smart-phone, tablet or camera phone. How could you grade it quickly and informatively?
- You want your students to use their mobile devices to capture evidence of their progress on a school project: what ethical considerations should you consider first?

show their progress towards the UK national teachers' standards. However, the students were very reluctant to do so, their students assumed the PDA was a phone and they felt very uncomfortable using it in the light of the schools' bans on students' use of mobile phones. Ferrer and Martí (2012) had a bit more success with teacher trainees in Spain. They describe a student teacher taking photos of mushrooms in the forest to illustrate a text-based assignment on teaching natural sciences. Drama trainees used cameras on their mobile phones and Glogster, a poster creation app, to evidence the process of creating a theatre play and then used the phones again to blog reflections on their learning. As Ferrer and Martí (2012) point out, using mobile devices like this, essentially to create multimedia mPortfolios, allows students to present evidence from informal, outside class settings such as field or concert trips as well as from the more usual classroom-based teaching and learning experiences. Participation from their student teachers though was limited, while Ferrer and Martí (2012) describe this in terms of only them just starting out, it seems likely to me that the current sociocultural climate in schools in Spain also militates against trainees' everyday use of mobile devices.

Thus, with the mobile phone bans and the rigid assessment structures seen in schools today, the promise shown in the early studies described above for using mobile or smartphones to support summative assessments has not yet been capitalised on. McFarlane (2015) attributes the lack of schools developing more 1:1 handheld computing initiatives to the mismatch between mobile device use and current assessment practice with high stakes assessments, such as national school leaving and university entrance examinations, that rely on handwriting skills. Indeed, Dede (2010) makes the point that we are more likely to ban the use of technological applications and representations from high stakes testing, rather than aim to measure students' abilities to use these tools, applications and media effectively. Is there, therefore, a need to develop new assessment mechanisms relevant to twenty-first century students that allows them to make the most of the potential of the mobile phone or tablet PC so often found in their purse or pocket?

9.4 The need to develop new assessment mechanisms for the BYOD era

There are a number of issues with current summative assessment practices that have led to calls internationally for change. In their report reflecting on the current situation and possible courses of action Hill and Barber (2014) point out some key contrasts between what we aspire for from student assessment in schools and what we actually have. For example, while we aim to create assessments that provide meaningful information on learning outcomes, we actually have over-reliance on grades or levels that reveal little about what the student can do. The feedback these provide to schools on student performance is typically provided too late and is too broad-brush to be of value in improving learning and teaching. Also we need assessments that accommodate the full range of outcomes valued in those leaving school but actually have tests and examinations that are dominated by questions assessing low-level cognitive processes. These fail to capture such valued outcomes as practical, laboratory and field work, speaking and listening abilities, higher-order cognitive processes and a range of inter- and intra-personal competencies. Such processes and competencies, increasingly seen as critical to equip young people with the skills required to be ongoing learners who can navigate today's ever-changing world of work and find fulfilment in their lives are the so-called 21st century skills (Hill and Barber, 2014).

The international response to the 21st century skills concept has been strong. Dede (2010) identifies four bodies from Europe and the USA each presenting slightly different conceptual frameworks for 21st century skills. The P21 Partnership for 21st Century Learning[1] that comprises a number of US states and companies including Ford, Lego, Pearson, Walt Disney, Intel, plus education, play and elearning businesses is one of the largest. In addition to these four there is also the Assessment and Teaching of 21st Century Skills (ATC21S) group in Australia. Each of these bodies represents different combinations of respected academic, government funded, third sector and industrial organisations. This multiplicity of initiatives led Oldfield et al. (2012) to conclude that exactly what constitutes '21st century skills' depended on who you asked; however, some themes are clearly common to all proposed frameworks. These include skills in digital literacy, communication, collaboration, critical thinking and problem solving, creativity and innovation. Listed like this, as Oldfield et al. (2012, p. 22) noted, 'these "21st century skills" often appear to align with the "higher-order" thinking skills identified in Bloom's Taxonomy of Educational Objectives'. We, therefore, need to be looking to assessments that can capture these skills.

This is where digital technology and mobile devices can help. As one 21st-century elementary school teacher put it:

> *Time to move forward and leave standardized testing in the past where it belongs and encourage students to use their phones productively. They have the world at their fingertips and a tool in their pocket that allows them to explore, create and communicate. If we want students to be capable, forward thinking leaders we must teach them to be so.*
>
> *(Dyck, 2015)*

Dyck (2015) adds that her school in Canada is abandoning traditional report cards in favour of continuous reporting through student online portfolios, parental emails, and daily snapshots into learning. Her views above are supported by numerous academics and researchers in Europe. Redecker and Johannessen (2013) point out how 21st-century assessment strategies need to go beyond testing factual knowledge to capture the less tangible themes underlying all key competences outlined in the European Parliamentary Recommendation on Key Competences for Lifelong Learning (European Parliament, 2006). They go on to highlight how practical tasks using mobile devices can be developed for comprehensive assessment in a variety of authentic contexts, particularly scientific inquiry, analysis, interpretation and reflection (Redecker and Johannessen, 2013). From Australia, Masters (2013) recognises the transformational potential of new technologies in his report on the imperatives, principles and challenges in reforming educational assessment for the Australian Council for Educational Research. He believes that future impact of new and emerging technologies will include enabling assessments to take place anywhere, anytime and in ways consistent with an understanding of learning as an ongoing, lifelong process. This would be alongside the creation of enhanced assessment environments through use of multimedia, greater interactivity and increased personalisation of assessments. While Masters (2013) also calls attention to the potential of using digital technology to provide more automated diagnosis of individuals' misunderstandings accompanied by timely feedback to the learners in a form that guides further action, Hartnell-Young (2016) reminds of the important role that the teachers have to play in implementing and taking forward any innovation. It is only where teachers and stakeholders work together, as in the 'rolling summit' on assessment reform and innovation organised by the Australian Council for Educational Research, that real, transformative progress can be made. However, in acknowledging the potential for mobile devices to support new ways of collecting data to support assessment of valued skills we need to take care, for, as Masters (2013) noted, advances in technology also have far-reaching implications for the collection, storage, analysis, interpretation and reporting of assessment information. The implications of using mobile devices for assessment anytime in authentic contexts are discussed in the next section.

9.5 Possible implications of using mobile devices for assessment

Many of the ethical questions arising over using mobile devices for school-based assessment such as the merging of formal and informal contexts and access to personal information have already been discussed in detail in Chapter 7. So here I will focus only on the associated collection and storage of data that has been uploaded either via mobile devices or desktop PCs for assessment purposes together with how that data is used.

Indeed, as Timmis et al. (2015) point out, data flow within the education sector, at classroom, institution and national levels, is already prolific. It is likely to increase further: the Open University, UK have identified learning analytics, the application of data and its analysis, not just to monitor progress but also to improve learners' results as one of the key trends in learning that appeared during the last year (Institute of Educational Technology, 2016). However, not only does this raise ethical issues about the degree of consent students may have over the collection and use of such data, equally important are the issues of how they can access, own and/or control their own personal data (Timmis et al., 2015). Timmis et al. (2015) add further concerns over the current rate of development of learning analytic technologies that outpaces that of technologies that share control with students through, for example, the use of portfolios and social software. This could potentially result in over-controlled, impersonal educational environments.

Furthermore, taking things to extremes, we should note My LifeSpace, one of several future mobile learning scenarios generated at discussion workshops sponsored by the UK Joint Information Systems Committee. MyLifeSpace envisages a 'whole of life' assessment strategy supported by data capture using mobile devices and associated cloud-based data storage (Wishart and Green, 2010). It describes the wholesale collection of life experiences, school and work experiences accompanied by prompts to generate learning and reflection from these experiences. It is much bigger than an ePortfolio and incorporates all of the things that a student generates throughout their learning and life journeys, inside and outside school. In the life space, there are virtual stores for different types of information, split into separate areas, such as: qualifications, work experience, assignments and a personal area. However, these areas are not completely separate and are likely to be cross-linked. Documentary evidence, text, audio and video, will be transferred to and from the life store silo store by mobile devices. Apps on the mobile device will help students remember that they are learning all the time, at school or college, at work, touring or at home and to prompt them to record that learning. The process will be multi input, through voice, camera or touch. The app will help learning as it responds to the way that a student organises their work. With appropriate viewing permissions set, a tutor, assessor or employer will visit a student's life store and gain a more rounded picture of their skills and abilities than is currently available.

While such a scenario fulfils Whitelock and Watt's (2008) call for a pedagogically driven model for e-assessment that can allow students to take more control of their own learning and become more reflective, storing such a wealth of data is obviously questionable practice. Also, how would we ensure students rose to such a huge challenge? Yet another, equally unwelcome, alternative is the automated scenario which Masters (2013) envisaged where learning analytics tools use uploaded data to drive teachers' feedback. Timmis et al. (2015) also note the risk that developments in digital technologies will drive assessment methods that will, in turn, drive teaching and learning practices. They propose that one way to mitigate the risk of technology driven assessment practices is for interdisciplinary teams to work together, to foreground the inherent tensions in their different beliefs with respect to technology enhanced learning.

9.6 Conclusion

As Sahin and Mentor (2016) note, using mobile devices, assessment can now take place at any location; a contemporary classroom could be contexts that are not bounded by physical classroom walls, such as when commuting, in kitchens or museums. Indeed, the exploratory studies into school-based assessment using mobile devices described above show the potential value in using them to record student progress. This progress can be captured in different places, outside as well as inside the classroom, and in different modes providing a rich picture of the development of a student's knowledge and skills. This information can, and is, being used by teachers to assess their students' learning formatively. However, by and large, summative assessments tend to rely on more traditional methods such as completing a test paper in the school exam hall. Such one-off assessments capture a student's knowledge at one point in time and several bodies, especially those responsible for developing 21st century skills, are now questioning their use. In an educational climate where skills such as creativity, collaboration, communication and critical thinking are prized, with evidence of ability in their use being sought for entry into employment, there is an exciting future for mobile device-based assessments. These would focus on evaluating and recording the process of learning instead of merely on the product. Additionally, if we were indeed able to change modes of assessment to those more suitable for assessing 21st century skills, education professionals' concerns such as the issues of plagiarism and cheating described in Chapter 8 would not be such a barrier to implementing mobile learning in schools. However, that said, we must remain mindful of the potential to over-collect assessment data and be careful to ensure its ethical and responsible use.

Questions

- Thinking of your specialist subject, design an assessment task that uses a student's smartphone, tablet or camera phone. How could you grade it quickly and informatively?
- You want your students to use their mobile devices to capture evidence of their progress on a school project: what ethical considerations should you consider first?

- Are 21st century skills of communication, collaboration, critical thinking and creativity taught or assessed in your workplace? If yes, how is that managed and if not, should they be?

Annotated further reading

- Reforming educational assessment

Masters, G. (2013) Reforming Educational Assessment: Principles, challenges, imperatives. *Australian Education Review*, Number 57. Melbourne: ACER. http://research.acer.edu.au/aer/12/

This research review, undertaken on behalf of the Australian Council for Educational Research, reviews research into school-based assessment and, as an outcome, argues for assessment reform by practitioners and policy-makers to better support learning. It outlines the current pressures for reconceptualising assessment in schools observing that traditional assessment methods are often not well aligned with current understandings of learning and do not capitalise on the current transformative potential of new technologies. In addition, they are of limited value for assessing deep understandings, life skills that develop only over extended periods of time or more personalised and flexible forms of learning. Masters (2013) presents five design principles for an effective Learning Assessment System alongside consideration of the most likely practical challenges to the implementation of such a system. These challenges include: the changing of widely held perceptions about educational assessment; the development of deep understandings of how learning occurs within specific learning domains; the promotion of more coherent systems of assessment across a range of educational contexts and the promotion of higher levels of assessment literacy across the profession.

Note

1 www.p21.org/

10 Recommendations for teaching via mobile learning opportunities and future scenarios

As readers will have learned mobile learning has appeared in many guises over the past fifteen years or so. Each initiative contains exciting teaching and learning opportunities yet teachers need to be well prepared in order to capitalise on them. In this chapter I present a number of conclusions and recommendations for practice drawn from both the findings of the developments reported in the preceding chapters and other published experiences of mobile learning initiatives. The chapter also presents three different possible scenarios: the first, where all schools supply handheld devices; the second, where schools allow students to bring their own; and the third, where mobile devices whether phones or tablets are banned from classroom use, with accompanying questions to stimulate reflection on their implications for teachers and teaching. First though, there are several issues that have not yet been addressed in any detail in this book and their presence within, and impact on, the field of mobile learning needs to be acknowledged. Foremost amongst these are usability and accessibility; clearly the technology needs to be usable, i.e. fit for purpose and easily operated by the target age group. Furthermore, we need to be aware that there will always be students, the differently able, the disadvantaged and those whose parents don't permit them, who will not have access to the same digital tools in the same way as most of the class. While there was no space in this book to address challenges for the differently able, recommendations in respect of the issues of usability and equal access are discussed briefly in the next section.

10.1 Usability and access issues

So many mobile learning initiatives report promising outcomes but essentially fail to deliver with statements like 'but if the Wi-Fi had been less flaky', 'if the screen had been bigger', 'if the batteries had lasted longer', 'if the tablets had been delivered on time', 'if the school had invested in skilled maintenance' regularly appearing. Angela McFarlane, reporting from her experience of the early mobile learning initiatives where the mobile devices (PDAs) used were technologically challenged compared to today's smartphones, sensibly advises that mobile devices intended to be used in schools for learning should be:

- robust with a battery that lasts all day;
- compatible with the school learning platform;
- able to run software that is in common use in school;

- affordable (with spares for loan); and
- personal to the user.

In addition, to ensure learning opportunities that effectively cross subject, real to virtual and/or home to school boundaries, a school should invest in technical support, adequate Wi-Fi and professional development (McFarlane, 2015). Wang (2016) notes that such technical issues, in particular the lack of future planning for increased Wi-Fi use, still colour teachers' perceptions in today's classrooms. Surveying over 150 primary and secondary school teachers attending a recent mobile learning event in Hong Kong elicited concerns about the instability of schools' Wi-Fi networks as a result of concurrent usage by students and teachers (Wang, 2016). Also the teachers had concerns about the often time-consuming nature of dealing with technological problems and about a lack of within-school support with colleagues focused only on the potential for mobile devices to result in disruption. Such a narrow focus is widely shared and, as noted in Chapter 8, schools can end up banning the devices rather than thinking through their potential for supporting learning. Like Wang (2016), I feel that exploration and action research on the educational use of mobile technology is being hampered by these restrictive institutional policies and school cultures. In addition, as Vosloo (2012) points out, this actually results in limited opportunities for teachers to learn how to incorporate mobile technologies into their classroom practice. Allaying colleagues' concerns as to the usability of mobile devices takes time. Indeed, McFarlane (2015) emphasises the need to allow time for a cultural shift as to how the new devices will be used in school as the teachers need time to learn from each other and enabling students to use the new tools becomes part and parcel of school practice.

With respect to user access to the devices it seems likely that the concept of a 1:1 initiative is aspirational; there will always be a few students who forget to charge their device or even forget it entirely. Some parents cannot and others don't wish to contribute towards of the cost of a mobile device. Accidents happen and a change of focus within the field of mobile learning itself to build more group work around devices in class could not only address this issue but also enable students who don't have access to appropriate digital tools to engage in collaborative learning opportunities. The Bike Baron game-based case study, *Raising standards in boys' writing using gaming*, reported in Chapter 3, Section 3.2 and the stop-motion animation creation activity briefly described in Chapter 9, Section 9.1 are both examples of small group work centred on a single mobile device. However, much has been said earlier about mobile learning offering opportunities for personalised learning, as in the case study *Personalising inquiry learning*, Chapter 3, Section 3.3 or as one of the key pedagogical principles behind mobile learning discussed in Chapter 5, Section 5.3. One-to-one tuition is clearly beneficial; however, the BYOD class teacher needs also to prepare for different contingencies. In practice, they are likely to have classroom ecology of digital tools ranging from the desktop against the back wall to the phone in a student's pocket via a mix of tablets and laptops with different operating systems. Where a school follows an OPD model the teacher can at least rely on everyone having the same version of an app yet, as already noted, malfunction and missing devices can still occur. Jahnke et al. (2014) found in their study of iPad adoption in Danish primary and secondary schools that such common classroom activity breakdowns result in mobile devices adding instead of reducing complexity. Also that such breakdowns can arise from learning and social challenges as well as technological problems. Jahnke et al. (2014) described teaching practice with iPads as moving away from an established, common routine and turning into a design project where the teacher juggles many different design elements. At least though, with the BYOD model, the students are familiar with their own devices and how to deal with minor technical hiccups. That said, we should also note that the digital divide can occur in many forms including knowledge of functionality and skills in or experience of using digital tools as well as, more simply, in possessing them or not (Van Dijk and Hacker, 2003). However, as seen from the wealth of available examples that I reviewed for inclusion in this book, schools and teachers are clearly becoming more attuned to capitalising on the potential benefits of mobile learning and orchestrating a variety of learning opportunities in both inside and outside school contexts. In the next section I therefore outline recommendations synthesised from these examples for teaching in schools via mobile learning.

10.2 Recommendations for teaching via mobile learning opportunities

Throughout this book I have tried to include a wide range of mobile learning examples sourced from schools across the globe. In the next sub-section I outline the benefits to learning most frequently reported in these examples and, in the following one, the associated challenges found so that teachers know what to plan for. The third sub-section includes recommendations about ethical issues teachers need to be alerted to when engaging students in learning via mobile devices, and the fourth sub-section includes recommendations for evaluation opportunities for, as US teachers experienced in iPad use reported to Kim (2014), teaching with mobile devices requires ongoing evaluation. They used their evaluation skills first to identify differences between using traditional tools and the iPads in order to determine the most influential benefits for learning they should be planning for and, second, to appraise the potential of the available apps for use in teaching. The final sub-section comprises helpful questions to support planning for a mobile learning initiative developed as a consequence of another iPad project, this time from Wales, reported by Beauchamp and Hillier (2014).

10.2.1 *Capitalise on key learning opportunities*

To make a success of a mobile learning initiative, teachers should have a clear vision of the learning purposes underpinning the proposed device use and the anticipated learning outcomes. As introduced in Section 2.2 and developed in Sections 5.2 and 5.3, there are several key affordances built into mobile devices that signal learning opportunities that teachers should aim to be capitalising on. These include:

- the essential portability of the device enabling it both to be carried between contexts and shared between students;
- multimedia functionality enabling video and animation as well as information in different modes such as text, images, sounds and voice;
- communication in this range of modes by connecting to the internet and/or other devices;
- location-awareness, giving directions and background information about nearby objects;
- data capture whether images, sound, voice or video for later use; and
- a vast range of dedicated, educational apps.

As seen in the case study examples presented in Chapters 3 and 4, teachers mix and match these learning opportunities whether inside or outside the classroom to make the most of the different tools. This enables them to create active and constructive learning opportunities where they can relate subject knowledge to be taught to authentic locations or activities and to reinforce learning through a variety of engaging, creative endeavours. For example, the two case studies taken from those displayed by Apple on its 'Classroom Stories' website *Using iPads 1:1 'The Secret Garden grows into an immersive experience'* (see p.33) and *Using iPads 1:1 'Heart anatomy with a digital pulse'* (see p.39) both include a particularly wide range of learning opportunities centred on just the one topic. Also as discussed in Chapter 9 this creative potential enables teachers to use the artefacts their students have produced using their mobile devices to support formative assessment and the ongoing evaluation and reflection needed (Kim, 2014) to successfully juggle the different lesson elements (Jahnke et al., 2014).

As a science teacher, I see the camera on mobile devices as central to the benefits that mobile learning can bring to the science classroom. Through taking photos, making animations and filming video clips students can support the visualisation of, and reinforce their learning of, dynamic scientific processes. This also enables us to study those processes that are otherwise too far away, too fast, too slow, too expensive, too small or too large to see at first hand. They can also be effectively used to record key learning events such as demonstrations and role plays in class for later playback to support further learning dialogue or even revision for examinations (Ekanayake and Wishart, 2014b).

McFarlane (2015) also notes that to maximise the benefits of personal ownership of mobile devices in schools both pedagogical approaches and teaching styles must accommodate a more autonomous learner style. One particular challenge to this is that the curriculum itself needs to accommodate this new attitude to learner responsibility for the approach to learning. Furthermore, our schools are quite likely to have been running along the same curricular principles for many years with time allocated to particular teaching subjects. Therefore, lesson planning to include mobile learning opportunities that could well cross subject as well as physical boundaries needs to involve the whole school. McFarlane (2015) also points out that the most successful mobile learning projects she observed combine the use of the device to access curriculum content and to produce student work in a variety of media with lessons being planned to take advantage of both use of and production of content.

Also, as covered in detail in Chapter 6, engaging teachers in professional development to ensure they have had time to practise with new technologies and are aware of the potential benefits outlined above to aim for is essential. Pegrum et al.'s (2013) recommendations on professional development for mobile learning initiatives include ensuring that protected time is made available, whether for teachers to attend formal training sessions or simply to play with the devices and to research apps and how they work. Though, that said, Pegrum et al. (2013) helpfully remind us that any training should maintain a focus on pedagogy ahead of the technology. Like others (McFarlane et al., 2009; Anthony and Gimbert, 2015; Beauchamp et al., 2015) they recommend building a professional learning community across the school and/or district. Such communities can be a sustainable professional development model for mobile learning that encourages collaboration, saves time and energy and avoids people 'reinventing the wheel'.

Lastly, we shouldn't forget the importance of ensuring ease of access to technical support for both teachers and students. The state of affairs whereby teachers routinely plan two lessons, one for the case where the Wi-Fi is working and a second in case it isn't, is burdensome and impacts negatively on schools' willingness to adopt mobile learning. McFarlane (2015) adds that good integration with existing technologies in the school aids the smooth adoption of mobile devices into routine teaching and learning and that time needs to be allowed for teachers to trial new lessons and to learn from each other. When this works the impact can be dramatic: in the Scotland iPad pilot, Burden et al. (2012) found that, over the course of their evaluation period, daily technology use during lessons rocketed from being reported by 10% of the students to 80%. Clearly, teachers are becoming better at juggling (Jahnke et al., 2014); however, with devices such as mobile phones that carry a weight of expectations there are likely challenges ahead. From their study of OPD schools in California, Philip and Garcia (2015) concluded that the difference in expectations of both students and staff as to how mobile phones could be used in school creates conflict. Students could not imagine why they would be allowed mobile phones if through filtering and class rules they were to be stripped of much of what made them phones. Whereas teachers feared their potential for disruption and could only conceive of allowing mobile devices into schools that were primarily meant for what they deemed as learning. As a result, neither side was satisfied with the mobile learning initiative, for issuing a mobile device for school and limiting its associated freedom fundamentally alters the meaning of the device. So, how can teachers make a success of a mobile learning initiative?

10.2.2 *Plan ahead for challenges*

It is essential to plan ahead to avoid the mismatched expectations just mentioned above and to prepare for a culture shift in established pedagogy. Challenges such as disruption, whether simply to the established teaching approach, disturbances produced by device notifications or off-task behaviour on the part of students have constantly dogged mobile learning initiatives. There are regular stories in the international media to alarm teachers; however, much less established research as to the frequency and causes of problems. Chapter 8 in this book, however, discusses increasingly serious issues associated with children and young people's use of mobile devices and the internet such as cyberbullying, sexting and cheating as well as disruption through off-task behaviour, incoming notifications and calls. While we need to take care to condemn the behaviour and not the device, Kaya's (2013) small-scale study from Turkey showed that if mobile devices are issued without professional development and school recommendations as to apps to use, young people will take advantage of their teachers' ignorance to use them inappropriately.

When faced with inappropriate use a teacher's usual response is to ban or confiscate the device involved; however, that does nothing towards teaching students about responsible use of technology and means the teachers themselves lose opportunities to learn how to incorporate mobile technology into classroom practice (Vosloo, 2012). Indeed, some teachers in Kim's (2014) study perceived that having the iPads available served as an opportunity to develop student understanding of responsible use of technology as well as skills to access, evaluate, create and communicate information using technology. However, the same teachers also reported that guiding students to use iPads in the classroom entails having clear communication with them about classroom rules, expectations and consequences. Also they needed to continuously remind students of this need for responsible use of iPads in the classroom.

One commonly found and recommended way forward is to make sure all possible stakeholders (teachers, students, parents, administrators and support staff) are engaged in developing a responsible use policy for mobile devices at school. Dyson et al. (2013) suggest that such a policy should aim to address any problems foreseen without limiting the implementation of this 'unique learning approach' (p. 411). The need to equip students with mobile learning skills, including awareness of ethical and responsible device use, to enable them to manage lifelong and workplace learning challenges is paramount. Some examples of such school policies from the early BYOD adopting schools are discussed in Section 7.2; however, engaging students in developing their own makes the lines of responsibility clear.

There are also, of course, technical challenges and, as well as the group learning strategies discussed earlier in this chapter, I recommend that the school keeps some spare, older or cheaper devices charged to use when students forget or break their own. Also, not to aim to follow the latest learning trend until it has been well tried and tested on a range of platforms. Simple apps like Socrative® and Kahoot® that have been designed to be accessible to classrooms and other learning environments worldwide are much more likely to run seamlessly with a class than, say, the latest augmented reality tool that requires plenty of both memory on the device and available bandwidth to run. Crucially, don't forget to test all the functions needed in the location where the devices are to be used: many a teacher has fallen foul of the 'but it worked perfectly when I tested it at home' rule.

There is good news ahead; McFarlane (2015) found that the time taken to manage the devices in a mobile learning initiative drops as they become established. However, there are also serious questions as to privacy and other ethical challenges when employing personal devices for formal, classroom learning that teachers need to consider and prepare for.

10.2.3 *Be aware of ethical considerations*

Ethical considerations arising in school-based mobile learning are discussed in detail in Chapter 7. They are, by and large, linked to the capacity of mobile devices to transcend what were once fixed information boundaries. These boundaries range from home to school, from private to public, from the formal to informal, from inside school to outside class and from the virtual to the real. Also they can be prompted by the way the internet can act as a multiplier with students intentionally or unintentionally sharing what was once, much more contained information. However, in Chapter 6, ways forward for professional development for teachers and mobile learning researchers engaging with mobile devices in schools that address these ethical challenges were presented. For example, those centred on developing ethics frameworks can be tailored for individual school circumstances.

In addition, Dyson et al. (2013) have developed a holistic framework for ethical mobile learning that includes the following considerations that educators should be aware of. Somewhat ambitiously but clearly with worthwhile aims, it includes:

- mobile learning as everyday practice;
- a positive ethic of responsibility for teachers and support personnel;
- a personal responsibility for students;
- agreed protocols;

- culturally appropriate practice;
- mobile etiquette; and
- appropriate response training to unethical behaviour for all stakeholders.

That said though, it is encouraging to note Bjerede and Bondi's (2012) finding from a 5th Grade classroom in the USA, using Android-based 7" tablets, that the students quickly established a culture of responsible use of their devices. Bjerede and Bondi (2012) found that, without complex and expensive device management software (just some basic internet filtering) and with limited technical support, the students were more than capable of using the devices responsibly in support of their learning and for their own personal purposes.

In respect of actual policies for responsible and ethical mobile device use, Dyson et al. (2013) add the need to encourage their ownership through their co-development with students and other stakeholders, institution-wide dissemination, training and implementation and also their regular review. This latter comment indicates that, as experienced mobile learning professionals, Dyson et al. (2013) are aware of how the pace of ongoing development of new technologies and apps results in the need to monitor and update teachers' plans for mobile learning opportunities. Thus the final recommendation I would like to highlight is the need for ongoing evaluation.

10.2.4 *Ongoing evaluation is particularly important*

Teachers are action researchers, regularly planning and implementing changes in their teaching practice according to perceived classroom need and new teaching strategies encountered and then weighing up the outcomes of the changes. They need to be skilled evaluators to detect whether any and all of a short teaching activity, a lesson or a sequence of lessons is achieving the desired learning outcomes. Indeed, when a dozen US secondary school teachers experienced in teaching with iPads were asked about the knowledge, skills and motivation needed to use them successfully, they all reported evaluation (of lessons, teaching resources and digital tools) was an essential skill (Kim, 2014).

However, that said, as discussed in Chapter 5, there are a number of specific challenges in evaluating mobile learning. These include the mobile nature of the learning activity itself leading to challenges in tracking it across locations and contexts. In addition, such activities may well involve multiple participants in different locations who are using a variety of personal devices and/or school hardware. Accessing students' personal devices, even if being used for school, can be ethically questionable unless everyone (students, teachers and parents) is agreed as to what is acceptable. One bonus though is that the devices themselves can be used to capture and store data to be used in evaluating and assessing learning. Indeed, as discussed in Chapter 9, there are many apps available, both those that can be used, like classroom response systems, for on-the-spot formative assessment and those that record progress over time to enable learning analytics to take place. Even basic camera phones without internet access can be used, as seen in the Sri Lankan case study *Using camera phones in small groups: 'The diversity of leaves'* reported in Chapter 3, by teachers to evaluate learning through the images students captured. Indeed, where a subject being taught such as design technology, bakery, physical education or dance itself involves learning about performance or process evaluation, the mobile phone camera can play a key role. Through capturing, replaying and discussing video students and teachers can review the skill or process being taught and work on improvements.

One aspect of ongoing evaluation that concerns teachers though is their need to monitor whether their students are on- or off-task and the small size of mobile device screens means teachers cannot immediately spot what apps students are using. Even when students are fully trained and signed up to responsible use policies teachers remain concerned for possible inappropriate use 'under their watch'. Many schools have Wi-Fi filtering systems; however, as pointed out in Chapter 8, they can themselves cause teachers problems and don't help to teach students about responsible phone or tablet use outside school. My last recommendation, therefore, is that schools consider investing in tools that enable teachers, even the students, to see each other's screens. These range from the sophisticated Netop Vision classroom software tools to the freely available Google Cast for Education and include those designed specifically for a particular device such as Apple TV with Airplay for iPads and Samsung School for their Android-based Galaxy tablets. Some work only through being connected to the same Wi-Fi network, yet others can also 'cast' screens via the internet if needed. Alternatively, teachers could plan in more group work where one or two students in a group are working with mobile devices in specific roles, e.g. researcher, camera person, and the other roles in the group, e.g. editor, writer, rely on them to stay on-task.

10.2.5 *Questions to support teachers and schools in planning*

Beauchamp and Hillier (2014, p.39) created this succinct table of questions (Table 10.1) that schools and teachers considering a mobile learning initiative need to address to support planning effectively for it. The questions in the table have been collated from their experience of working with students, their parents, teachers and allied education professionals to evaluate an iPad initiative in six primary schools in Wales. Intended as a checklist of things to consider before investing in iPads it includes questions that teachers, other school staff, governors, and indeed school councils, should first ask when considering investing in iPads or other mobile technologies. I reproduce it overleaf in its original form with their permission as its practical, down-to-earth nature may well be more directly helpful to practising teachers and school leaders than many of the more theoretical points I have covered hitherto.

It is my belief that with thorough planning for three key areas – first, teaching, learning and assessment strategies; second, responsible and ethical student behaviour; and third, the devices themselves with their software and maintenance needs – schools can effectively deploy mobile devices to support student (and teacher) learning. It is the fact that things can and, without sufficient preparation, do go wrong that currently leads to Male and Burden's (2014) description of the use of mobile devices in schools as 'access denied'. Schools and stakeholders internationally are persisting in seeing the technology rather than the curriculum and the increasingly outdated assessment structures as the root of the problem.

10.3 Future thinking

In this section I conclude this book by presenting three possible visions for mobile learning in secondary schools; each is actually in place in a number of schools today but there is no collective agreement as to whether it represents the way forward. Each scenario is

Table 10.1 Questions to support teachers and schools in planning (Beauchamp and Hillier, 2014; p.39)

Who	What	Where	When	How
Who is going to use the mobile devices? (Staff, students, in what order?)	What areas of learning/subjects/age groups will we focus on – if any – when first introduced or when more iPads bought?	Where are they going to be used? (what years; locations – on site and off site)	When are they going to be used? (timetables or ad hoc)	How are they going to be used?
	What other resources will you/we need? (e.g. infrastructure or hardware, such as covers or leads)		When will you/we need additional infrastructure (e.g. Apple TV or charging trolleys)? [Budget planning cycle]	How does this relate to our School Improvement Plan?
	What do iPads do better than our existing resources?			How will they improve our provision?
Who will monitor use of iPads?	What difference do you/we feel they will make?	Where shall we look for impact?	When do we get feedback/check if we need more iPads?	How will we get feedback on effectiveness?
Who is going to provide training (LA, outside agency, members of staff or students)?				How will we measure the impact? (e.g. teacher, students and parent survey; governor visits?)
Who will charge, store and book out iPads as needed?	What equipment will we need to add Apps and charge iPads?	Where are they going to be charged and stored?	When are they going to be charged?	
Who will add Apps?	What budget are we going to use? (Devolved to a certain amount?)			How are we going to pay for Apps?
Who is going to provide training/feedback/support to parents?	What training/feedback/support to parents are we going to provide?	Where are we going to provide training/feedback/support to parents?	When are we going to provide training/feedback/support to parents?	How are we going to inform and involve parents?
Who will formulate rules (including safe use online and around the school) of use?	What (positive) rules if any will we introduce?	Where will rules be displayed – if at all?	When will we introduce rules?	How will rules be formulated? (Bottom up or top down?)
Who will amend relevant policies/home-school agreements?				How will this impact on other ICT resources (such as ICT suites or fixed PCs)?

accompanied by questions to trigger reflection on or discussion of the scenario and, through that, support the reader in planning ahead for decisions about implementing mobile learning themselves.

10.3.1 *OPD*

School A follows the National Curriculum and its 206 Year 7 boys and girls (aged 11–12) are taught in mixed ability subject groups of 28–31. It lies in the countryside centrally to the villages it serves and students have access outside the classroom to playing fields and a small nature area.

With support from the district and advice over how to manage hardware and software maintenance School A has purchased sufficient A5 size tablets for use by all of the incoming Year 7 (11–12 year olds) and their teachers. They have been assigned on a 1:1 basis to individual students but they must be kept in school charging trolleys outside of school hours. However, the teachers can take theirs home, and they were also given them six months before the tablets were made available to students and the different teaching departments have made time available in their bi-weekly meetings to plan what apps to use and how. The school is currently updating its Acceptable Use Policy (AUP) for ICT use in school.

- What apps or other hardware do you think the school should consider obtaining?
- Who should be contributing to the redesigned AUP?
- What plans should the school make to help this initiative become sustainable?
- Should the classroom teachers help ensure the devices are maintained and used appropriately and, if so, how?
- What suggestions for teaching activities can you contribute?
- What concerns would you expect teachers in the school to have?

10.3.2 *BYOD*

School B also follows the National Curriculum; however, it is bigger and has a more suburban location than school A. It takes students, both male and female, aged 11–18 from across the south of the city and prepares them for further education on leaving school via both vocational and academic routes. It has some outside playground; however, students have to travel to the sports field for PE and games.

Following a survey of its student population, School B has realised that 36% of its students have bought or been given tablets, also 74% have access to internet-connected smartphones and a further 13% have mobile phones with cameras. It has, therefore, decided to allow students to use their preferred mobile device in school and to encourage teachers to create teaching and learning activities to help students use their mobile devices productively.

- What would you include in the school's responsible use policy?
- What apps or other hardware do you think the school should consider obtaining?
- Students are complaining about receiving malicious comments online from others in the school, what can you do?
- How could the BYOD initiative be evaluated? What data should be collected and how?
- What suggestions for teaching activities can you contribute?
- What concerns would you expect teachers in the school to have?

10.3.3 *Mobile devices are banned*

School C is a smaller girls only independent school with 692 students aged from 13 to 18 years of age. It prepares students for the International Baccalaureate as well as national qualifications. Like school B it is based on the city outskirts but has more extensive grounds.

School C also has a small boarding house on its site and is very concerned with its role 'in loco parentis'. With parental permission boarders can bring mobile devices to the school but neither they nor the day students may use them in class or during breaks when in the main school buildings. Teachers feel unable to use mobile devices to look up facts or news in class or open school areas because of this ban. It is not widely flouted by students either as devices confiscated on sight are often not returned for several days.

- What other ICT hardware do you think the school should consider obtaining?
- Parents are complaining about their children receiving malicious texts from others in the school, what can you do?
- What concerns would you expect teachers in the school to have?
- What further research would the school need to see to change its policy?

Finally, in this section, two or three more questions based on these school scenarios for the reader to consider are:

- Which of the above three schools would you like to work at, or work with, and why is that?
- Will your answer to the last point about *why* be sustainable for the foreseeable future? What can we do to make things more sustainable?

10.4 Conclusion

From my experience of a wide range of mobile learning initiatives, and reviewing even more for this book, my conclusion is that mobile devices are here to stay and, as teachers, we should capitalise on the potential they can offer to support learning. The more we expect them to be used productively in class, the more opportunities there will be to educate students in using them responsibly. However, I am very aware that they also offer potential for disaster and teachers need both guidance and support with planning for their use. I hope that this book in some way helps with this. We should bear in mind, though, that one of the potential teaching scenarios created at an early mobile learning workshop run on behalf of the International Association of Mobile Learning was 'Dealing with the unexpected consequences of complexity'. Certainly the BYOD scenario in the previous section can appear alarmingly complex to those inexperienced in managing even one branded device and it takes a real vote of confidence in your class to let them manage the technology themselves. However, as we have seen, many teachers do indeed feel able to take this step which is great news. There can be, though, no one particular recommended pedagogy for mobile learning; it is up to us as teachers to pick and choose according to need, to orchestrate, even to juggle teaching strategies while being mindful of possible pitfalls. Functions and apps on mobile devices can support teachers with planning for, implementing and, in particular, evaluating lessons.

Furthermore, to carry this out this effectively, in the light of the changing contexts and technologies inherent within mobile learning, senior leaders and stakeholders need to recognise that teachers must be supported in professional learning communities and with time made available to pilot and evaluate the new challenges. Lastly, to finish on a positive note, Chiu (2015) showed that Hong Kong secondary school teachers' anxiety about using mobile devices in teaching was reduced through practical experience with the devices themselves. He compared a group of language and humanities teachers with a group from maths and science. However, while both groups showed significantly less anxiety after the adoption year, the analysis also showed that only the mathematics and science teacher group significantly improved their perceived ease of use of employing mobile devices in teaching (Chiu, 2015). Given that, in sourcing examples for this book, I came across disproportionately more case studies of mobile learning in science than in other subjects, there are clearly even more challenges ahead for the others. However, we must pull together and support each other for future challenges lie ahead for us all. These will include students with wearable devices that a class teacher cannot pick out from normal clothing or accessories and, quite possibly, pico-projection, where a mobile device projects its screen onto surrounding walls or furniture.

Annotated further reading

- An evaluation of an iPad implementation

Beauchamp, G. and Hillier, E. (2014) *An Evaluation of iPad Implementation Across A Network of Primary Schools in Cardiff.* Cardiff, UK: School of Education–Cardiff Metropolitan University.

Link to project report available at: www.cardiffmet.ac.uk/education/research/Documents/iPadImplementation2014.pdf.

This report evaluates the implementation of iPads in six primary schools from different areas across Cardiff, the capital city of Wales. The main focus of the study was to explore how the iPads were introduced and implemented, as well as to assess the impact they had on the attitudes and motivations of teachers, parents and students. It provides a rich description of the implementation with plenty of illustrations and practical advice. Key themes identified in the evaluation were: the importance of both informal and formal methods of iPad training for staff; high levels of teacher, student and parent enthusiasm and motivation; ease of use; enhancement of pupil independence; and how the iPad supports various methods of assessment. In addition, all teachers reacted positively to having students assist them with the iPads and, in many cases, encouraged them to support other students in the class as well. Conclusions and recommendations relevant for school districts worldwide are offered to enhance teaching and learning opportunities with an iPad or similar tablet.

- Identifying emerging issues in mobile learning

Wishart, J. and Green, D. (2010) Identifying emerging issues in mobile learning in further and higher education: A report to JISC.

Link to the report available at: www.bristol.ac.uk/media-library/sites/education/migrated/docu-ments/emergereport.pdf.

While this report describes the results of a series of discussion workshops where experienced practitioners explored visions of how mobile technologies will influence practice in Higher Education (HE) and Further Education (FE) in the near future, readers from the school education sector may well be interested in some of the more futuristic scenarios it contains. The workshop series was funded by the UK's Joint Information Systems Committee (JISC) as part of the Users and Innovation research programme. This exploration focused on identifying emerging issues for the sector arising from the increasingly likely large-scale use of smartphones, PDAs and camera phones by learners in HE and FE, both on campus and in the workplace. It was carried out through scenario generation using three different futures prediction tools in three workshops.

References

Admiraal, W., van Vugt, F., Kranenburg, F., Koster, B., Smit, B., Weijers, S. and Lockhorst, D. (2016) Preparing pre-service teachers to integrate technology into K–12 instruction: Evaluation of a technology-infused approach. *Technology, Pedagogy and Education*, 26(1), 105–120.

Ahmed, S. and Parsons, D. (2013) Abductive science inquiry using mobile devices in the classroom. *Computers & Education*, 63, 62–72.

Albury, K. (2016) Sexting, schools and surveillance: Mediated sexuality in the classroom. In G. Brown and K. Browne (Eds) *The Routledge Research Companion to Geographies of Sex and Sexualities* (pp.359–368). Abingdon: Routledge.

Allen, L. (2015) Sexual assemblages: Mobile phones/young people/school. *Discourse: Studies in the Cultural Politics of Education*, 36(1), 120–132.

Andrews, T., Dyson, L.E., Smyth, R. and Wallace, R. (2011) The ethics of m-learning: Classroom threat or enhanced learner agency? In *Proceedings of the 10th World Conference on Mobile and Contextual Learning (mLearn 2011)* (pp.295–230). Beijing, China.

Andrews, T., Dyson, L.E. and Wishart, J. (2013) Supporting practitioners in implementing mobile learning and overcoming ethical concerns: A scenario-based approach. In *QScience Proceedings of the 12th World Conference on Mobile and Contextual Learning (mLearn 2013)* (10). Doha, Qatar: CNAA.

Andrews, T., Dyson, L. and Wishart, J. (2015) Advancing ethics frameworks and scenario-based learning to support educational research into mobile learning. *International Journal of Research & Method in Education*, 38(3), 320–334.

Anthony, A.B. and Gimbert, B. (2015) Higher education partnerships for learning with mobile technologies in P-12 environments. In Y. Zhang (Ed.) *Handbook of Mobile Teaching and Learning* (pp.517–533). Springer International Publishing.

Arrigo, M., Di Giuseppe, O., Fulantelli, G., Gentile, M., Merlo, G., Seta, L. and Taibi, D. (2010) *Mobile Technologies in Lifelong Learning: Best Practices*. Palermo, Italy: Italian National Research Council.

Aubusson, P., Schuck, S. and Burden, K. (2009) Mobile learning for teacher professional learning: Benefits, obstacles and issues. *ALT-J Research in Learning and Teaching*, 17(3), 233–247.

Ayres, D., Tyrrell, C. and Poon, K. (2013) Mobile technology: A study on the impact on the role of the initial teacher training (ITT) tutor. *Research in Teacher Education*, 3(1), 27–32.

Baran, E. (2014) A review of research on mobile learning in teacher education. *Educational Technology & Society*, 17(4), 17–32.

Batchelor, J. and Botha, A. (2009) *Liberating Learning*. Paper presented at the Educational Association of South Africa, Amanzimtoti, South Africa.

Batchelor, J., Herselman, M., Traxler, J. and Fraser, W. (2012) Emerging technologies, innovative teachers and moral cohesion. In P. and M. Cunningham (Eds) *IST-Africa 2012 Conference Proceedings*. Dar es Salaam, Tanzania: IIMC International Information Management Corporation.

Beatty, I.D., Gerace, W.J., Leonard, W.J. and Dufresne, R.J. (2006) Designing effective questions for classroom response system teaching. *American Journal of Physics*, 74(1), 31–39.

Beauchamp, G., Burden, K. and Abbinett, E. (2015) Teachers learning to use the iPad in Scotland and Wales: A new model of professional development. *Journal of Education for Teaching*, 41(2), 161–179.

Beauchamp, G. and Hillier, E. (2014) *An Evaluation of iPad Implementation Across a Network of Primary Schools in Cardiff*. Cardiff: School of Education-Cardiff Metropolitan University. Retrieved 18.7.2016 from: www.cardiffmet.ac.uk/education/research/Documents/iPadImplementation2014.pdf.

Beauchamp, T.L. and Childress, J.F. (1983) *Principles of Biomedical Ethics*. Oxford: Oxford University Press.

Beland, L.P. and Murphy, R. (2015) *Ill Communication: Technology, distraction & student performance*. CEP Discussion Paper No 1350. London: London School of Economics.

Bergmann, J. and Sams, A. (2012) *Flip Your Classroom: Reach every student in every class every day*. Washington, DC: International Society for Technology in Education.

Bjerede, M. and Bondi, T. (2012) *Learning is Personal: Stories of Android tablet use in the 5th grade*. A Learning Untethered Project. Retrieved 1.3.2017 from: www.learninguntethered.com/wp-content/uploads/2012/08/Learning-is-Personal.pdf.

Black, P.J. and Wiliam, D. (1998) Inside the black box: Raising standards through classroom assessment. *Phi Delta Kappan*, 80(2), 139–148.

Blume, H. (2015, 16 April) L.A. school district demands iPad refund from Apple. *Los Angeles Times*. Retrieved 9.2.2017 from: www.latimes.com/local/lanow/la-me-ln-ipad-curriculum-refund-20150415-story.html.

Bober, M. (2010) *Games Based Experiences for Learning*. Bristol: Futurelab. Retrieved 18.7.2016 from: www.nfer.ac.uk/publications/FUTL11/FUTL11.pdf.

Bonaiuti, G., Calvani, A. and Piazza, D. (2015) Increasing classroom engagement and student comprehension through the use of clickers: An Italian secondary school experience. *REM–Research on Education and Media*, 5(1), 95–108.

Botha, A. (Ed.) (2012) Mobile Learning Curriculum Framework, CSIR Meraka Collaboration (in press). Retrieved 11.11.16 from: https://mobimooc.wikispaces.com/Mobile+Learning+Curriculum+Framework.

Botha, A., Batchelor, J., Traxler, J., de Waard, I. and Herselman, M. (2012) Towards a mobile learning curriculum framework. In P. and M. Cunningham (Eds) *IST-Africa 2012 Conference Proceedings*. Dar es Salaam, Tanzania: IIMC International Information Management Corporation.

Brown, E. (Ed.) (2010) *Education in the Wild: Contextual and location-based mobile learning in action*. A report from the STELLAR Alpine Rendezvous workshop series. Nottingham: University of Nottingham Learning Sciences Research Institute (LSRI).

Brown, T.H. (2005) Towards a model for m-learning in Africa. *International Journal on E-Learning*, 4(3), 299–315.

Burden, K., Hopkins, P., Male, T., Martin, S. and Trala, C. (2012) *iPad Scotland Final Evaluation Report*. Hull: University of Hull. Retrieved 18.7.2016 from: https://xmascotland.wufoo.eu/forms/scottish-mobile-personal-device-evaluation-2012/.

Burden, K. and Hopkins, P. (2016) Barriers and challenges facing pre-service teachers use of mobile technologies for teaching and learning. *International Journal of Mobile and Blended Learning*, 8(2), 1–20.

Burden, K., Schuck, S. and Aubusson, P. (2012) m-Research: Ethical issues in researching young people's use of mobile devices. *Youth Studies Australia*, 31(3), 17.

Campbell, S.W. (2006) Perceptions of mobile phones in college classrooms: Ringing, cheating, and classroom policies. *Communication Education*, 55(3), 280–294.

Canvas (2016) Classroom ban on personal tech due to fears of distraction. Retrieved 11.03.2017 from: www.canvaslms.com/news/press-releases/canvas-uk-classroom-ban-on-personal-tech-due-to-fears-of-distraction.

Carmichael, P. and Youdell, D. (2007) Using virtual collaboration environments for educational research: Some ethical considerations. *Research Intelligence*, 100, 26–29.

Carskadon, M.A. (2011) Sleep in adolescents: The perfect storm. *Pediatric Clinics of North America*, 58(3), 637–647.

Century, J. and Levy, A. (2004) *Institutionalization and Sustainability: Think tank bringing theory of and research on sustainability to practice*. Research and Evaluation Report. Newton, MA: Center for Science Education. Retrieved 23.09.16 from:http://scalemsp.wceruw.org/files/research/Products/CenturyLevy_BringingTheorySustainabilityPractice.pdf.

Cerezo, F., Arnaiz, P. and Gimenez, A.M. (2016) Online addiction behaviors and cyberbullying among adolescents. *Anales de Psicología*, 32(3), 761.

Cerratto-Pargman, T. and Milrad, M. (2016) Beyond innovation in mobile learning. In J. Traxler and A. Kukulska-Hulme (Eds) *Mobile Learning: The Next Generation* (pp.154–178). London: Routledge.

Chen, Y.S., Kao, T.C. and Sheu, J.P. (2003) A mobile learning system for scaffolding bird watching learning. *Journal of Computer Assisted Learning*, 19, 347–359.

Cheng, F. and Haagen, L. (2015) Mobilizing the middle kingdom: Bringing m-learning to a Chinese high school. In Y. Zhang (Ed) *Handbook of Mobile Teaching and Learning* (pp.457–485). Springer International Publishing.

Cheung, W.S. and Hew, K.F. (2009) A review of research methodologies used in studies on mobile handheld devices in K-12 and higher education settings. *Australasian Journal of Educational Technology*, 25(2), 153–183.

Chigona, A. and Chigona, W. (2008) MXit up in the media: Media discourse analysis on a mobile instant messaging system. *The African Journal of Information and Communication*, 2008(9), 42–57.

Chiu, T.K.F. (2015) Adoption of mobile learning in schools: Impact of changes in teacher values. Paper in D. Churchill, T.K.F. Chiu and N. J. Gu (Eds.) *Proceedings of the International Mobile Learning Festival 2015* (pp.448–467). Hong Kong: University of Hong Kong.

Chou, C.C., Block, L. and Jesness, R. (2012) A case study of mobile learning pilot project in K-12 schools. *Journal of Educational Technology Development and Exchange*, 5(2), 11–26.

Clark, W., Logan, K., Luckin, R., Mee, A. and Oliver, M. (2009) Beyond Web 2.0: Mapping the technology landscapes of young learners. *Journal of Computer Assisted Learning*, 25(1), 56–69.

Clarke, B. and Svanaes, S. (2015) *Updated Review of the Global Use of Mobile Technology in Education.* London: Techknowledge for Schools. Retrieved 02.02.2017 from: http://smartfuse.s3. amazonaws.com/mysandstorm.org/uploads/2016/01/T4S-FKY-Literature-Review-11.12.15-1.pdf.

Clarke, J. (2013) Augmented reality, multimodal literacy and mobile technology: An experiment in teacher engagement. In *QScience Proceedings of the 12th World Conference on Mobile and Contextual Learning (mLearn 2013)* (28). Doha, Qatar: CNAA.

CommonSense Media (2009) *35% of Teens Admit to Using Cell Phones to Cheat.* San Francisco, CA: CommonSense Media. Retrieved 6.1.2017 from: www.commonsensemedia.org/about-us/ news/press-releases/35-of-teens-admit-to-using-cell-phones-to-cheat.

Connor, R. (2015) *Tablets and Connectivity 2015 Full Report English Schools.* London: British Educational Suppliers Agency. Retrieved 18.7.2016 from: www.besa.org.uk/sites/default/files/ tab2015_0.pdf.

Cooper, K., Quayle, E., Jonsson, L. and Svedin, C.G. (2016) Adolescents and self-taken sexual images: A review of the literature. *Computers in Human Behavior,* 55, 706–716.

Cornelius, S. and Shanks, R. (2017) Expectations and challenges: The implementation of mobile devices in a Scottish primary school. *Technology, Pedagogy and Education,* 26(1), 19–31.

Costanzo, M. and Handelsman, M.M. (1998) Teaching aspiring professors to be ethical teachers: Doing justice to the case study method. *Teaching of Psychology,* 25(2), 97–102.

Cramer, M. and Hayes, G. (2010) Acceptable use of technology in schools: Risks, policies, and promises. *IEEE Pervasive Computing,* 9(3), 37–44.

Cristol, D. and Gimbert, B. (2013) Academic achievement in BYOD classrooms. In *QScience Proceedings of the 12th World Conference on Mobile and Contextual Learning (mLearn 2013)* (15). Doha, Qatar: CNAA.

Crompton, H. (2013) A historical overview of mobile learning: Toward learner-centered education. In Z.L. Berge and L.Y. Muilenburg (Eds) *Handbook of Mobile Learning* (pp.3–14). Florence, KY: Routledge.

Crompton, H. and Burke, D. (2015) School culture for the mobile digital age. *Media Education – Studi, ricerche, buone pratiche,* 6(2), 208–223.

Davies, N. (2013) Ethics in Pervasive Computing Research. *IEEE Pervasive Computing,* 12(3), 2–4.

Dede, C. (2010) Comparing frameworks for 21st century skills. *21st Century Skills: Rethinking How Students Learn,* 20, 51–76.

Deinhammer, J. (2016) *A Heart Anatomy Lesson with a Digital Pulse.* Cupertino, CA: Apple Inc. Retrieved 26.8.2016 from: www.apple.com/education/teach-with-ipad/classroom/heart-anatomy/.

de Waard, I., Koutropoulos, A., Keskin, N., Abajian, S.C., Hogue, R., Rodriguez, C.O. and Gallagher, M.S. (2011) Exploring the MOOC format as a pedagogical approach for mlearning. In *MLearn2011: Proceedings of 10th World Conference on Mobile and Contextual Learning* (pp.138–145).

Dooney, L. (2016, 7 November) Hundreds of students caught cheating in NCEA exams in 2015, figures show. *Stuff Education.* Wellington, NZ: Fairfax Media. Retrieved 6.1.2016 from www. stuff.co.nz/national/education/86164797/Hundreds-of-students-caught-cheating-in-NCEA-exams-in-2015-figures-show.

Dyck, L. (2015) *Comment on Option 3: Actually USE the smartphones.* In S. McLeod's blog, Technology, Leadership and the Future of Schools. Retrieved 3.2.2107 from: http://dangerous-lyirrelevant.org/2015/05/option-3-actually-use-the-smartphones.html.

Dyson, L.E., Andrews, T., Smyth, R. and Wallace, R. (2013) Towards a holistic framework for ethical mobile learning. In Z. Berg and L. Muilenberg (Eds) *The Routledge Handbook of Mobile Learning* (pp.405–416). New York & London: Routledge.

Dyson, L.E., Wishart, J. and Andrews, T. (*in press*) Ethical issues surrounding the adoption of mobile learning in the Asia Pacific region. In H. Farley, A. Murphy and L.E. Dyson (Eds) *Making mlearning Last? Harnessing Trends and Challenging Orthodoxies.* Springer International Publishing.

Educause (2015) *Current Topics: M-learning and mobility.* Retrieved 10.7.2015 from: www.educause.edu/eli/programs/learning-technologies.

Ekanayake, T.M.S.S.K.Y. (2011) *The Potential of Mobile Phones to Support Science Teachers in Sri Lanka: A focus on pedagogy.* Unpublished doctoral dissertation. University of Bristol, UK.

Ekanayake, T.M.S.S.K.Y. and Wishart, J.M. (2014a) Developing teachers' pedagogical practice in teaching science lessons with mobile phones. *Technology, Pedagogy and Education,* 23(2), 131–150.

Ekanayake, S.Y. and Wishart, J. (2014b) Mobile phone images and video in science teaching and learning. *Learning, Media and Technology,* 39(2), 229–249.

Ertmer, P.A. (1999) Addressing first- and second-order barriers to change: Strategies for technology integration. *Educational Technology Research and Development,* 47(4), 47–61.

European Parliament (2006) Lifelong learning – key competences. Recommendation 2006/962/ EC. Retrieved 2.2.2017 from: http://eur-lex.europa.eu/legal-content/EN/TXT/?uri=URISERV: c11090.

Farrow, R. (2011) Mobile learning: a meta-ethical taxonomy. In P. Isiais and I. Arnedillo-Sanchez (Eds) *IADIS International Conference proceedings, Mobile Learning 2011* (pp.102–110). IADIS Press.

Ferko, A. and Koreňová, L. (2015) Some possibilities for using mobile learning in mathematics. *Mathematica V,* 15. Retrieved 8.1.2017 from: http://math.ku.sk/data/konferenciasub/ CPSMC2015/Mathematica_V_print_2015.pdf#page=18

Ferrer, G.T. and Martí, M.C. (2012) M-portfolios: Using mobile technology to document learning in student teachers' e-portfolios. *eLearning Papers,* 32(1), 1–5.

Fies, C. and Marshall, J. (2006) Classroom response systems: A review of the literature. *Journal of Science Education and Technology,* 15(1), 101–109.

Fleschler Peskin, M., Markham, C.M., Addy, R.C., Shegog, R., Thiel, M. and Tortolero, S.R. (2013) Prevalence and patterns of sexting among ethnic minority urban high school students. *Cyberpsychology, Behavior, and Social Networking,* 16(6), 454–459.

Forbes, S. (2016) *BYOD and Secondary Schools.* Abingdon: RM Education. Retrieved 15.9.2016 from: www.techandlearning.uk/download/rm-education-byod-and-secondary-schools/.

Gado, R., Ferguson, R. and van't Hooft, M. (2006) Inquiry-based instruction through handheld-based science activities: Preservice teachers' attitude and self-efficacy. *Journal of Technology and Teacher Education,* 14 (3), 501–529.

Gamble, A.L., D'Rozario, A.L., Bartlett, D.J., Williams, S., Bin, Y.S., Grunstein, R.R. and Marshall, N.S. (2014) Adolescent sleep patterns and night-time technology use: Results of the Australian Broadcasting Corporation's Big Sleep Survey. *PloS One,* 9(11), e111700.

Garrett, N.A. (2010) Student mobile technologies: Implications for classroom management poli- cies and procedures. In *Proceedings of Ed-MEDIA: World Conference on Educational Multimedia & Technology 2010* (pp.1699–1704). Waynesville, NC: AACE.

GDE (2011) *Guidelines on the Management and Usage of ICTs in Public Schools in Gauteng.* South Africa: Gauteng Department of Education. Retrieved 24.11.2016 from: http://schoolnet.org. za/GDE/docs/guidelines.pdf.

Gibson, J.J. (1979) *The Ecological Approach to Visual Perception.* Boston, MA: Houghton Mifflin.

Grimus, M. and Ebner, M. (2016) Mobile phones and learning perceptions of Austrian students aged from 11 to 14 years. In *Proceedings of Ed-MEDIA: World Conference on Educational Media & Technology 2016* (pp.112–121). Waynesville, NC: AACE. Retrieved 9.2.2017 from: https:// www.learntechlib.org/p/172940.

GSMA (2015) *Children's use of mobile phones: A special report 2014.* London and Tokyo: GSMA and NTT DOCOMO Inc. Retrieved 14.07.2016 from: http://stakeholders.ofcom.org.uk/ binaries/research/media-literacy/children-parents-nov-15/childrens_parents_nov2015.pdf.

Hammersley, M. and Traianou, A. (2012) *Ethics in Qualitative Research: Controversies and contexts.* London: Sage.

Hansen, F.A., Kortbek, K.J. and Grønbæk, K. (2010) Mobile urban drama for multimedia-based out-of-school learning. In *Proceedings of the 9th International Conference on Mobile and Ubiquitous Multimedia* (17). New York, NY: Association for Computing Machinery.

Hartnell-Young, E. (2008) Mobile phones for learning in mainstream schooling: Resistance and change. In *Proceedings of mLearn 2008: The Bridge from Text to Context* (pp.160–167). Wolverhampton: University of Wolverhampton.

Hartnell-Young, E. and Heym, N. (2008) *How Mobile Phones Help Learning in Secondary Schools.* Coventry: Becta.

Hartnell-Young, E. (2016) Technology to improve assessments of learning in class, school and nation. In A. Marcus-Quinn and T. Hourigan (Eds) *Handbook on Digital Learning for K-12 Schools* (pp. 329-339). Springer International Publishing.

Haßler, B., Major, L. and Hennessy, S. (2016) Tablet use in schools: A critical review of the evidence for learning outcomes. *Journal of Computer Assisted Learning*, 32, 139–156.

Helm, T. (2013, 27 July) Schools ask parents to stump up £200 for iPads. *The Guardian.* Retrieved 25.11.2016 from: www.theguardian.com/education/2013/jul/28/ipad-tablet-computer-school- parents.

Herrington, J., Oliver, R. and Reeves, T. (2003) Patterns of engagement in authentic online learning environments. *Australian Journal of Educational Technology*, 19(1), 59–71.

Herro, D., Kiger, D. and Owens, C. (2013) Mobile technology. *Journal of Digital Learning in Teacher Education*, 30(1), 30–40.

Hill, P. and Barber, M. (2014) *Preparing for a Renaissance in Assessment.* London: Pearson. Retrieved 20.1.17 from https://research.pearson.com/articles/preparing-for-a-renaissance- inassessment.html.

Hinduja, S. and Patchin, J.W. (2012) *School Climate 2.0: Preventing cyberbullying and sexting one classroom at a time.* Thousand Oaks, CA: Corwin Press.

Hobby, R. (2016, 9 August) Back to school bill: pencil case, pens, rubber … and a £785 iPad. *The Guardian.* Retrieved 15.1.17 from: www.theguardian.com/education/2016/aug/09/back- to-school-bill-ipad-technology-parents.

Hodkinson, H. and Hodkinson, P. (2005) Improving schoolteachers' workplace learning. *Research Papers in Education*, 20(2), 109–131.

Horvath, M.A.H., Alys, L., Massey, K., Pina, A., Scally, M. and Adler, J.R. (2013) *Basically... Porn is Everywhere: A rapid evidence assessment on the effects that access and exposure to pornography has on children and young people.* Project Report. Office of the Children's Commissioner for England, London, UK. Retrieved 10.01.2017 from: http://eprints.mdx.ac.uk/10692/1/BasicallyporniseverywhereReport.pdf.

Howard, D.E., Lothen-Kline, C. and Boekeloo, B.O. (2004) Using the case-study methodology to teach ethics to public health students. *Health Promotion Practice*, 5, 151–159.

Hu, Y. and Huang, R. (2013) The effects of iPad-based classroom response system in secondary school. In *Advanced Learning Technologies (ICALT): Proceedings of IEEE 13th International Conference on Advanced Learning Technologies* (477–478). IEEE.

Huizenga, J., Admiraal, W., Akkerman, S. and Dam, G. t. (2009) Mobile game-based learning in secondary education: Engagement, motivation and learning in a mobile city game. *Journal of Computer Assisted Learning*, 25, 332–344.

Hur, J.W., Shen, Y.W., Kale, U. and Cullen, T.A. (2015). An exploration of pre-service teachers' intention to use mobile devices for teaching. *International Journal of Mobile and Blended Learning*, 7(3), 1–17.

Hwang, G.J. and Hsun-Fang Chang, H.F. (2011) A formative assessment-based mobile learning approach to improving the learning attitudes and achievements of students. *Computers & Education*, 56(4), 1023–1031.

Institute of Educational Technology (IET) (2016) *Trends in Learning Report.* Milton Keynes: The Open University. Retrieved 2.2.2017 from: www.open.ac.uk/research/main/news/trends-learning-2016-report.

Irving, K., Sanalan, V. and Shirley, M. (2009) Physical science connected classrooms: case studies. *Journal of Computers in Mathematics and Science Teaching*, 28(3), 247–275.

Jahnke, I., Svendsen, N.V., Johansen, S.K. and Zander, P-O. (2014) The dream about the magic silver bullet – the complexity of designing for tablet-mediated learning. In P. Bjørn, and D. McDonald (Eds) *Group'14: Proceedings of the 18th ACM International Conference on Supporting Group Work* (pp. 100–110). New York, NY: Association for Computing Machinery.

Jere-Folotiya, J., Chansa-Kabali, T., Munachaka, J.C., Sampa, F., Yalukanda, C., Westerholm, J., Richardson, U., Serpell, R. and Lyytinen, H. (2014) The effect of using a mobile literacy game to improve literacy levels of grade one students in Zambian schools. *Educational Technology Research and Development*, 62(4), 417–436.

Jones, A.C. (2006) Affective factors in learning with mobile devices. In M. Sharples (Ed.) *Big Issues in Mobile Learning: Report of a workshop by the Kaleidoscope Network of Excellence Mobile Learning Initiative.* Nottingham: University of Nottingham.

Kamtsiou, V., Koskinen, T., Naeve, A., Pappa, D. and Stergioulas, L. (2007) A glimpse at the future of technology enhanced-professional learning: trends, scenarios and visions. In A. Boonen and W. Van Petegem (Eds) *European Networking and Learning for the Future. The EuroPACE Approach.* Heverlee, BE: EuroPACE ivzw-Garant Publishers.

Kang, J.M., Shim, K.C., Dong, H.K., Gim, W.H., Son, J., Kwack, D.O., Oh, K.H. and Kim, Y.J. (2014) Practical use of the Classroom Response System (CRS) for diagnostic and formative assessments in a high school life science class. *Journal of the Korean Association for Science Education.* 34(3), 273–283.

Karsenti, T. and Fievez, A. (2013) *The iPad in Education: Uses, benefits, and challenges – A survey of 6,057 students and 302 teachers in Quebec (Canada).* Montreal, QC: CRIFPE. Retrieved 3.2.2017 from: http://karsenti.ca/ipad/iPad_report_Karsenti-Fievez_EN.pdf.

Katz, J.E. (2005) Mobile phones in educational settings. In K. Nyiri (Ed.) *A Sense of Place* (pp.305–317). Vienna: Passagen Verlag.

Kay, R.H. (2009) Examining gender differences in attitudes toward interactive classroom communications systems (ICCS). *Computers & Education,* 52(4), 730–740.

Kay, R., and Knaack, L. (2009) Exploring the use of audience response systems in secondary school science classrooms. *Journal of Science Education and Technology,* 18(5), 382–392.

Kaya, S. (2013) *Science Teachers' Perspectives on Benefits and Problems Faced Using Tablet Computers in Science Education: The story from a secondary school in Turkey.* Unpublished MSc dissertation, University of Bristol, UK.

Kearney, M., Schuck, S., Burden, K. and Aubusson, P. (2012) Viewing mobile learning from a pedagogical perspective. *Alt-J Research in Learning Technology,* 20, 14406.

Kearney, M., Burden, K. and Rai, T. (2015) Investigating teachers' adoption of signature mobile pedagogies. *Computers & Education,* 80, 48–57.

Keengwe, J., Schnellert, G. and Jonas, D. (2014) Mobile phones in education: Challenges and opportunities for learning. *Education and Information Technologies,* 19(2), 441–450.

Khalid, M.S., Kilic, G., Christoffersen, J. and Purushothaman, A. (2015) Barriers to the integration and adoption of iPads in schools: A systematic literature review based on the philosophy of 'Think Global, Act Local.' In *Proceedings of Global Learn Berlin 2015* (pp.335–345). Fern Universität in Hagen, Regionalzentrum Berlin: Association for the Advancement of Computing in Education (AACE).

Khaniya, T. (2006) Use of authentic materials in EFL classrooms. *Journal of Nepal English Language Teachers' Association,* 11(1–2), 17–23.

Kiger, D., Herro, D. and Prunty, D. (2012) Examining the influence of a mobile learning intervention on third grade math achievement. *Journal of Research on Technology in Education,* 45(1), 61–82.

Kim, J. (2014) *Voices of Middle and High School Teachers on the Knowledge, Skills, and Motivation Needed When Using iPads in Teaching.* Unpublished doctoral dissertation. Boston University. Retrieved 18.2.2017 from: http://hdl.handle.net/2144/11105.

Kimbell, R. (2008) e-Assessment in project e-scape. *Design and Technology Education: An International Journal,* 12(2), 66–76.

Kimbell, R. (2012a) The origins and underpinning principles of e-scape. *International Journal of Technology and Design Education,* 22(2), 123–134.

Kimbell, R. (2012b) Evolving project e-scape for national assessment. *International Journal of Technology and Design Education,* 22(2), 135–155.

Kolb, L. (2008) *Toys to Tools: Connecting student cell phones to education.* Eugene, OR: International Society for Technology in Education (ISTE).

Koole, M.L. (2009) A model for framing mobile learning. In M. Ally (Ed.) *Mobile Learning: Transforming the delivery of education and training* (pp.25–47). Athabasca, Canada: Athabasca University Press.

Kukulska-Hulme, A. and Traxler, J. (2005) *Mobile Learning – A Handbook for Educators and Trainers.* London: Routledge.

Kwok, K., Ghrear, S., Li, V., Haddock, T., Coleman, P. and Birch, S.A. (2016) Children can learn new facts equally well from interactive media versus face to face instruction. *Frontiers in Psychology*, (7), 1603.

Kyriacou, C. and Zuin, A. (2016) Cyberbullying of teachers by students on YouTube: challenging the image of teacher authority in the digital age. *Research Papers in Education*, 31(3), 255–273.

Lai, A.F. and Chen, C.H. (2013) Mobile-based peer assessment app and elementary students' perception: Project works of computer curriculum as an example. In *Proceedings of Advanced Learning Technologies (ICALT)* (pp.489–490). IEEE.

Lally, V., Sharples, S., Tracy, F., Bertram, N. and Masters, S. (2012) Researching the ethical dimensions of mobile, ubiquitous and immersive technology enhanced learning (MUITEL): A thematic review and dialogue. *Interactive Learning Environments*, 20(3), 217–238.

Lee, H., Feldman, A. and Beatty, I.D. (2012) Factors that affect science and mathematics teachers' initial implementation of technology-enhanced formative assessment using a classroom response system. *Journal of Science Education and Technology*, 21(5), 523–539.

Lee, M. and Levins, M. (2016) *BYOT and the Digital Evolution of Schooling*. Armidale, AUS: Douglas and Brown.

Lenhart, A. (2009) *Teens and Sexting: How and why minor teens are sending sexually suggestive nude or nearly nude images via text messaging*. Washington, DC: Pew Research Centre. Retrieved 9.1.2017 from: www.pewinternet.org/2009/12/15/teens-and-sexting/.

Lenhart, A., Ling, R., Campbell, S. and Purcell, K. (2010) *Teens and Mobile Phones*. Washington, DC: Pew Research Center. Retrieved 12.12.2016 from: http://pewinternet.org/Reports/2010/Teens-and-Mobile-Phones/Summary-offindings.aspx.

Lin, S.F. and Lai, C.L. (2016) Bullying in Hong Kong schools. In P.K. Smith, K. Kwak and Y. Toda (Eds) *School Bullying in Different Cultures: Eastern and Western Perspectives*. Cambridge: Cambridge University Press.

Livingstone, S., Haddon, L., Görzig, A. and Ólafsson, K. (2011) *Risks and Safety on the Internet: The perspective of European children. Full Findings*. LSE, London: EU Kids Online.

Livingstone, S. and Smith, P.K. (2014) Annual Research Review: Harms experienced by child users of online and mobile technologies: The nature, prevalence and management of sexual and aggressive risks in the digital age. *Journal of Child Psychology and Psychiatry*, 55(6), 635–654.

Liu, C., Chen, S., Chi, C., Chien, K.P., Liu, Y. and Chou, T.L. (2016) The effects of clickers with different teaching strategies. *Journal of Educational Computing Research, Online First*, 0735633116674213.

Looi C.K., Wong L.-H., So H.-J., Seow P., Toh Y., Chen W., Norris C. and Soloway E. (2009) Anatomy of a mobilized lesson: Learning my way. *Computers & Education*, 53, 1120–1132.

Looi, C.K., Zhang, B., Chen, W., Seow, P., Chia, G., Norris, C. and Soloway, E. (2011) 1: 1 mobile inquiry learning experience for primary science students: A study of learning effectiveness. *Journal of Computer Assisted Learning*, 27(3), 269–287.

Maas, A. (2011, 27 October) Orewa College iPad plans move ahead. *Stuff Education*. Retrieved 25.11.2016 from: www.stuff.co.nz/national/education/5859716/Orewa-College-iPad-plans-move-ahead.

Mac Mahon, B., Ó Grádaigh, S. and Ghuidhir, S.N. (2016) iTE: Student teachers using iPad on a Second Level Initial Teacher Education Programme. *International Journal of Mobile and Blended Learning*, 8(2), 21–34.

Maeng, J.L. (2016) Using technology to facilitate differentiated high school science instruction. *Research in Science Education, Online First*, 1–25.

Male, T. and Burden, K. (2014) Access denied? Twenty-first-century technology in schools. *Technology, Pedagogy and Education*, 23(4), 423–437.

Malliou, E., Savvas, S., Sotiriou, S., Miliarakis, A. and Stratakis, M. (2004) The MOTFAL project: Mobile technologies for ad hoc learning in J. Attewell and C. Savill-Smith (Eds) *Mobile Learning: Anytime everywhere. A book of papers from MLEARN 2004*. London: Learning and Skills Development Agency.

de-Marcos, L., Hilera, J.R., Barchino, R., Jiménez, L., Martínez, J.J., Gutiérrez, J.A., Gutiérrez, J.M. and Otón, S. (2010) An experiment for improving students' performance in secondary and tertiary education by means of m-learning auto-assessment. *Computers & Education*, 55(3), 1069–1079.

Mascheroni, G. and Cuman, A. (2014) *Net Children Go Mobile Final Report, Deliverables D6.4 and D5.2*. Milan: Educatt. Retrieved 8.1.2016 from: http://netchildrengomobile.eu/reports/

Masters, G. (2013) Reforming Educational Assessment: Principles, challenges, imperatives. *Australian Education Review*, Number 57. Melbourne: ACER. Retrieved 02.02.2017 from: http://research.acer.edu.au/aer/12/

Mattila, P., and Fordell, T. (2005) *MOOP–Using m-learning environment in primary schools*. Paper presented at MLEARN 2005, Cape Town, South Africa.

Mayer, R.E. (1997) Multimedia learning: Are we asking the right questions? *Educational Psychologist*, 32, 1–19.

McAfee (2013) *Digital Divide: How Teens are Keeping Parents in the Dark*. Press Release. Retrieved 6.1.2017 from: http://newsroom.mcafee.com/press-release/digital-divide-how-teens-are-keeping-parents-dark.

McFarlane, A. (2015) *Authentic Learning for the Digital Generation: Realising the potential of technology in the classroom*. London: Routledge.

McFarlane, A., Triggs, P. and Ching Yee, W. (2009). *Researching Mobile Learning: Overview. A Report for Becta*. Coventry, UK: Becta Retrieved 28.4.2016 from http://dera.ioe.ac.uk/1473/.

McGuire, L., Roberts, G. and Moss, M. (2004) *Final Report to QCA on the eVIVa Project 2002 – 2004*. Retrieved 19.1.2017 from: http://rubble.heppell.net/archive/eviva/media/Eviva_Final_Report_2004-feb2008.pdf.

Meek, J. (2006) *Adopting a Lifecycle Approach to the Evaluation of Computers and Information Technology*. Unpublished PhD Thesis. School of Electronic, Electrical and Computer Engineering, University of Birmingham.

Merchant, G. (2012) Mobile practices in everyday life: Popular digital technologies and schooling revisited. *British Journal of Educational Technology*, 43, 770–782.

Metcalf, S. J., and Tinker, R.F. (2004) Probeware and handhelds in elementary and middle school science. *Journal of Science Education and Technology*, 13(1), 43–49.

Meyer, A.P.B. (2015) iPads in inclusive classrooms: Ecologies of learning. In P. Isaías, J.M. Spector, D. Ifenthaler and D.G. Sampson (Eds) *E-Learning Systems, Environments and Approaches* (pp.25–37). New York, NY: Springer.

Mifsud, L. (2002) Alternative learning arenas – pedagogical challenges to mobile learning technology in education. In *Proceedings of IEEE International Workshop on Wireless and Mobile Technologies in Education, WMUTE 2002* (pp.112–116). Växjö, Sweden. IEEE.

Mifsud, L. (2014) Mobile learning and the socio-materiality of classroom practices. *Learning, Media and Technology*, 39(1), 142–149.

Milrad, M., Wong, L.H., Sharples, M., Hwang, G.J., Looi, C.K. and Ogata, H. (2013) Seamless learning: An international perspective on next-generation technology-enhanced learning. In Z.L. Berge and Y.L. Muilenburg (Eds) *Handbook of Mobile Learning* (pp. 95–108). Abingdon: Routledge.

Mitchell, A., Patrick, K., Heywood, W., Blackman, P. and Pitts, M. (2014) *National Survey of Australian Secondary Students and Sexual Health 2013*. Melbourne: Australian Research Centre in Sex Health and Society & La Trobe University. Retrieved 10.1.2017 from: https://members. youthcoalition.net/sites/default/files/articles-external/National%20Survey%20of%20Australian%20 Secondary%20Students%20and%20Sexual%20Health.pdf.

Monks, C.P., Robinson, S. and Worlidge, P. (2012) The emergence of cyberbullying: A survey of primary school pupils' perceptions and experiences. *School Psychology International*, 33(5), 477–491.

Moore, M.G. (1997) Theory of Transactional Distance. In D. Keegan (Ed.) *Theoretical Principles of Distance Education* (pp.22–38). New York: Routledge Studies in Distance Education.

Moss, K. and Crowley, M. (2011) Effective learning in science: The use of personal response systems with a wide range of audiences. *Computers & Education*, 56(1), 36–43.

Moura, A. (2015) iPad program in K-12 education: Pilot year. In Y. Zhang (Ed.) *Handbook of Mobile Teaching and Learning* (pp.601–616). Springer International Publishing.

Munezawa, T., Kaneita, Y., Osaki, Y., Kanda, H., Minowa, M., Suzuki, K., Higuchi, S., Mori, J., Yamamoto, R. and Ohida, T. (2011) The association between use of mobile phones after lights out and sleep disturbances among Japanese adolescents: A nationwide cross-sectional survey. *SLEE*, 34(8), 1013–1020.

Murray, P. (2006) *Can PDA's make a difference?* Paper presented at Australian Computers in Education Conference (ACEC) 2006, Cairns, Queensland, Australia.

Mwapwele, S.D. and Roodt, S. (2016) The extent of usage of mobile devices for learning outside the classroom in a secondary school in Tanzania. In *Proceedings of the International Conference on Information Resources Management (CONF-IRM 2016)*, (65).

Naismith, L., Lonsdale, P., Vavoula, G. and Sharples, M. (2004) *Report 11: Literature Review of Mobile Technologies in Learning*. Bristol: Futurelab. Retrieved 24.10.2016 from: www.nfer.ac. uk/publications/FUTL15.

National Children's Bureau/Association for School and College Leaders (NCB/ASCL) (2016) *Keeping Young People in Mind*. Retrieved 8.1.2016 from: www.ascl.org.uk/utilities/document-summary.html?id=D91C5B0A-72A6-4117-96A9B343E51FB296.

Naylor, A. and Gibbs, J. (2015) Using iPads as a learning tool in cross-curricular collaborative initial teacher education. *Journal of Education for Teaching*, 41(4), 442–446.

Ng, W. and Cumming, T.M. (Eds) (2015) *Sustaining Mobile Learning: Theory, research and practice*. Abingdon: Routledge.

Ng, W. and Nicholas, H. (2013) A framework for sustainable mobile learning in schools. *British Journal of Educational Technology*, 44 (55), 695–715.

Nikou, S.A. and Economides, A.A. (2013). Mobile assessment: State of the art. In Z.L. Berge and L.Y. Muilenburg (Eds) *Handbook of Mobile Learning* (pp.346–355). Florence, KY: Routledge.

Nordmark, S. and Milrad, M. (2012) Mobile Digital Storytelling for Promoting Creative Collaborative Learning. In *Proceedings of the Seventh IEEE International Conference on Wireless, Mobile, and Ubiquitous Technology in Education, WMUTE 2012*. Takamatsu, Japan. IEEE.

O'Bannon, B.W. and Thomas, K.M. (2015) Mobile phones in the classroom: Preservice teachers answer the call. *Computers & Education*, 85, 110–122.

O'Malley, C., Vavoula, G., Glew, J.P., Taylor, J., Sharples, M. and Lefrere, P. (2003) *Guidelines for Learning/Teaching/Tutoring in a Mobile Environment*. MOBllearn project report, D4.1. Retrieved 11.06.2017 from: https://hal.archives-ouvertes.fr/hal-00696244/document

Obringer, S.J. and Coffey, K. (2007) Cell phones in American high schools: A national survey. *Journal of Technology Studies*, 33(1), 41–47.

Ofcom (2015) *Children and Parents: Media Use and Attitudes Report*. London: Ofcom. Retrieved 14.17.2016 from: http://stakeholders.ofcom.org.uk/binaries/research/media-literacy/children-parents-nov-15/childrens_parents_nov2015.pdf.

Oldfield, A., Broadfoot, P., Sutherland, R. and Timmis, S. (2012) *Assessment in a Digital Age: a research review*. Bristol: University of Bristol. Retrieved 27.01.2017 from: www.bris.ac.uk/media-library/sites/education/documents/researchreview.pdf.

de Oliveira, D.R. and Maia, L.D.S.L. (2016) Mobile technologies and pedagogical practices: An analysis of ways to use mobile devices in public schools. *Minutes of the 3rd Meeting on Games and Mobile Learning* (pp.110–118). Coimbra, Portugal: University of Coimbra.

Oliver, B. (2005) Mobile blogging, 'Skyping' and podcasting: Targeting undergraduates' communication skills in transnational learning contexts. *Microlearning*, 107(4), 587–600.

Oller, R. (2012) *The Future of Mobile Learning* (Research Bulletin). Louisville, CO: Educause Center for Analysis and Research. Retrieved 4.07.2015 from: https://net.educause.edu/ir/library/pdf/ERB1204.pdf.

Olumide, A.O., Adebayo, E. and Oluwagbayela, B. (2016) Gender disparities in the experience, effects and reporting of electronic aggression among secondary school students in Nigeria. *BMJ Global Health*, 1(3), e000072.

Ott, T., Haglind, T. and Lindström, B. (2014) Students' use of mobile phones for school work. In M. Kalz and Y. Bayyurt (Eds) *Mobile as Mainstream – Towards Future Challenges in Mobile Learning* (pp.69–80). Cham, Switzerland: Springer International Publishing.

Pachler, N. (2010) Research methods in mobile and informal learning: Some issues. In G. Vavoula, N. Pachler and A. Kukulska-Hulme (Eds) *Researching Mobile Learning: Frameworks, tools and research designs* (2nd ed.). Oxford: Peter Lang.

Pachler, N., Bachmair, B., Cook, J. and Kress, G. (2010) *Mobile Learning: Structures, agency, practices*. New York, NY: Springer.

Papert, S. (1980) *Mindstorms: Children, computers, and powerful ideas*. New York: Basic Books, Inc.

Park, Y. (2011) A pedagogical framework for mobile learning: Categorizing educational applications of mobile technologies into four types. *The International Review of Research in Open and Distributed Learning*, 12(2), 78–102.

Parsons, D. and Adhikari, J. (2016) Bring Your Own Device to secondary school: The perceptions of teachers, students and parents. *The Electronic Journal of e-Learning*, 14(1), 66–80.

Parsons, D., Wishart, J. and Thomas, H. (2016) Exploring mobile affordances in the digital classroom. In I. Arnedillo-Sanchez and P. Isiais (Eds) *Proceedings of IADIS 2016 12th International Conference on Mobile Learning* (pp.43–50). IADIS Press.

Passey, D. and Zozimo, J. (2014) *Research Report: A training needs analysis to support mobile learning and information and communication technology teacher training in MLEARN partner countries.* Lancaster: Lancaster University. Retrieved 21.10.2016 from: http://eprints.lancs. ac.uk/78695/.

Passey, D. and Zozimo, J. (2016) *Research Report: Outcomes from a training programme to support mobile learning and information and communication technology teacher training in MLEARN partner countries.* Lancaster: Lancaster University. Retrieved 21.10.2016 from: http://eprints.lancs.ac.uk/69448/4/Passey_Zozimo_MLEARN_Research_Report_WP5_1_final. pdf.

Patchin, J. W. (2013) *Cyberbullying Research: 2013 Update.* Cyberbullying Research Center, USA. Retrieved 08.01.2017 from: http://cyberbullying.org/cyberbullying-research-2013-update.

Pea, R.D. (2002) *Learning Science through Collaborative Visualization over the Internet.* Paper presented at Nobel Foundation Virtual Museums Symposium, Stockholm, May 26–29.

Pegrum, M., Oakley, G. and Faulkner, R. (2013) Schools going mobile: A study of the adoption of mobile handheld technologies in Western Australian independent schools. *Australasian Journal of Educational Technology,* 29(1), 66–81.

Perry, D. (2003) *Handheld Computers PDAs in Schools.* Coventry: British Educational Communications and Technology Agency. Retrieved 6.11.2016 from: http://dera.ioe.ac.uk/ 1644/7/becta_2003_handhelds_report_Redacted.pdf.

Pew Research Center (2016) *Smartphone Ownership and Internet Usage Continues to Climb in Emerging Economies.* Washington, DC: Pew Research Center. Retrieved 2.5.2016 from: www.pewglobal.org/files/2016/02/pew_research_center_global_technology_report_final_ february_22__2016.pdf.

Philip, T. M. and Garcia, A. (2015) Schooling mobile phones: Assumptions about proximal benefits, the challenges of shifting meanings, and the politics of teaching. *Educational Policy,* 29(4), 676–707.

Phippen, A. (2016) *Children's Online Behaviour and Safety: Policy and Rights Challenges.* London: Palgrave Macmillan.

Piaget, J. (1952) *The Origins of Intelligence in Children.* New York: International Universities Press.

Pimmer, C. and Gröhbiel, U. (2013) *The affordances of social mobile media for boundary crossing.* Paper presented at the Swiss Society for Research in Education Conference: Integrating formal and informal learning, Lugano, Switzerland, August 21–23.

Pintus, A., Carboni, D., Paddeu, G., Piras, A. and Sanna, S. (2004) Mobile lessons: Concept and applications for 'on-site' geo-referenced lessons. In J. Attewell and C. Savill-Smith (Eds) *Mobile Learning: Anytime everywhere. A book of papers from MLEARN 2004* (pp.163–165). London: Learning and Skills Development Agency.

Porter, G., Hampshire, K., Milner, J., Munthali, A., Robson, E., de Lannoy, A., Bango, A., Gunguluza, N., Mashiri, M., Tanle, A. and Abane, A. (2016) Mobile phones and education in Sub-Saharan Africa: From youth practice to public policy. *Journal of International Development,* 28, 22–39.

Power, T., Shaheen, R., Solly, M., Woodward, C. and Burton, S. (2012) English in action: School based teacher development in Bangladesh. *Curriculum Journal,* 23(4), 503–529.

Purcell, K., Heaps, A., Buchanan, J. and Friedrich, L. (2013) *How teachers are using technology at home and in their classrooms.* Washington, DC: Pew Research Center's Internet & American Life Project.

Quinn, C. (2000) mlearning: Mobile, wireless, in-your-pocket learning. *LiNE Zine.* Retrieved 21.07.2015 from: www.linezine.com/2.1/features/cqmmwiyp.htm.

Ranieri, M. and Bruni, I. (2013) Empowering creativity in young people through mobile learning: An investigation of creative practices of mobile media uses in and out of school. *International Journal of Mobile and Blended Learning (IJMBL)*, 5(3), 17–33.

Redecker, C. and Johannessen, Ø. (2013) Changing assessment – Towards a new assessment paradigm using ICT. *European Journal of Education*, 48(1), 79–96.

Resnick, L.B. (1987) The 1987 presidential address: Learning in school and out. *Educational Researcher*, 16(9), 13–54.

Richards, R.B. (2014) *Exploring the Relationship between Teachers' Formative Assessment Beliefs and Practices through Integration of Mobile Screencasting*. Unpublished doctoral dissertation, Columbia University, USA.

Ringrose, J., Gill, R., Livingstone, S. and Harvey, L. (2012) *A Qualitative Study of Children, Young People and 'Sexting': A report prepared for the NSPCC*. London: NSPCC.

Şahin, F. and Mentor, D. (2016) Using mobile phones for assessment in contemporary classrooms. In D. Mentor (Ed.) *Handbook of Research on Mobile Learning in Contemporary Classrooms* (pp.116–138). Hershey, PA: IGI Global.

Sakellariou, T. and Carroll, A. (2012) Rates of cyber victimization and bullying among male Australian primary and high school students. *School Psychology International*, 33(5), 533–549.

Seppälä, P. and Alamäki, H. (2003) Mobile learning in teacher training. *Journal of Computer Assisted Learning*, 19(3), 330–335.

Sharples, M. (2000) The design of personal mobile technologies for lifelong learning. *Computers & Education*, 34(3–4), 177–193.

Sharples, M. (2002) Disruptive devices: Mobile technology for conversational learning. *International Journal of Continuing Engineering Education and Life Long Learning*, 12(5–6), 504–520.

Sharples, M. (Ed.) (2006) *Big Issues in Mobile Learning: Report of a workshop by the Kaleidoscope Network of Excellence Mobile Learning Initiative*. Nottingham: University of Nottingham.

Sharples, M. (2007) Evaluation methods for mobile learning. In N. Pachler (Ed.) *Research Methods in Informal and Mobile Learning: Towards a research agenda* (pp.12–13). London, UK: WLE Centre, Institute of Education.

Sharples, M. (2009) Methods for evaluating mobile learning. In G.N. Vavoula, N. Pachler, and A. Kukulska-Hulme (Eds) *Researching Mobile Learning: Frameworks, tools and research designs* (pp.17–39). Oxford: Peter Lang Publishing Group.

Sharples, M. (2010) Foreword. In E. Brown (Ed.) *Education in the Wild: Contextual and location-based mobile learning in action. A report from the STELLAR Alpine Rendez-Vous Workshop series* (pp.4–6). Nottingham: Learning Sciences Research Institute, University of Nottingham.

Sharples, M. (2013) Mobile learning: Research, practice and challenges. *Distance Education in China*, 3(5), 5–11.

Sharples, M., Scanlon, E., Ainsworth, S., Anastopoulou, S., Collins, T., Crook, C., Jones, A., Kerawalla, L., Littleton, K., Mulholland, P. and O'Malley, C. (2015) Personal inquiry: Orchestrating science investigations within and beyond the classroom. *Journal of the Learning Sciences*, 24(2), 308–341.

Sharples, M., Taylor, J. and Vavoula, G. (2007) A theory of learning for the mobile age. In R. Andrews and C. Haythornthwaite (Eds) *The Sage Handbook of E-learning Research* (pp.221–247). London: Sage Publications.

Sheard, M.K., Chambers, B. and Elliott, L. (2012) *Effects of Technology-Enhanced Formative Assessment on Achievement in Primary Grammar.* York: Institute for Effective Education, University of York. Retrieved 18.01.2016. from: http://eprints.whiterose.ac.uk/75089/1/QfLGrammarReport_Sept2012.pdf.

Sheninger, E. (2016) *Asking the Right Questions About Mobile Learning.* Personal Blog. Retrieved 14.07.2016 from: http://esheninger.blogspot.co.uk/2016/07/asking-right-questions-about-mobile.html

Smith, H., Ng, K.H., Walker, K., Underwood, J., Heldt, S., Fitzpatrick, G., Luckin, R., Good, J., Wyeth, P. and Benford, S. (2007) Reconstructing an informal mobile learning experience with multiple data streams. In G. Vavoula, A. Kukulska-Hulme and N. Pachler (Eds) *Proceedings of Workshop Research Methods in Informal and Mobile Learning* (pp.29–34), London: WLE Centre, Institute of Education.

So, K.K.T. (2004) Applying wireless technology in field trips: A Hong Kong experience. *Australian Educational Computing*, 19 (2), 3–7.

Sparkes, R. (2016) *The Secret Garden Grows into an Immersive Experience.* Cupertino, CA: Apple Inc. Retrieved 18.7.2016 from: www.apple.com/uk/education/teach-with-ipad/classroom/secret-garden/.

Spinello, R.A. (2003) *Case Studies in Information Technology Ethics* (2nd ed.). Upper Saddle River, NJ: Prentice Hall.

Spinuzzi, C. (2005) The methodology of participatory design. *Technical Communication.* 52(2), 163–174.

Stern, S. (2004) Studying adolescents online: A consideration of ethical issues. In E.A. Buchanan (Ed.) *Readings in Virtual Research Ethics: Issues and controversies.* Hershey, PA: Idea Group.

Swan, K., van't Hooft, M., Kratcoski, A. and Unger, D. (2005) Teaching and learning with mobile computing devices: Closing the gap. In H. van der Merwe and T. Brown (Eds) *Mobile Technology: The Future of Learning in Your Hands, mLearn 2005 Book of Abstracts* (pp. 157–161). Cape Town, SA: 4th World Conference on mlearning.

Syvänen, A. and Nokelainen, P. (2005) Evaluation of the technical and pedagogical mobile usability. In J. Attewell and C. Savill-Smith (Eds) *Mobile Learning Anytime Everywhere: A book of papers from MLEARN 2004* (pp.191–195). London: Learning and Skills Development Agency (LSDA).

Syvänen, A., Pehkonen, M., and Turunen, H. (2004) Fragmentation in mobile learning. In J. Attewell and C. Savill-Smith (Eds) *Learning with Mobile Devices: Research and Development. A book of papers from MLEARN 2003* (pp.155–166). London: Learning and Skills Development Agency (LSDA).

Taylor, J. (2006). Evaluating mobile learning: What are appropriate methods for evaluating learning in mobile environments? In M. Sharples (Ed.) *Big Issues in Mobile Learning: Report of a workshop by the Kaleidoscope Network of Excellence Mobile Learning Initiative.* Nottingham: University of Nottingham.

Thomas, K. and Muñoz, M.A. (2016) Hold the phone! High school students' perceptions of mobile phone integration in the classroom. *American Secondary Education*, 44(3), 19–37.

Thomas, K.M., O'Bannon, B.W. and Bolton, N. (2013) Cell phones in the classroom: Teachers' perspectives of inclusion, benefits, and barriers. *Computers in the Schools*, 30(4), 295–308.

Thomas, K.M., O'Bannon, B.W. and Britt, V.G. (2014) Standing in the schoolhouse door: Teacher perceptions of mobile phones in the classroom. *Journal of Research on Technology in Education*, 46(4), 373–395.

Thomas, R.M. (2008) *What Schools Ban and Why*. Westport, CT: Praeger.

Timmis, S., Broadfoot, P., Sutherland, R. and Oldfield, A. (2015) Rethinking assessment in a digital age: Opportunities, challenges and risks. *British Educational Research Journal*, 42(3), 454–476.

Tirocchi, S. (2015) Mobile phones at school: Bad student behaviour or an innovative resource? *Media Education – Studi, ricerche, buone pratiche*, 6(2), 308–320. Retrieved 15.7.2016 from: http://riviste.erickson.it/med/wp-content/uploads/08_Tirocchi_II_2015_fin.pdf.

Traxler, J. (2007) Defining, discussing and evaluating mobile learning: The moving finger writes and having writ…. *The International Review of Research in Open and Distributed Learning*, 8(2). Retrieved 21.7.2016 from: www.irrodl.org/index.php/irrodl/article/view/346/875.

Traxler, J. (2011) Introduction. In J. Traxler and J. Wishart (Eds) *Making Mobile Learning Work: Case Studies of Practice*. Bristol: ESCalate. Retrieved 21.7.2016 from: http://escalate.ac.uk/8250.

Traxler, J. and Bridges, N. (2004) Mobile learning – the ethical and legal challenges. In J. Attewell and C. Savill-Smith (Eds) *Mobile Learning: Anytime Everywhere. A Book of Papers from MLEARN 2004* (pp.203–208). London: Learning and Skills Development Agency (LSDA).

Traxler, J. and Kukulska-Hulme, A. (2005) Evaluating mobile learning: Reflections on current practice. In H. van der Merwe and T. Brown (Eds) *Mobile Technology: The Future of Learning in Your Hands, mLearn 2005 Book of Abstracts* (pp.157–161). Cape Town, SA: 4th World Conference on mlearning.

Trilling, B. and Fadel, C. (2009) *21st Century Skills: Learning for Life in Our Times*. Hoboken, NJ: John Wiley & Sons.

Turner, J. (2016) Mobile learning in K-12 education: Personal meets systemic. In D. Churchill, J. Lu, T. K. Chiu and B. Fox (Eds) *Mobile Learning Design: Theories and Application*. Singapore: Springer.

UNESCO (2015) *ICT in Education » Mobile Learning*. Paris: UNESCO. Retrieved 24.7.2015 from: www.unesco.org/new/en/unesco/themes/icts/m4ed/.

Utsumi, S. (2010) Cyberbullying among middle-school students: Association with children's perception of parental control and relational aggression. *Japanese Journal of Educational Psychology*, 58(1), 12–22.

Vahey, P. and Crawford, V. (2002) *Palm Education Pioneers Program: Final evaluation report*. Menlo Park, CA: SRI International. Retrieved 5.4.2016 from: http://palmgrants.sri.com/PEP_Final_Report.pdf.

Van den Abeele, M., Campbell, S.W., Eggermont, S. and Roe, K. (2014) Sexting, mobile porn use, and peer group dynamics: Boys' and girls' self-perceived popularity, need for popularity, and perceived peer pressure. *Media Psychology*, 17(1), 6–33.

Van Dijk, J. and Hacker, K. (2003) The digital divide as a complex and dynamic phenomenon. *The Information Society*, 19(4), 315–326.

van 't Hooft, M. (2006) *Usability issues*. Posting on the CIDER Mobile Learning SIG forum, 26 May 2006. Retrieved 14.2.2017 from: http://cider.athabascau.ca/CIDERSIGs/mobilelearning/mlearndiscussion/talkback/1148656719.

Vath, R., Bobrowsky, W., Soloway, E., Blumenfeld, P., Krajcik, J., Meriweather, A., Sarrat, P. and Wise, S. (2005) *Supporting Teachers using Palm Computers: Examining classroom practice over time*. Paper presented at National Educational Computing Conference, Philadelphia, June 2005. Retrieved 24.4.2016 from: http://www.umich.edu/~hiceweb/downloads/Vath_etal_NECC2005.pdf.

Vavoula, G. and Sharples, M. (2009) Meeting the challenges in evaluating mobile learning: A 3-level evaluation framework. *International Journal of Mobile and Blended Learning*, 1, 54–75.

Vavoula, G., Sharples, M., Rudman, P., Meek, J. and Lonsdale, P. (2009) MyArtspace: Design and evaluation of support for learning with multimedia phones between classrooms and museums. *Computers & Education*, 53(2), 286–299.

Verizon (2012) *New National Survey Finds that More Than a Third of Middle School Students Use Mobile Devices for Homework; Yet Mobile-Device Use Is Still Not Common in Classrooms.* Retrieved 5.9.2016 from:www.verizon.com/about/news/press-releases/new-national-survey-finds-more-third-middle-school-students-use-mobile-devices.

Visser, R.D., Evering, L.C. and Barrett, D.E. (2014) # TwitterforTeachers: The implications of Twitter as a self-directed professional development tool for K–12 teachers. *Journal of Research on Technology in Education*, 46(4), 396–413.

Vosloo, S. (2012) Mobile learning and policies: Key issues to consider. UNESCO Working Series on Mobile Learning. Paris: UNESCO. Retrieved 30.10. 2016 from: http://unesdoc.unesco.org/images/0021/002176/217638E.pdf.

Vygotsky, L.S. (1978) *Mind in Society: The development of higher psychological processes.* Cambridge, MA: Harvard University Press.

Wadsworth, Y. (1998) What is Participatory Action Research? *Action Research International*, Paper 2. Retrieved 24.10.2016 from: www.aral.com.au/ari/p-ywadsworth98.html.

Wang, T. (2016) Overcoming teachers' concerns – Where are we in the harnessing of mobile technology in K-12 classrooms in Hong Kong? In D. Churchill, J. Lu, T.K. Chiu, and B. Fox (Eds) *Mobile Learning Design* (pp.239–248). Singapore: Springer.

West, M. (2012) *Mobile Learning for Teachers. Global themes.* Paris: UNESCO. Retrieved 3.5.2016 from: http://unesdoc.unesco.org/images/0021/002164/216452E.pdf.

West, M. and Vosloo, S. (2013) *Policy Guidelines for Mobile Learning.* Paris: UNESCO. Retrieved 6.2.2017 from: http://unesdoc.unesco.org/images/0021/002196/219641e.pdf.

Wexler, S., Brown, J., Metcalf, D., Rogers, D. and Wagner, E. (2008) *Mobile Learning: What is it, why it matters, and how to incorporate it into your learning strategy.* Retrieved 10.7.2015 from: www.elearningguild.com/research/archives/index.cfm?id=132&action=viewonly.

White, T. and Martin, L. (2014) Mathematics and mobile learning. *TechTrends*, 58(1), 64–70.

Whitelock, D. and Watt, S. (2008) Reframing e-assessment: Adopting new media and adapting old frameworks. *Learning, Media & Technology*, 33(3), 151–154.

Whyley, D. (2006) *Learning2Go.* Retrieved 5/12/2006 from: www.learning2go.org/.

Wiliam, D. and Thompson, M. (2008) Integrating assessment with instruction: What will it take to make it work? In C.A. Dwyer (Ed.) *The Future of Assessment: Shaping teaching and learning* (pp.53–82). Mahwah, NJ: Lawrence Erlbaum Associates.

Willard, N.E. (2007) *Cyberbullying and Cyberthreats: Responding to the challenge of online social aggression, threats, and distress.* Champaign, IL: Research Press.

Williams, C. (2012) *Raising Standards in Boys' Writing using the iPad for Gaming.* Personal Blog MrAndrewsOnline 24 June 2012. Retrieved 18.07.2016 from: http://mrandrewsonline.blogspot.co.uk/2012/06/raising-standards-in-boys-writing-using.html.

Williams, P.J. and Kimbell, R. (Eds) (2012) Special Issue on e-Scape, *International Journal of Technology and Design Education*, 22(2), May 2012.

Wingkvist, A., and Ericsson, M. (2009) Sharing experience from three initiatives in mobile learning: Lessons learned. In S.C. Kong et al. (Eds) *Proceedings of the 17th International Conference on Computers in Education* (pp.613–617). ICCE 2009.

Winters, N. (2006) What is mobile learning? In M. Sharples (Ed.) *Big Issues in Mobile Learning: Report of a workshop by the Kaleidoscope Network of Excellence Mobile Learning Initiative* (pp.5–9). Nottingham: University of Nottingham.

Wishart, J. (2008) Challenges faced by modern foreign language teacher trainees in using handheld pocket PCs (Personal Digital Assistants) to support their teaching and learning. *ReCALL*, 20(03), 348–360.

Wishart, J. (2009) Ethical considerations in implementing mobile learning in the workplace. *International Journal of Mobile and Blended Learning*, 1(2), 76–92.

Wishart, J. (2010) The need to plan ahead for social and ethical challenges in contextual and location-based learning. In E. Brown (Ed.) *Education in the Wild: Contextual and location-based mobile learning in action.* (STELLAR Alpine Rendez-Vous workshop series). Nottingham: Learning Sciences Research Institute.

Wishart, J. (2013) *Ethical Considerations Emerging in the Study of Mobile Learning.* Paper presented at the International Symposium on Digital Methodologies in Educational Research, Lancaster. May 2013.

Wishart, J. (2016) Using the cameras on mobile phones, iPads and digital cameras to create animations in science teaching and learning. In H. Crompton and J. Traxler (Eds) *Mobile Learning and STEM: Case Studies in Practice* (pp.17–28). London: Routledge.

Wishart, J. (2017) Exploring how creating stop-motion animations supports student teachers in learning to teach science. *Journal of Research on Technology in Education*, 49(1–2), 88–101.

Wishart, J. and Green, D. (2010) *Identifying Emerging Issues in Mobile Learning in Further and Higher Education: A report to JISC.* Retrieved 5.11.16 from: www.bristol.ac.uk/media-library/sites/education/migrated/documents/emergereport.pdf.

Wishart, J. and Triggs, P. (2010) MuseumScouts: Exploring how schools, museums and interactive technologies can work together to support learning. *Computers & Education*, 54(3), 669–678.

Wishart, J., Ramsden, A. and McFarlane, A. (2007) PDAs and handhelds: ICT at your side and not in your face. *Technology, Pedagogy and Education*, 16(1), 95–110.

Wong, G.K. (2016) A new wave of innovation using mobile learning analytics for flipped classroom. In D. Churchill, J. Lu, T.K. Chiu and B. Fox (Eds) *Mobile Learning Design: Theories and Application.* Singapore: Springer.

World Bank (2015) *Mobile Cellular Subscriptions (per 100 people).* International Telecommunication Union, World Telecommunication/ICT Development Report and database. Retrieved 07.02.2017 from: http://data.worldbank.org/indicator/IT.CEL.SETS.P2

Wu, W.H., Wu, Y.C.J., Chen, C.Y., Kao, H.Y., Lin, C.H., and Huang, S.H. (2012) Review of trends from mobile learning studies: A meta-analysis. *Computers & Education*, 59(2), 817–827.

Wyeth, P., Fitzpatrick, G., Good, J., Smith, H., Luckin, R., Underwood, J., Ng, K.H., Walker, K. and Benford, S. (2008) Learning through treasure hunting: The role of mobile devices. In I. Arnedillo-Sanchez (Ed.) *Proceedings of the IADIS International Conference on Mobile Learning* (pp.27–34). Algarve, Portugal: IADIS Press.

Yarnall, L., Shechtman, N. and Penuel, W.R. (2006) Using handheld computers to support improved classroom assessment in science: Results from a field trial. *Journal of Science Education and Technology*, 15(2), 142–158.

Zhang, B., Looi, C.K. Chen, W. Tan, N. Seow, S.K., Oh, T.T. and Chung, T.M. (2006) *Using mobile learning technologies for primary environmental education in Singapore schools.* Paper presented at International Science Education Conference, Singapore, 22–24 November 2006.

Zimmer, M. (2010) "But the data is already public": On the ethics of research in Facebook. *Ethics in Information Technology,* 12, 313–325.

Zurita, G. and Nussbaum, M. (2004) A constructivist mobile learning environment supported by a wireless handheld network. *Journal of Computer Assisted Learning,* 20(4), 235–243.

Index